# ARCHAEOLOGY AND ANTHROPOLOGY

# Archaeology and Anthropology

edited by

*Duncan Garrow and Thomas Yarrow*



Oxbow Books
*Oxford and Oakville*

*Published by*
Oxbow Books, Oxford, UK



ISBN 978-1-84217-387-9

Cover photo by Chuck Choi
(detail of *Riverlines* by Richard Long, Hearst Tower, New York City)

*This book is available direct from:*

Oxbow Books, Oxford, UK
*(Phone: 01865-241249; Fax: 01865-794449)*

*and*

The David Brown Book Company
PO Box 511, Oakville, CT 06779, USA
*(Phone: 860-945-9329; Fax: 860-945-9468)*

*or from our website*

www.oxbowbooks.com

A CIP record for this book is available from the British Library

Library of Congress Cataloging-in-Publication Data

Archaeology and anthropology / edited by Duncan Garrow and Thomas Yarrow.
p. cm.
Includes bibliographical references.
ISBN 978-1-84217-387-9
1. Forensic archaeology. 2. Forensic anthropology. I. Garrow, Duncan. II. Yarrow, Thomas.
GN69.A73 2010
301--dc22

2010011870

*Printed in Great Britain by*
Short Run Press, Exeter

# Contents

# List of figures

# Notes on the contributors

MATT EDGEWORTH is a research associate at the University of Leicester. He studied for his degree and PhD in archaeology and anthropology at the University of Durham. He has worked mostly for commercial archaeological units, directing numerous fieldwork projects. He is the author of *Acts of Discovery* (Archaeopress 2003) and editor of *Ethnographies of Archaeological Practice* (Altamira 2006).

STEPHAN FEUCHTWANG is a Professor in the Department of Anthropology, at the London School of Economics. Since 1966 he has undertaken research on popular religion and politics in China resulting in a number of publications on charisma, place, temples and festivals. He is currently undertaking research on the comparison of civilisations and empires.

PAOLA FILIPPUCCI is a college lecturer in social anthropology at Murray Edwards College, Cambridge. She has a first degree in archaeology and her current research on the social memory of war and post-war reconstruction in Eastern France has an archaeological element through her membership of a team specializing in Great War archaeology (see http://www.no-mans-land.info/).

CHRIS FOWLER is a lecturer in later prehistoric archaeology at the School of Historical Studies, Newcastle University. He has written a number of publications on concepts of the body and person in anthropology and archaeology, and specialises in British Neolithic and early Bronze Age archaeology.

DUNCAN GARROW is a lecturer at the School of Archaeology, Classics and Egyptology, University of Liverpool. His research interests include the Mesolithic-Neolithic 'transition' in north-west Europe; Iron Age and Roman material culture; long-term histories of depositional practice and interdisciplinary approaches to material culture.

CHRIS GOSDEN is Professor of European Archaeology at the School of Archaeology, University of Oxford. His research interests include the relationship between anthropology and archaeology, and interdisciplinary understandings of human intelligence. He is currently involved in projects investigating Celtic Art in Iron Age and Roman Britain, 'Englishness' within the Pitt-Rivers Museum, and material culture in Borneo.

TIM INGOLD is Professor of Social Anthropology at the University of Aberdeen. His ethnographic focus is on the circumpolar North, and he has written on hunting and pastoralism, human-animal relations, evolutionary theory, language and tool use, environmental perception and skilled practice. His current research is on the comparative anthropology of the line, exploring issues on the interface between anthropology, archaeology, art and architecture.

Gavin Lucas is a lecturer in archaeology at the University of Iceland. His research interests lie in archaeological theory and the archaeology of the modern world. He is the author of *Critical Approaches to Fieldwork* (2001), *An Archaeology of Colonial Identity* (2004) and *The Archaeology of Time* (2005) as well as co-editor with Victor Buchli of *Archaeologies of the Contemporary Past* (2001).

Lesley McFadyen is currently undertaking research at the Universidade do Porto, studying the material culture and architecture of Chalcolithic enclosure sites in Portugal. Her research works across chronology and geography, and engages with evidence for the Mesolithic, Neolithic and Bronze Age, particularly in Britain, France and Portugal. Her main interests include the experience of building and construction in prehistory, and how architecture connected to landscape and material culture in the past.

David Robinson is a lecturer at the University of Central Lancashire. His research focuses upon the material enculturation of the landscape and environment from spatial and temporal perspectives. He has conducted fieldwork in the United Kingdom, India, Spain, and California, the latter of which was the focus of his PhD dissertation on rock-art, landscapes, and taskscapes. He is currently focusing on excavating rock-art in South-Central California and approaches to colonial and post-colonial archaeology, while continuing to examine prehistoric material practices.

Mike Rowlands is Professor of Anthropology and Material Culture at University College, London. He has undertaken both archaeological and ethnographic research and has published influential works on a range of subjects including material culture, heritage, nationalism, and long term social and cultural change.

Marilyn Strathern is Emeritus Professor of Social Anthropology at the University of Cambridge. Her research, principally undertaken in Papua New Guinea and England, has led to the publication of numerous articles and books including on issues of kinship, society, gender and the New Reproductive Technologies.

Julian Thomas is Professor of Archaeology at the University of Manchester. His research is concerned with the Neolithic archaeology of Britain and Europe, and with the theory and philosophy of archaeology.

Thomas Yarrow is a lecturer in social anthropology and human geography in the School of Environment, Natural Resources and Geography, University of Wales, Bangor. He has worked in contract archaeology and has written extensively on archaeological fieldwork practice. His current research focuses on contested ideas of development and modernity around a large scale resettlement project in Ghana.

# Acknowledgements

This volume has been some time in the making. The original impetus to re-visit the relationship between archaeology and anthropology emerged through discussions and debates loosely centred around the archaeological 'theory group', held in the Department of Archaeology, University of Cambridge from around 2002 to 2006. We would like to acknowledge an intellectual debt to all those who participated in these discussions – the sum of which is not reducible to the many (and now rather dispersed) parts that contributed to this. Within the group, over a period of time, frustration grew at the tendency to imagine archaeology's difference from anthropology in terms of a 'deficit'. These frustrations found productive expression through a conference on 'Archaeological Anthropology: experiments in inter-disciplinarity' held at the McDonald Institute for Archaeological Research, University of Cambridge, in May 2005. We would like to express our gratitude to the Department of Social Anthropology, Cambridge and to the McDonald Institute for their assistance (financial and otherwise) in organising that event. We would also like to thank participants and contributors to the event, who stimulated further reflection, and facilitated the emergence of a more coherent intellectual agenda around this theme. In this regard, it is particularly important to acknowledge the input of Manuel Arroyo, Matei Candea and Mark Knight, who gave talks on the day which are not directly represented within the current volume. In the process of turning those proceedings into this edited volume, we have been helped considerably by Clare Litt at Oxbow Books, and by Anwen Cooper and Chantal Conneller. Finally, we would also like to express our sincere thanks to the sixteen anonymous reviewers who gave invaluable feedback on the individual papers.

# 1

# Introduction: archaeological anthropology

*Duncan Garrow and Thomas Yarrow*

## *Introduction*

This book explores the disciplinary relationship between anthropology and archaeology. In doing so, the papers collected within it confront a series of fundamental issues of contemporary relevance to both subjects including the theorisation of temporality and materiality, the construction of disciplinary epistemologies, and the nature of inter-disciplinary encounter.

Archaeology and anthropology arose from a common project which aimed to understand human social and cultural diversity in its totality; since their inception there has been considerable intellectual traffic between the two disciplines. However, in recent years the balance of this relationship has shifted. Whilst the 'post-processual'[1] turn in archaeology has been accompanied by a vigorous interest in anthropological theory and ethnographic insight, anthropological interest in archaeology has waned. Within a range of theoretical and geographical contexts, this has led to a situation in which archaeology has been a net 'importer' of anthropological ideas and descriptions, leading to what a number of archaeologists have described as a theoretical 'trade deficit' (Gosden 1999, Tilley 1996). In this context theoretical convergence seems, paradoxically, to have diminished collaborative possibilities.

This book explores possible reasons for the development of this imbalance, and looks at what it can tell us about the construction of knowledge in both disciplines. Its aim is not to seek synthesis or consensus but to shed critical light on the ways in which disciplinary commitments variously frame, enable or constrain the exploration of what it means to be human, both in the present and in the past. It also asks why this perception of asymmetry persists and what it might reveal about the disciplinary theories and practices of archaeology and anthropology. Anthropologically informed archaeological accounts have become commonplace in recent decades, as archaeologists have sought to exploit ethnographic descriptions as ways of understanding past societies by analogy (e.g. Parker Pearson and Ramilisonina 1998, Schmidt 2000, Wylie 1985) as well as for the wider theoretical possibilities that anthropological approaches open up (e.g. Fowler 2004, Jones 1997, Parker-Pearson and Richards 1994).[2] By contrast, contributors to this volume seek to chart new territory in opening out the possibilities for an 'archaeological anthropology', by which we mean forms of collaboration and relationship that do not straightforwardly reproduce existing understandings of disciplinary hierarchy and asymmetry.[3]

It is important to acknowledge that this book focuses predominantly on the ways in which this relationship has played out in the context of British institutional and theoretical contexts (although see especially Lucas, and Robinson, this volume). Nonetheless, it picks up on wider issues concerning the underlying epistemological foundations of archaeology and anthropology, and the possibilities and problems for collaborative relationships between these. The American 'four-fold' system (of cultural, physical and linguistic anthropology, and archaeology) has often been held up as a model for such collaboration. However Segal and Yanigisako's (2005) recent account points to a situation in the US that is more similar to the European academic context than archaeologists and anthropologists have often cared to admit, characterised, as they and other contributors to the volume suggest, by misunderstandings, ruptures and profound theoretical differences.

We frame the volume as an experimental endeavour in the sense that the form of inter-disciplinary relationship we have in mind does not as we understand it entail the application of 'known' forms of disciplinary expertise to common and agreed upon problems. Indeed for many of the contributors this has entailed a leap of faith; an attempt to reach beyond their own understandings and assumptions of the epistemological and ontological bases of archaeology and anthropology in order to re-perceive the relationships and boundaries between these in new terms.

Importantly the list of contributors to this volume includes people working in both archaeological and anthropological institutional contexts. However, for many, their theoretical and substantive interests blur any neat distinction between the two disciplines. This is reflected in the complex range of disciplinary identities represented by the authors: some were originally trained as archaeologists and have since undertaken mostly ethnographic or anthropologically informed research (Rowlands, Filippucci); others have been led by research from anthropology towards archaeology (Yarrow, Ingold) or from archaeology towards anthropology (Fowler, Robinson); and many have undertaken forms of research that itself transcends any neat categorisation into either discipline (McFadyen, Lucas). We highlight this institutional and theoretical diversity not so much as a representational claim, as for the way in which authors' biographies highlight the fluid and contextual ways in which disciplinary distinctions are evoked and the variety of ways in which people experience, assert or alternatively transcend such boundaries. From this point, it not only follows that archaeology and anthropology represent internally contested and heterogeneous forms of knowledge (Segal and Yanagisako 2005), but also that the boundaries between these can take many forms – a point elaborated by a number of the contributors. Writing of interdisciplinary relations more generally, Barry, Borne and Weszkalnys make the important point that

> Disciplinary boundaries and contents are neither inherently fixed nor fluid; rather they are relational and in formation... (Barry, Born, and Weszkalnys 2008: 27).

For our purposes, it follows that even if it is important to appreciate the sociological and institutional ways in which institutional differences are upheld, the distinctions we are talking about do not delimit sociologically or institutionally discrete groups of people (see also Edgeworth, and Lucas this volume).

Contributors to this volume seek to re-appraise the relationship between the two disciplines in the light of contemporary theoretical debates and preoccupations within both. Although many of the authors are concerned to interrogate the existence and consequences of perceived disciplinary asymmetries, they do so from perspectives that in different ways challenge the widespread belief (within archaeology and anthropology alike) that archaeology has less to offer in the way of theoretical and substantive interest. In framing the problem in these terms, this volume builds on existing accounts of the relationship between archaeology and anthropology but diverges from these in important ways. It thus marks a departure from previous work, which has generally conceived the relationship between the two disciplines in relatively abstract historical and/or theoretical terms. Whilst contributors engage with these theoretical and historical legacies, they focus on how such differences variously manifest themselves in contemporary scholarly attempts to understand human social and cultural diversity.

In his influential book *Anthropology and Archaeology: a changing relationship* (1999), Gosden argues for a re-appraisal of the relationship between archaeology and anthropology along less hierarchical lines, a position that many of the contributors to this volume share. However, Gosden's book is itself conceived as 'an account of anthropological concepts and trends which may be of use to archaeologists' (1999: xi). Thus, to extend his own metaphorical conception of the relationship between these disciplines, the book functions as a major 'importer' of anthropological ideas. From the perspective of a rather different set of theoretical preoccupations, earlier works by Hodder (1982) and Orme (1981) are both founded on, and contribute to, a similar sense of asymmetry. In seeking to move away from the universalising and generalising impulses of earlier processual archaeologists, Hodder set out 'to achieve a more comprehensive review than is at present available of the use of ethnographic data and anthropological concepts' (1982: 9). Orme's interest in the relationship between archaeology and anthropology reinscribed a similar sense of asymmetry by casting anthropology as a source of 'structured comparative studies' (1981: i) from which archaeologists may draw in order 'to look beyond the horizons of their own culture when they seek to understand the raw material of their discipline' (1981: i). In all these accounts anthropology is therefore seen as a source of theoretical inspiration and substantive knowledge for archaeologists, whilst the concomitant possibility of archaeological knowledge inspiring anthropological scholarship is largely overlooked (see Holtorf 2000, Van Reybrouck 2000).

By contrast, the accounts within this volume aim to address the relationship between archaeology and anthropology in ways that seek to speak to debates within both. As Edgeworth points out in his paper, it can be very revealing to highlight the metaphors chosen to describe that relationship. Within the thirteen papers gathered here, we find the following terms used: bridge, blockage, field, pool, hole, wall, connection, disconnection, siblings, rift, fracture, imbalance, trade-deficit, asymmetry, symmetry, locale, spaces, terrain, fuzzy domain, blind-spot, absence, gap. Whilst contributors quite naturally offer a varied and sometimes very different set of perspectives on the nature of the relationship between archaeology and anthropology, a key point to emerge through these is that prevailing ideas within both disciplines have acted to mitigate against an appreciation of what anthropologists might learn from archaeology.

In this context, the question then becomes: how might we render the subject of archaeology relevant *to* anthropology? How do the theories and practices of archaeologists already challenge those of anthropology, or how could they be made to do so? On the other hand, what is it about anthropological descriptions and accounts that make those of archaeologists seem surplus to requirement? Indeed it is the seeming intractability of these problems that provides the very reason for pursuing them. In rendering archaeology anthropologically relevant it may be that anthropology rejuvenates itself in the process, bringing home fresh conceptual 'provisions' (Rosga 2005) in the form of new contexts and conceptual usages.

From the perspective of anthropology, calls for renewed engagement with archaeology, have been relatively few and far between. Ethnographies of archaeological practice constitute one notable area in which engagement has taken place (e.g. Edgeworth 2003, 2006, this volume, Shankland 1996, Yarrow 2003, 2006). However issues of disciplinarity have been relatively un-theorised in this context. At least until the recent 2009 Association of Social Anthropologists conference convened around the theme of 'Anthropological and archaeological imaginations: past, present and future', Ingold has been a notable exception in his insistence and demonstration of how archaeology might inform anthropology. In an editorial for *Man* (1992), he suggested that social and cultural anthropology, together with biological anthropology and archaeology, form a necessary unity and that unless these subjects are brought closer together, we will fail to understand how the practical skills of language, speech, memory and cognition are all developmentally embodied in the human organism through processes that operate at radically different time-scales. Life, he argues, entails the passage of time in ways that anthropological frameworks are ill equipped to understand. From this perspective time and landscape are seen as potentially unifying themes, that archaeologists are uniquely capable of illuminating:

> The specific contribution of archaeology lies in its ability to demonstrate the essential temporality of the landscape regarded as no mere backdrop to human history, but as forever coming into being in and through the activities of the people who live in it ... Archaeologists reading the landscape as historians read documents are alone able to give the

> landscape back to the people to whom it belongs ... Thus anthropology needs archaeology if it is to substantiate its claims to be a genuinely historical science (1992: 694).

Although many of the contributors to this volume are broadly in sympathy with this perspective, a number of them also demonstrate some of the ways in which acknowledgement of difference need not lead to resolution or agreement. Thus, we would argue that a re-appraisal of the relationship between archaeology and anthropology does not entail simply putting 'the other side' across, by showing how archaeological concepts or findings may be of use to anthropologists. Rather it entails analysis and appraisal of the ways in which 'sides' are drawn up in the first place. It follows that we are in agreement with Hodder, when he suggests:

> A productive link between archaeology and anthropology emerges only in a limited space. At a particular contingent moment, there is desire for interaction. What is also of note is that potential for interaction is greatest where the two disciplines are sovereign and bring their own expertise and questions to the table (Hodder 2005: 138).

Tilley (1996) notes that debates about the disciplinary relationship between archaeology and anthropology have generally taken place in relatively abstract terms, and have often recycled idealised representations of what archaeology and anthropology are about. If one result of this has been to reinforce and entrench a boundary, then another has been a general failure to overlook internal diversity on both 'sides'. We would also add that these stereotypical portrayals have acted to stabilise and regulate interactions in ways that have tended to mitigate against new and unpredictable forms of collaboration. Some time ago, Wagner described the problem that 'anthropology is theorised and taught as an effort to rationalise contradiction, paradox and dialectic rather than to trace out and realize their implications' (1975: x). In framing our discussion in terms of an attempt to understand disciplinary differences is there a danger that we reify and codify the practices of both archaeologists and anthropologists and in doing so lend them an unwanted sense of solidity?

By focusing on the myriad ways in which archaeologists and anthropologists are practically and theoretically entwined, we hope not. Our interest is not so much in 'the' relationship between archaeology and anthropology as in the nature of actual and possible relationships between archaeologists and anthropologists. Accordingly contributors examine wider issues of disciplinary difference in the context of particular ethnographic and archaeological research. In doing so, they trace out disciplinary and inter-disciplinary contradictions, paradoxes and dialectics as these are realised in relation to specific kinds of analytic and descriptive problems. In this sense, disciplines are not taken to inhere in codified norms, or bodies of knowledge (cf. Segal and Yanagisako 2005). Rather they are seen as particular forms of embodied practice through which people variously relate to one another and to the artefacts and people they seek to understand.

While this approach leads to a sense of the diversity of disciplinary relationships and interfaces that exist, it also underscores the point that self-awareness about disciplinary forms, methods and assumptions need not equate to self-consciousness or self-referentiality in ways that obscure the various people and artefacts that we study. Ingold cautions against this possibility, alerting us to the danger that within anthropology, the post-structural turn has led to a situation in which increasingly texts '...are studied not for the light they throw upon the world but for what they reveal about the practices of anthropologists themselves and the doubts and dilemmas that surround their work' (Ingold 2007: 89). Such dangers notwithstanding, we follow Riles and Jean-Klein (2005) in suggesting that care for anthropology's disciplinary identity need not be to the detriment of care for those we study. By extension we would add that an explicit understanding of archaeological theory should reveal rather than foreclose understanding of the specific artefacts, sites – and by extension people – that they study. If both archaeology and anthropology are necessarily 'mediative' (Wagner 1975), creating 'cultures' and 'societies' for people who may not imagine – or may not have imagined – their own lives in these terms, then there is no necessary trade-off between appreciation of the forms of inventions that our disciplines take, and appreciation of the inventiveness of those we study. As Wagner suggests, if we do not invent by extending our concepts and categories, then we conceal the inventiveness of others, reducing them to static models.

The anthropologist Viveiros de Castro (2003) argues that the lack of 'native' interpretation (by which he means the interpretation of whoever anthropologists happen to study) has the great advantage of allowing the proliferation of anthropological interpretation of this lack. Extending this argument, it could be suggested that the substantive asymmetry that is often imagined between the discursivity of anthropological subjects and archaeology's lack thereof is not quite the problem that it is often imagined to be. Indeed lack of discourse could from this perspective be imagined as a resource, in the sense that it acts as an imaginative stimulus (a point elaborated in different ways by Lucas, McFadyen, and Yarrow, this volume).

This approach departs from an increasingly widespread view of inter-disciplinary collaboration in which disciplines are taken to be self-evidently distinct bodies of knowledge to be applied as complementary forms of expertise, the whole supposedly emerging as more than the sum of its disciplinary parts. As Barry, Borne and Weszkalnys (2008) argue, this understanding arises as a relatively recent response to intensifying demands for research to be integrated into the wider economy and society, feeding from and into new forms of governmentality. From this view, particularly widespread amongst policy-makers, disciplinary difference is taken as a starting point. As Strathern puts it:

> Interdisciplinarity is premised on the subsequent merging of what once had distinct origins and looks ... to an undivided future (2004: 38).

Earlier concerns with the relationship between archaeology and anthropology arose in a time before which 'inter-disciplinarity' had been elevated from a means of producing new forms of knowledge to an explicit end in itself. Nonetheless earlier scholars have also tended to see the theoretical and methodological differences between these disciplines as the essential problem facing the possibility of collaboration. For example the archaeologist Orme suggested that 'it is feared that the lack of common ground makes it impossible to create a scientific link between the two subjects' (1981: 2), whilst contributors to an edited volume on 'areas of mutual interest' (Spriggs 1977) similarly elucidated how theoretical differences mitigate against the pursuit of common themes.

By contrast, contributors to this volume move towards to an understanding of the activities and interests that constitute such differences in the first place. Here theoretical and methodological distinctions are not seen as barriers to collaboration but as the very factors that enable it. This does not simply equate to the idea that both disciplines have distinctive and complementary theories, through which common problems are pursued. Indeed as some of the contributors suggest, the very 'problems' with which archaeologists and anthropologists grapple are different. In a context in which archaeology and anthropology increasingly draw their inspiration from a common body of theory (Gosden 1999), it might be that their differences are not straightforwardly theoretical.

While the papers collected in this volume shed new light on the relationship between archaeology and anthropology, we also suggest that they contribute to wider discussions of inter-disciplinarity. They do so not by providing general models of disciplinary difference or normative prescriptions for how such encounters should or might take place; rather they contribute to the more modest but arguably more important goal of understanding the disciplinarily specific ways in which such encounters occur. Just as it has been argued (among others by anthropologists) that multi-culturalism runs the risk of reducing culture to forms of difference that are knowable and prescribable in advance (e.g. Benson 1996), when inter- (and multi-) disciplinarity becomes an end point to which, crucially, large sums of money are often attached, then ends become means and all that any given discipline can do is exemplify that difference (cf. Strathern 2004). Whilst this volume emphatically highlights the potential generativity of such disciplinary differences, we would join with Strathern in her recent insistence that the explication of such difference should be taken as an end point rather than a starting point of analysis.

* * *

Perhaps inevitably given the scope of the volume, the papers collected within it engender profound differences of opinion and perspective. Nonetheless, a number of central themes can be discerned within the papers collected below, which intersect at various different levels.

One of the central themes is that of *the transformation of ideas* – the notion that in the movement of ideas between archaeology and anthropology concepts can and often do change, reinvigorating old debates and reinvigorating themselves in the process. Fowler, for example, traces the concept of personhood as it has flowed between the two subjects; Filippucci discusses the impact that archaeological ideas about material traces might have on anthropological thinking; Gosden highlights the benefits that archaeology's sophisticated powers of description might have to offer; and Robinson considers the transformations through which archaeological and ethno-historical evidence must go in order to ensure that a satisfactory account (which incorporates both) can be reached. Perhaps most radically, and somewhat against the grain of many of the other contributors, Ingold's suggestion is that the disciplines of archaeology and anthropology must themselves profoundly change in order to dissolve the unhelpful foundational distinction between past and present.

Alongside these discussions of the transformative flow of ideas between archaeology and anthropology, several papers consider the notion that *history* might also productively be included in this relationship, creating a trialectic flow of ideas (see, for example, papers by Lucas, Feuchtwang and Rowlands, Filippucci, and Robinson). In terms developed in Strathern's concluding remarks, this common concern with history emerges in these papers as a form of 'boundary object'; a construct or concept that is imbued with enough shared meaning to facilitate its translation across those worlds without reducing the difference between these.

The second central thread we wish to highlight – *the conceptualisation of theoretical frameworks* – is closely related to these discussions of interdisciplinary flow. A number of papers within the volume argue that similarities and differences between the two disciplines not only arise from the existence (or absence) of common theoretical frameworks, but also derive from the ways in which 'theory' is discussed, and the place that explicit conceptual frameworks are taken to occupy within the processes by which archaeologists and anthropologists seek to understand and explain. Hence discourses about 'theory' as much as the theories 'themselves' have taken different paths within archaeological and anthropological debates. For example, in their discussions of the concept of 'absence' within archaeology, both Lucas and Yarrow explore how, in the long term, similar theoretical concepts have been made to do different work within archaeology and anthropology. Fowler highlights similar issues in his discussion of the effects on 'theories' as they move in both directions.

A third theme encompasses one area in which archaeology has generally always been seen as having something to bring to the academic table, that of *temporality*. McFadyen discusses the fact that archaeology's long-term vision provides it with unique insight into processes of change, Feuchtwang and Rowlands explore the potential of accounts in which different and multiple conceptualisations of time are included, whilst Ingold considers the possibility of a hybrid discipline which no longer worries about things being 'old' or 'contemporary'.

Perhaps inevitably in any discussion of a relationship, our fourth theme – *the boundary between the two disciplines*, and the manner in which it has been, or might be, conceptualised – is addressed directly by a number of the authors, and also by Strathern and Thomas in their commentary pieces. Both Yarrow and Lucas, for example, consider the important historical and contemporary effects of each discipline's conceptualisation of itself in relation to the other, while Edgeworth describes the productive effects of his own (and others') 'transgression' of that boundary. Thomas argues that we are perhaps wrong to erect a boundary, when that boundary is inevitably fluid and hard to pin down, whilst Ingold suggests that we could perhaps knock it down altogether. Strathern, on the other hand, considers potential 'boundary objects' (both material and immaterial) which might successfully be used in negotiations between the two.

A fifth and final theme developed within a number of papers is that of *absence*. Lucas, McFadyen, Strathern, Thomas and Yarrow all highlight the notion of absence as a central metaphor in the archaeology/anthropology relationship, discussing how conceptualisations of archaeology as having a lack of evidence in comparison to anthropology have led to a perceived *asymmetry* between the two disciplines. Whilst many have viewed this asymmetry in negative terms, Yarrow argues that, in fact, it can be an extremely productive position (a point also discussed by Strathern, Thomas and Lucas). From a slightly different perspective, McFadyen questions our conceptions of absence/presence in the material record, and how we see the relationship between 'past' people and 'present' things; Robinson highlights the fact that perceived absences in both the ethno-historical and archaeological records can actually be complementary rather than contradictory; while Filippucci outlines what she feels archaeology has been able to teach her about her own (and by implication anthropology's) conceptions of the 'fragmented' or 'partial' specifically in relation to social memory.

* * *

Ingold has suggested that anthropology is 'philosophy with the people in' (1992: 696), highlighting the ways in which the concepts that anthropologists generate and the theoretical issues that they seek to resolve arise out of their encounters with people through the process of ethnography. Perhaps from this perspective archaeology could similarly be seen as 'philosophy with the things in', in the sense that the source of its theoretical generativity will always be precisely in the ways in which the artefacts that archaeologists excavate elude and 'stretch' the ideas and concepts with which it starts.

Clearly this is not to suggest that each discipline confines its *interests* to these domains. Archaeologists do not for the most part study things as an end in itself: they examine these things in order to shed light on the contexts in which they were used and the meanings and uses that people gave them. Anthropologists on the other hand primarily adopt an ethnographic methodology that privileges the discursive and non-discursive ways in which people relate to one another, on the basis of speaking and relating to people as 'participant observers'. However if 'people' are in this sense a methodological starting point, this often leads to consideration of the ways people think 'through' these things (Henare, Holbraad, and Wastell 2007) and to a focus on the ways in which artefacts enable and support the relations that they have with one another (e.g. Gell 1997, Miller 1987).

Thus we suggest that archaeology and anthropology do not provide symmetrical or complementary perspectives on a common set of problems. Rather contributors to this volume illustrate how the different epistemological problems that they routinely face lead to different forms of 'routine reflexivity' (Wagner 1975), regardless of the specific theoretical interests at stake. Common theoretical positions have been drawn into the resolution of different sets of epistemological issues arising from the ways in which archaeology and anthropology make the world available to themselves. For all that archaeologists and anthropologists might themselves call an absolute ontological separation between 'people' and 'things' into theoretical doubt (e.g. Bateson 1972, Ingold 1990, Jones 2002, Knappett 2002), their own methodological and epistemological practices do ultimately *start* from this difference (see also Hicks in press, Lucas in press).

We began our *Introduction* by noting that archaeology and anthropology arose from a common project, which aimed to understand human social and cultural diversity. While the paths of these two subjects may have diverged somewhat over the past century or so, this broad goal, ultimately, arguably remains the same for both. Our aim in this book, as we have said already, is not to bring the two subjects 'back together'; given the often productive tensions that disciplinary differences engender, this would seem problematic. However, we certainly do hope that by examining in detail the relationship between the two subjects and the various methods and theories that each employs – in imagining an 'archaeological anthropology' – this volume will raise some interesting questions and future possibilities for both disciplines.

*Notes*

1 'Post-processual' archaeology was a movement which began in the early 1980s (see Trigger 2006, Ch. 8 for a summary). Essentially, post-processual archaeologists began to incorporate post-modern thought into archaeological theory. Amongst many things, they sought to recover past meanings and symbolism, viewed material culture as 'active' within society, and self-consciously recognised archaeology as a subjective interpretive process.

2 The journal *Anthropological Archaeology*, founded in 1982, has published a range of papers describing and demonstrating how anthropological descriptions and approaches can be of use to archaeologists. As Gosden (1999) notes, these have generally been undertaken in ways that extend 'processualist' concerns to use ethnography as the basis of describing and documenting cross-cultural generalisations about human behaviour.

3 In a recent paper Hodder (2005) uses this term in making a similar challenge to the asymmetrical way in which these disciplines are conventionally imagined to relate.

## *References*

Barry, A., G. Born, and G. Weszkalnys 2008. Logics of interdisciplinarity. *Economy and Society* 37: 20–49.

Bateson, G. 1972. *Steps to an Ecology of Mind.* Chicago and London: University of Chicago Press.

Benson, S. 1996. Asians Have Culture, West Indians Have Problems: Discourses in Race Inside and Outside Anthropology. In T. Ranger, Y. Samad, and O. Stuart (eds) *Culture, Identity and Politics*. Aldershot: Avebury.

Edgeworth, M. 2003. *Acts of Discovery: An Ethnography of Archaeological Practice.* Oxford: Archaeopress.

Edgeworth, M. 2006. *Ethnographies of Archaeological Practice: Cultural Encounters, Material Transformations.* Lanham, New York, Toronto and Oxford: Altamira Press.

Fowler, C. 2004. *The Archaeology of Personhood: An Anthropological Approach.* New York and London: Routledge.

Gell, A. 1997. *Art and Agency: An Anthropological Theory*. Oxford: Oxford University Press.

Gosden, C. 1999. *Anthropology and Archaeology: a Changing Relationship*. London: Routledge.

Henare, A., M. Holbraad, and S. Wastell. 2007. *Thinking Through Things: Theorising Artefacts Ethnographically*. London and New York: Routledge.

Hicks, D. in press. The Material Culture Turn. In D. Hicks and M. Beaudry (eds) *The Oxford Handbook of Material Culture Studies*. Oxford: Oxford University Press.

Hodder, I. 1982. *The Present Past: An Introduction to Anthropology for Archaeology*. London: Batsford.

Hodder, I. 2005. An Archaeology of the Four-Field Approach in Anthropology in the United States. In D. A. Segal and S. J. Yanagisako (eds) *Unwrapping the Sacred Bundle: reflections on the disciplining of anthropology*, 126–140. Durham and London: Duke University Press.

Holtorf, C. 2000. Making Sense of the Past Beyond Analogy. In A. Gramsch (ed.) *Vergleichen als archäologische Methode: Analogien in den Archäologien*, 165-175. Oxford: Archaeopress.

Ingold, T. 1990. Society, Nature and the concept of Technology. *Archaeological Review from Cambridge* 9: 5–18.

Ingold, T. 1992. Editorial. *Man (New Series)* 27: 693–696.

Ingold, T. 2007. Anthropology is Not Ethnography. *Proceedings of the British Academy* 154: 69–92.

Jones, A. 2002. *Archaeological Theory and Scientific Practice.* Cambridge: Cambridge University Press.

Jones, S. 1997. *The Archaeology of Ethnicity: Constructing Identities in the Past and Present.* London and New York: Routledge.

Knappett, C. 2002. Photographs, Skeumorphs and Marionettes. Some thoughts on Mind, Agency and Object. *Journal of Material Culture* 7: 97–117.

Lucas, G. in press. Fieldwork and Collecting. In D. Hicks and M. Beaudry (eds) *The Oxford Handbook of Material Culture Studies*. Oxford: Oxford University Press.

Miller, D. 1987. *Material Culture and Mass Consumption.* Oxford: Basil Blackwell.

Orme, B. 1981. *Anthropology for Archaeologists: An Introduction.* London: Gerald Duckworth.

Parker Pearson, M. and Ramilisonina 1998. Stonehenge for the ancestors: the stones pass on the message. *Antiquity* 72: 308–26.

Parker Pearson, M. and C. Richards (eds) 1994. *Architecture and Order: Approaches to Social Space.* London: Routledge.

Riles, A., and Jean-Klein, I. 2005. Introducing Discipline: Anthropology and Human Rights Administrations. *Political and Legal Anthropology Review* 28: 173–202.

Rosga, A. 2005. The Traffic in Children: The Funding of Translation and the Translation of Funding. *Political and Legal Anthropology Review* 28: 173–202.

Schmidt, R. A. 2000. Shamans and northern cosmology: the direct historical approach to mesolithic sexuality. In R. A. Schmidt and B. L. Voss (eds) *Archaeologies of Sexuality*. London and New York: Routledge.

Segal, D. A., and S. J. Yanagisako. 2005. Introduction. In D. A. Segal and S. J. Yanagisako (eds) *Unwrapping the Sacred Bundle: reflections on the disciplining of anthropology*. Durham and London: Duke University Press.

Shankland, D. 1996. Çatalhöyük: the anthropology of an archaeological presence. In I. Hodder (ed.) *On the Surface: Çatalhöyük 1993–1995*. Cambridge: McDonald Institute for Archaeological Research and the British Institute of Archaeology at Ankara, 349–58.

Spriggs, M. 1977. *Archaeology and anthropology: areas of mutual interest*. Oxford: British Archaeological Reports.

Strathern, M. 2004. *Commons and Borderlands: Working Papers on Interdisciplinary, Accountability and the Flow of Knowledge*. Oxford: Sean Kingston Publishing.

Tilley, C. 1996. *An Ethnography of the Neolithic: Early Prehistoric Socieities in Scandanavia*. Cambridge: Cambridge University Press.

Trigger, B. 2006. *A history of archaeological thought* (second edition). Cambridge: Cambridge University Press.

Van Reybrouck, D. 2000. Beyond ethnoarchaeology? A critical history on the role of ethnographic analogy in contextual and post-processual archaeology. In A. Gramsch (ed.) *Vergleichen als archäologische Methode: Analogien in den Archäologien*, 39-52. Oxford: Archaeopress.

Viveiros de Castro, E. 2003. (anthropology) AND (science). *Manchester Papers in Social Anthropology* 7.

Wagner, R. 1975. *The Invention of Culture*. Chicago and London: University of Chicago Press.

Wylie, A. 1985. The Reaction Against Analogy. *Advances in Archaeological Theory and Method* 8: 63–111.

Yarrow, T. 2003. Artefactual persons: the relational capacities of persons and things in the practice of excavation. *Norwegian Archaeological Review* 36, 65-73.

Yarrow, T. 2003. Sites of Knowledge: Different Ways of Knowing an Archaeological Excavation. In M. Edgeworth (ed.) *Ethnographies of Archaeological Practice: Cultural Encounters, Material Transformations*. Lanham, New York, Toronto and Oxford: Altamira Press.

2

# Not knowing as knowledge: asymmetry between archaeology and anthropology

*Thomas Yarrow*

## *Asymmetry*

This paper explores the widespread understanding that archaeology and anthropology exist in an asymmetrical relationship to one another characterized by an archaeological theoretical 'trade deficit'. While the paper questions the basis on which this asymmetry has been imagined, it also explores the effects that this has had. Through examining how archaeologists and anthropologists have historically imagined the relationship between these disciplines, the paper sets out to understand the implications of this asymmetry for both. Rather than seek to redress this asymmetry, it demonstrates how asymmetry has in fact been archaeologically productive, leading to an explicitness about archaeological procedures and their limits and concomitantly to an openness to other disciplinary insights. On the other hand, for anthropologists the perception of asymmetry simultaneously arises from and leads to assumptions that have foreclosed certain lines of enquiry, relating to a disciplinary narrowing of horizons.

In the introduction to *An Ethnography of the Neolithic*, Tilley starts by describing an archaeological fantasy that is revealing of wider assumptions both about the kinds of knowledge that archaeologists and anthropologists produce and about the relationships between these disciplines:

> I have sometimes imagined what it might be like to be transported back into the past in a time capsule, to arrive somewhere in Sweden during the Neolithic and to be able to observe what was really going on, stay for a couple of years and then return to the late twentieth century and write up my ethnography. I have thought how much richer, fuller and more sophisticated the account would be. I would actually know who made and used the pots and axes, what kind of kinship system existed, how objects were exchanged and by whom, the form and nature of ethnic boundaries, the details of initiation rites, the meaning of pot designs and the significance of mortuary ceremonies (Tilley 1996: 1).

Tellingly, whilst such archaeological fantasies of time-travel are common, the corresponding fantasy does not seem to capture the anthropological imagination: anthropologists, to my knowledge, do not often fantasize about the possibility of travelling forwards in time and viewing their own field-sites through the material remains of the people who once lived there. Why might this be? My suggestion is that the asymmetry is indicative of a wider perception, shared by archaeologists and anthropologists alike, that the 'partial' and 'fragmented' nature of archaeological evidence leaves archaeologists with less to say about the issues of social life taken to be at the heart of both disciplines (see also Lucas, and Filippucci, this volume).

Tilley himself deconstructs aspects of this common archaeological fantasy of time travel, arguing that archaeological and anthropological accounts are both constructed from different elements that need to be interpreted and made sense of in similar ways (cf. Lucas 2005). However, as he rightly points out, such fantasies are indicative of a wider *perception* of disciplinary asymmetry, that underscores the theoretical 'trade' between archaeologists and anthropologists: archaeologists commonly imagine themselves to lack the kinds of theories and insights that anthropologists can provide, and routinely draw on these in their descriptions and analyses of the past. Despite some notable exceptions (e.g. Ingold 1992, Layton 2008) anthropologists rarely seem to incorporate the ideas, theories or descriptions of archaeologists in their own accounts.

In pointing to the mutual entanglements of archaeology and anthropology, the archaeologist Gosden (1999) argues that it would be impossible to imagine the discipline of archaeology in the absence of anthropological writing on subjects such as gift exchange, kinship, symbolism and gender. By the same token he also suggests that archaeological writing has contributed to the discipline of anthropology in terms of an understanding of long-term chronology. Yet even if we accept that this is the case, an almost total lack of any explicit anthropological acknowledgement of this 'debt' remains puzzling.

Despite a long history of archaeological claims for the potential theoretical and substantive contribution of the discipline, a disciplinary 'trade deficit' (Gosden 1999, Tilley 1996) therefore seems to persist. As Tilley has noted, a concern with the 'mutual relationship' has taken place almost exclusively within archaeological discussions, suggesting that 'while most archaeologists read some anthropology, few anthropologists seem to read any archaeology' (1996: 2). Some time ago Rowlands and Gledhill similarly described this imbalance of interest, suggesting that Childe was 'the only archaeologist that many anthropologists in this country ever admit to having read' (1977: 144). Tellingly, archaeologically authored introductions to anthropology such as Orme's (1981) *Anthropology for Archaeologists*, Hodder's (1982a) *The Present Past* and more recently Gosden's *Archaeology and Anthropology* (1999), do not have their counterparts within anthropology.

Interestingly the recent theoretical convergences that have taken place around areas such as material culture, gender and the body do not seem to have fundamentally altered this relationship. While Hodder points to the origin of many of the theoretical frameworks that have informed these developments in disciplines such as philosophy and sociology, he notes that within archaeology '...there was still a "looking over ones shoulder" at cultural anthropology to see how translations and applications of the ideas had been made in a related discipline' (2005: 132).

The fact that anthropological accounts of the disciplinary relationship are rare is itself symptomatic of a perceived asymmetry on the part of anthropologists. Until recently, Ingold has been a notable exception in his insistence that 'anthropology needs archaeology if it is to substantiate its claims to be a genuinely historical science' (1992: 64). In the wake of the 2009 Association of Social Anthropology conference on 'Archaeological and Anthropological Imaginations: past, present and future', this may be set to change. Calls during this conference, by archaeologists and anthropologists, for an increasing anthropological sensitivity to archaeological thinking are clearly to be welcomed. Nonetheless, it is important to be sensitive to the terrain in which such exchanges take place and the asymmetries – actual or perceived – that have attended these.

Taking up one of the central themes of the volume, this paper explores the question of why this perception of asymmetry persists and asks what this might reveal about the disciplinary theories and practices of archaeology and anthropology. In pursuing this line of enquiry my intention is not to 'overcome' this asymmetry. Rather I want to examine its theoretical and practical consequences. This entails considering the possibility that an archaeological perception of absence – whether of data or theory – is itself constitutive of a distinctive disciplinary ontology and that as such it need not be considered in negative terms. Thus my aim is not simply to put 'the other side', by showing how archaeological concepts or findings may be of use to anthropologists. Instead my analysis highlights how archaeologists and anthropologists have imagined how 'sides' are drawn up in the first place. Rather than pre-suppose a distinction between 'archaeology' and 'anthropology' as the self-evident starting point of analysis, I suggest that this distinction is itself an artefact of various debates within and between these disciplines; as such it has taken a variety of different forms.

My own interest is not to highlight where archaeologists might fruitfully contribute theoretical or substantive insight (as other contributors to this volume do convincingly). Rather I want to argue that successive theoretical developments have been driven by a perception of disciplinary asymmetry with regards to anthropological knowledge practices. To borrow again from the imagery of theoretical 'trade', my intention is not to engage in this trade but to try to understand the underlying ideas and assumptions that have driven it.

In this way, I hope to contribute to a 'symmetrical' (Latour 1987, Latour 1993) understanding of the issue of asymmetry. Rather than take asymmetry as the taken for granted starting point of analysis I suggest that it needs to be accounted for in terms of an analysis of the practices, relationships and ideas that produce it. This entails an attempt to understand the ways in which a disciplinary sense of deficiency is itself constitutive of particular forms of interpretation and analysis and how a *perception* of absence has proved a stimulus to very different kinds of theorising.

## *Connections and disconnections*

Through an exploration of the shifting ways in which the relationship between archaeology and anthropology has been understood, I seek to highlight the different theoretical positions that have variously been used to explain and redress a sense of theoretical 'deficit'. In doing so, I do not propose to provide a comprehensive historical overview of disciplinary trends (see Gosden 1999, Hodder 1982a, Orme 1981, Trigger 1989) but rather seek to shed light on the *terms* within which the relationship between archaeology and anthropology has been explicitly conceived within archaeological and anthropological debates.

As a number of authors have argued (Gosden 1999, Ingold 1992, Orme 1981, Wylie 1985), the social evolutionism of the late nineteenth and early twentieth century provided a theoretical context in which the study of past and present societies were seen to be inextricably linked. In attempting to account for contemporary cultural and biological diversity archaeological and anthropological material was treated equally, in the sense that both shed light on the common processes of evolution by which that difference came about. In other words a single theoretical framework both necessitated and enabled the collection of different kinds of data. Because archaeology and anthropology were not at this point institutionalised as distinct disciplinary endeavours, the issue of their 'relationship' did not explicitly arise.

The formal distinction between archaeology and anthropology can be seen to arise from a set of methodological and institutional changes that took place during the beginning of the twentieth century: the creation of distinct departments and the formalization, differentiation and specialization of different fieldwork techniques acted as processes of 'mediation' and 'purification' (Latour 1993) through which the disciplinary distinction between archaeology and anthropology became increasingly solidified (Lucas in press).

As others have suggested, these distinctions were institutionalized and theoretically elaborated in different ways within North American and British traditions. In North America there has tended to be a closer relationship between archaeology and anthropology, a fact that Hodder (1982a: 38) attributes in part to the ways in which the presence of native American societies created awareness of the potential for using ethnographic analogies to explain archaeological phenomena. In this way the 'direct historic' approach developed in the 1930s and 1940s, based on the assumption that the accounts of ethnographers and ethno-historians could be fruitfully employed as a way of understanding archaeological remains within the same area (see also Robinson this volume). From this perspective Taylor claimed that the archaeologist was 'Jekyll and Hyde, claiming to 'do' history but 'be' an anthropologist' (1948: 6). Archaeology was squarely defined in anthropological terms, as part of the four-fold approach that persists today (Segal and Yanagisako 2005).

In the UK, by contrast, the functionalism of anthropologists such as Radcliffe-Brown and Malinowski led to the increasing institutionalization of disciplinary difference in ways that mitigated against collaboration. In the wake of Radcliffe-Brown's rejection of 'conjectural history', Childe (1946) sought to reinstate a sense of archaeology's distinctive contribution to the study of humanity, arguing that an understanding of the contemporary functions of particular social institutions has to be complemented by an understanding of their historical evolution in order to move beyond a descriptive technique to the classificatory science that he proposed should be the common aim of both. In this way the essential parity between archaeology and anthropology was seen to derive from methodological differences that acted to define a particular kind of collaborative relationship. Anthropological participant observation led to an integrative model of society that archaeologists could not hope to replicate on the basis of the archaeological record. Nonetheless, archaeological evidence was seen to enable an historical analysis of the development of social institutions that would provide 'a valid clue to the rank of a contemporary culture and its position in an evolutionary sequence' (Childe 1946: 250). Archaeology and anthropology were seen as 'complementary departments of the science of man related in the same way, as palaeontology and zoology in the science of life' (1946: 243).

In a similar vein the British archaeologist Hawkes (1954) proposed a form of collaboration that depended on the pursuit of common aims and objectives through complementary and distinctive forms of theory and methodology. Hawkes' famous 'ladder of inference' points to the paradox that whilst archaeology is defined in terms of the study of people in the past, the ideas, beliefs and social and political arrangements of these people have to be inferred in their absence. While he suggests that it is relatively easy to infer the techniques by which archaeological artefacts are produced and even the subsistence economies that would have prevailed, he is more pessimistic about the possibility of inferring information about social and political organisation on the basis of the kind of information that prehistorians have access to. Thus he asks rhetorically:

> If you excavate a settlement in which one hut is bigger than all others, is it a chief's hut so you can infer chiefship, or is it really a medicine lodge or a meeting hut for initiatives, or a temple? [...] How much could the archaeologist of the future infer, from his archaeology alone, of the Melanesian institutions studied by Malinowski? (1954: 161–162).

Hawkes' recognition of the limits of archaeological evidence led him to suggest that anthropologists could provide information on non-material aspects of culture that the archaeological record does not preserve. Anthropology, in other words, provided the means by which 'gaps' in the archaeological record could be 'filled in'. In this view anthropology not only provided information of use in the reconstruction of past societies, but also, by implication, a *model* of society and in this sense 'the making more fully anthropological' of the past was taken as the goal of archaeology.

In different ways, the accounts of both Childe and Hawkes thus locate an underlying asymmetry between archaeology and anthropology in the unequal access that these disciplines respectively have to 'society'. In the light of subsequent critiques, it could rightly be objected that this apparent asymmetry rests on a misunderstanding in so far as both these theories reify and objectify society as a knowable, tangible and holistic entity (see Holtorf 2000, Van Reybrouck 2000). Not only does this negate the theoretical and ethnographic work of anthropologists in making this entity appear, it also effectively places ethnographically informed knowledge beyond critical scrutiny as a form of 'information' or 'data'.

Whether or not we agree with the theoretical positions adopted by these archaeologists, however, is not really the point. Rather I want to direct attention beyond their own explicit understandings in order to suggest that this *perception* of asymmetry in fact had productive effects. In particular, the understanding that archaeological data was in certain respects deficient stimulated archaeologists to look beyond the discipline in search of new ideas and theories. In doing so, the understanding was that knowledge could be 'applied' from anthropologically 'known' contexts, to archaeological contexts that were less well known. Yet this language of 'application' conceals the extent to which archaeological borrowings of anthropological ideas change and extend them. Regardless of the view one takes of Hawkes' 'ladder of inference', it makes explicit limits to archaeological data and the interpretations these give rise to. By contrast, during the same period, anthropological faith in functionalist models and methods tended to preclude understanding of the limits to interpretation and analysis. Consequently both Hawkes' and Childe's assessment that these limits lay in the absence of historical consideration, went largely unheeded. A holistic vision of society had its counterpart in a holistic vision of the discipline of anthropology, in ways that precluded the historical dimension that archaeological accounts could have helped provide.

With the advent of 'processual' or 'new' archaeology during the 1960s, a rather different conception of the relationship between archaeology and anthropology developed. By contrast to the 'culture-history' approach of archaeologists such as Childe, processual archaeologists responded to a perceived disciplinary asymmetry by arguing that rather than simply contribute to the explanation of difference within particular locales, archaeologists should seek to generate general laws to explain broader processes of cultural evolution. For Binford, the North American archaeologist at the forefront of this approach, processualism was explicitly seen to provide a framework within which archaeology could make a more significant contribution to anthropology. In outlining his vision of 'Archaeology as Anthropology', Binford aimed, 'to escalate the role which the archaeological discipline is playing in furthering the aims of anthropology and to offer suggestions as to how we, as archaeologists, may profitably shoulder more responsibility for furthering the aims of our field' (1962: 217). In this view, anthropology was defined as the attempt to explain the total range of physical and cultural similarities and differences within the entire temporal span of human existence. Since most of the evidence for this difference was understood to be available only through an examination of archaeological material, this was seen to give archaeology an advantage in one key respect:

> We as archaeologists have available a wide range of variability and a large sample of cultural systems. Ethnographers are restricted to the small and formally limited extant cultural systems (1962: 224).

While Binford argued that archaeologists could not dig up social systems or ideology, he saw these limitations to be offset by the extensiveness of the archaeological record and its ability to enable examination of long-term processes of cultural change in ways that the ethnographic record does not allow. Moreover he was far less circumspect about the possibility of inferring reliable information about the functioning of extinct cultural systems on the basis of archaeological remains than many of his archaeological and anthropological contemporaries, suggesting that:

> Granted we cannot excavate kinship terminology or a philosophy but we can and do excavate the material items which functioned together with these more behavioural elements within the appropriate cultural sub-systems. The formal structure of artefact assemblages together with the between element contextual relationships should and do present a systematic and understandable picture of *the total extinct* cultural system (1962: 218–9).

Within America this processual or 'new' archaeology paved the way for increasing collaboration between archaeologists and anthropologists. In particular evolutionary anthropologists such as Lee and DeVore (1968) saw the potential for synergy in terms of their aims of understanding processes of cultural development through the generation of generalized laws. Thus in the introduction to *Man the Hunter* Lee and DeVore's (1968) proposition that the emergence of economic, social and ideological forms is as much a part of human evolution as developments in human anatomy and physiology, provides the context in which archaeological and anthropological approaches are seen to provide different forms of data on the same basic problems.

Within the UK, by contrast, the advent of the 'new' archaeology was accompanied by a conception of the relationship between archaeology and anthropology in rather different terms (cf. Gosden 1999, Hodder 1982a). While Clarke's 'analytic archaeology' shared many of the aims and objectives of Binford's processualism, his assertion that 'archaeology is archaeology is archaeology' (1968: 13), contrasted with Binford's view of 'anthropological archaeology'. Renfrew's 'social archaeology' (1984) was heavily influenced by American processualists such as Binford but also differed in highlighting the distinctiveness of an archaeological approach in terms of an emphasis on material culture. While Renfrew's (1973) edited volume *The Explanation of Culture Change* sought to bring archaeological and anthropological perspectives to bear on a set of common issues, the concluding remarks written by the structuralist anthropologist Edmund Leach serve to highlight how far apart – from an anthropological perspective, at least – these disciplines were imagined to be.

For Leach the search by processual archaeologists for general laws of cultural and social behaviour directly contradicted anthropological evidence for the infinite variability of social and cultural life, a view reflected in his candid assessment of the conference from which papers from the volume were drawn:

> All along contributors were making remarks that could only make sense if you were to take as given a unilinear theory of social development of a kind which the social anthropologists finally abandoned about forty years ago. As far as social anthropology is concerned, I appreciate your difficulty as archaeologists; you would like to use the data of ethnography to give fresh blood to your archaeological remnants. Used with great discretion I believe that ethnographic evidence can in fact help you to do this; but far too many of the participants at the seminar seemed to think that the analogies between ethnographic society and archaeological society are direct ... i.e. that 'primitive' societies from the 20th century can be treated as fossilized survivals from proto-historical or even palaeolithic times (Leach 1973: 761).

In this vein he denigrated the functionalism of such 'new' archaeology and the concomitant emphasis on economic subsistence, settlement patterns and demography, arguing these overlooked the more fundamental issue of what was 'in the minds of the actors' (1973: 769), namely, religion and politics.

Leach's critiques of the processual archaeology of the time were in many ways pertinent and despite his own assessment of the barriers to meaningful dialogue, his intervention was important in helping to push archaeological theory in new directions. Foreshadowing later post-processual archaeological critiques, he highlighted the problems of treating the ethnographic record as 'information' and of reducing 'primitive' contemporary societies to the status of fossilized survivals of an archaeological past. However in overstating the theoretical and methodological scope of anthropology (a point to which I return below), I suggest that Leach mistook the *perception* of deficit that archaeologists themselves articulated, with a literal absence of insight or understanding. Taking archaeological assessments of the 'partiality' of their data at face value, he overlooked the space that this *perception* creates for archaeological theorisation and imagination.

Whether or not we find the theories of processual archaeologists convincing is not really the point. What I want to highlight is rather the way in which an archaeological perception that kinship and philosophy are 'missing', opens up a space for ideas and data beyond the discipline. The middle range theory of processual archaeologists departs from earlier archaeological formulations such as those proposed by Childe and Hawkes in imagining ethnography not as a source of 'direct' analogies but as the basis upon which cultural universals could be derived. Nonetheless both constitute theoretical and analytical frameworks that effectively account for what archaeology is imagined to lack. Although the theoretical context had changed considerably, a holistic and systemic vision of society opened up archaeological interest in anthropology, whilst closing down anthropological interest in archaeology. Understanding society as a holistic entity, albeit one that was symbolically rather than functionally integrated, led to the anthropological perception of disciplinary self-sufficiency, leaving little space for archaeological ideas.

Against this backdrop, contributors to a conference that later appeared as a volume edited by Spriggs (1977a) sought to build a theoretical 'bridge'. Although different contributors had a range of perspectives on the form that this might take, the reconciliation of structuralism and Marxism was seen by many to provide a theoretical framework within which archaeological and anthropological perspectives could be reconciled. Spriggs, for example, advocated a form of structural Marxism suggesting that in contrast to the ahistorical structuralism of anthropologists such as Leach and Levi-Strauss this would create a more comprehensive theory, allowing the explanation of socio-cultural change in ways that 'could provide a useful framework for archaeologists, anthropologists and historians' (1977b: 5). In a similar vein Rowlands and Gledhill argued that in anthropology history was treated at best as 'background' and analysis of more dynamic social processes remained limited, and hence:

> At the present time ... the responsibility lies with archaeologists to develop theoretically the structural models that will be required to achieve recently stated aims concerning the explanation of long-term processes of change (1977: 155).

Marrying structuralist concerns with socially and culturally embedded systems of symbolisation and meaning with a Marxist concern with historical transformation, was thus seen by a number of British archaeologists of the late 1970s to create the theoretical context in which both archaeology and anthropology could contribute to the elucidation of long-term cultural change on the basis of equals. As with earlier paradigms, the development of a new theoretical framework came largely from within archaeology and was concerned to redress an existing relationship of theoretical inequality.

While Hodder's 'post-processual' or 'contextual' archaeology (1982a, 1982b) arose in a similar theoretical context, it took a rather different form. In critiquing the processual concern to develop universal laws of cultural change, Hodder drew extensively from anthropological theory and description. Yet anthropology was not seen (as it was for Binford) as a source of information from which to formulate empirically testable hypotheses relating to processes of cultural evolution. Rather ethnography was taken to constitute a heuristic resource, enabling archaeologists to step outside the western frameworks within which archaeological interpretation otherwise proceeds. In proposing that all interpretations of the past necessarily draw on theoretical and common sense assumptions of people in the present, Hodder implicitly recognised a disciplinary asymmetry: the present was knowable in ways that the past was not.

This provided the rationale for drawing on ethnographic analogies and undertaking ethno-archaeology 'in order to clothe the skeleton remains of the past in the flesh and blood of living, functioning, acting people' (1982b: 12). As such, Hodder continued to define archaeology partly in terms of anthropologically derived models of society, by which archaeological data was seen to offer less than the complete picture. This perception of the missing subject (see Lucas, this volume) stimulated a renewed interest in the conditions under which analogies could legitimately be asserted between past and present societies. In contrast to earlier theorists, Hodder also highlighted the possibilities of such absences and gaps in their own right. In particular he argued that lacking direct access to people, archaeologists are forced to concern themselves with the non-discursive aspects of culture, leading to a unique perspective on social and cultural processes: 'material things can say things which words cannot or do not' (1982b: 207), Hodder suggested, arguing in a related way that, 'As archaeologists we are not digging up what people said and thought but we are digging up a particular type of expression, which, through its ambiguity and subtlety, is powerful and effective' (1982b: 207).

Archaeological understandings of the relationship between archaeology and anthropology have therefore taken a variety of forms, reflecting different perspectives on what the aims and theoretical objectives of these disciplines should be. This account provides an admittedly partial view that is intended to illustrate some of the assumptions that have informed the ways in which archaeologists and anthropologists have imagined their relationships to one another. While different theorists have located this difference in a range of ways, my suggestion is that archaeology has tended to be defined (by archaeologists as well as anthropologists) in terms that make it appear to lack the kinds of insights, knowledge or data that anthropology can provide. I am not proposing that there is any inherent reason why this has to be the case, nor am I suggesting that it could not be otherwise. Nonetheless the account highlights how the perception of archaeological deficit has acted as a stimulus to make explicit the distinctive nature of archaeological theories and practices.

## *Asymmetry re-considered*

In his 'concluding remarks' discussed above, Leach (1973) explicates what he sees as some of the key disciplinary differences between archaeology and anthropology, in terms of a set of asymmetries. In particular he suggests that whilst anthropologists can observe the workings of social systems 'first hand', archaeologists are only capable of observing these on the basis of 'patterned residues' and hence their meaning must 'forever remain a mystery' (1973: 767). Archaeology, he suggests, is properly about the study of people, yet the nature of the archaeological record is such that most aspects of human behaviour remain absent: things may reflect the meanings that people give them but are not the meanings themselves; moreover since archaeological evidence is necessarily 'partial' many of these are lost. Thus archaeology's absence of people is seen as the basis of a theoretical asymmetry between the two: whilst anthropologists can study people directly, archaeologists can only study them on the basis of the things they left behind.

In the light of subsequent theoretical discussions, this view can be called into question on a number of different levels. In particular archaeologists, anthropologists and social studies of science have questioned both the absolute ontological separation of people and things (e.g. Henare, Holbraad, and Wastell 2007, Ingold 2000, Latour 1999, Law 1994, Strathern 1988, Strathern 1990), and the idea that the material world simply reflects passively the meanings and ideas of society (e.g. Gell 1997, Miller 1987, Miller 1998). If the thoughts and ideas of people do not end at their corporeal limits (Bateson 1972, Ingold 2000) then Leach's characterisation of the distinction between archaeology and anthropology as that between the study of people and the study of things, seems problematic. And if the material world actively participates in the construction of meaning and the distribution of agency (e.g. Holtorf 2002, Knappett 2002, Latour 1993) then a methodology that focuses on material culture seems at least in theory to have as much to say about that meaning as one that focuses on the spoken words and actions of 'people' (Hicks in press). Recent calls for a 'symmetrical' archaeology (Shanks 2007, Webmore 2007, Witmore 2007) make precisely this point.

Moreover, whilst Leach characterises the archaeological record as 'partial', subsequent theoretical discussions call into question his assumption that anthropologists themselves have access to the kinds of social 'wholes' that his account seems to presuppose. If, as a number of anthropologists have argued (e.g. Gupta and Ferguson 1997, Marcus 1998, Thornton 1988, Tyler 1986) the social 'whole' is an artefact of ethnographic description, as opposed to an actually existing empirical reality, then it would seem that Leach is guilty of conflating anthropological models, descriptions and theories with 'the people' these purport to explain. The archaeologist Groube (1977) makes a similar point about the abstraction necessarily entailed in ethnographic description, suggesting, after Durkheim, that 'the immobile man he studies is not man'. Seen in this light, anthropologists do not straightforwardly study 'people': they study the societies and cultures they belong to. As a comment on the process of synthesis and abstraction entailed in arriving at these analytic entities, Wagner suggested some time ago that in their representations of 'culture', anthropologists, 'keep the ideas, the quotations, the memoirs, the creations, and let the people go' (1975: 26).

Seen from this perspective it could be argued that anthropologists do not have a privileged position when it comes to studying people; they simply face a different set of interpretive issues. Whilst archaeologists may lament an absence of 'people', the presence of living, talking humans simply brings to light a different set of methodological and interpretive problems. Indeed the (broadly post-structuralist) writing of a number of anthropologists (e.g. Clifford 1986, Fortun 2001, Gupta and Ferguson 1997, Rabinow 1986) has increasingly made some of these evident, through calling into question the means by which anthropologists elicit and represent the meanings and beliefs of those they study. In place of the image of the social 'whole', anthropologists have pointed to the partial and selective view that ethnographic fieldwork necessarily entails, to the ways in which the subjectivity of the fieldworker conditions the nature of his/her findings, and to the necessarily selective process by which disparate utterances, situations and acts are pieced together through writing and analysis. From this perspective it would seem that rather than a relationship of asymmetry there in fact exists one of difference. Yet to argue in this way that disciplinary imbalance is illusory, is to fail to account for the importance of this *sense* of imbalance and the theoretical and practical consequences this has had (and arguably continues to have) for archaeologists and anthropologists respectively.

If archaeologists confront a different set of interpretive and methodological problems then they have also developed a distinct set of theoretical 'solutions'. Over the years, archaeologists have made these explicit in a variety of different ways, suggesting for example, that an archaeological perspective leads to a unique understanding of processes of social evolution (e.g. Binford 1962), long-term change (e.g. Rowlands and Gledhill 1977), and material culture (e.g. Hodder 1982b). In these various ways, archaeology has brought unique insights on the wider issue of what it means to be human.

To be clear, I am not suggesting that these ideas are inherently less interesting, significant or valid than the kinds of theories produced by anthropologists. Rather my suggestion is that many of these developments have been driven precisely by the *sense* that archaeology lacks certain kinds of knowledge. This sense of deficiency or lack has taken a variety of different forms. Clearly not all of these are equally useful and I am not straightforwardly advocating any one of them. My point is that much archaeological thinking constitutes a particular knowledge of absence, that is not the same as an absence of knowledge.

In making this point I wish to draw an analogy between archaeologists and the Baktamin of Papua New Guinea, for whom Strathern (re-interpreting the work of Frederik Barth) has suggested: 'the knowledge that they are lost is not, so to speak, lost knowledge, it is knowledge about absence, about forgetting and about an unrecoverable background' (1991: 97–8). Confronted by a sense of loss, Baktamin initiators, she suggests, are forced into making the knowledge that they retain work, not by filling in the gaps, but by borrowing from the knowledge of their neighbours and by making that which remains do the differentiating work it has to. In this way they are forced to make what is to hand carry the marks of a lost complexity:

> Perhaps seeing their own activities like so many particles of dust against a huge background of ignorance is what spurs their efforts. This ignorance is not of the unknowable: it is of what has been dropped from their repertoire, the intervening particles that once completed what is now left (1991: 98).

With this image of knowledge in mind, we might seek to reappraise the idea that the 'partiality' of archaeological data is the problem that many have imagined it to be. Although archaeological thinking has often been premised on an illusory conception of the 'completeness' of anthropologically informed models of society, the attendant sense of archaeological 'partiality' has been productive. As the preceding account demonstrates, it has acted as a wellspring for theoretical innovation, prompting archaeologists to re-imagine their own discipline in new terms and to critically appraise archaeological practices and assumptions; it has led to forms of analysis and theorising that are explicit in the acknowledgement of their own limits; and it has led to a focus on aspects of social life that are often overlooked.

As such, the *perception* of theoretical deficit has led to a kind of disciplinary reflexivity that anthropology has tended to lack. While many anthropologists would argue that the very strength of the discipline lies in its capacity to use other people's views of the world as a way of unpicking its own epistemological foundations, such openness has been largely absent in anthropological engagements with archaeology. Going against the grain of prevailing thought in both disciplines, my suggestion is that the perception of disciplinary asymmetry has actually been far more of a problem for anthropology than it has for archaeology.

## Acknowledgements

A number of people's comments and criticisms on earlier drafts of this paper have been of great help in formulating and refining the argument and in this respect I wish to thank Matt Candea, Chantal Conneller, Anwen Cooper, Chris Fowler, Duncan Garrow, Tim Ingold and Gavin Lucas. The article was written and researched with the support of a Leverhulme Early Career Fellowship.

## References

Bateson, G. 1972. *Steps to an Ecology of Mind.* Chicago and London: University of Chicago Press.

Binford, L. 1962. Archaeology as Anthropology. *American Antiquity* 28, 217–225.

Buchli, V. 2006. Architecture and Modernism. In C. Tilley, W. Keane, S. Kuchler, M. Rowlands, and P. Spyer (eds.) *Handbook of Material Culture*, 254–302. London: Sage.

Childe, V. G. 1946. Archaeology and Anthropology. *Southwestern Journal of Anthropology* 2, 243–251.

Clarke, D. 1968. *Analytic Archaeology*. London: Methuen.

Clifford, J. 1986. On Ethnographic Analogy. In J. Clifford and G. Marcus (eds.) *Writing Culture: The Poetics and Politics of Ethnography*, 98–122. Berkeley and Los Angeles: University of California Press.

Fabian, J. 1983. *Time and the other. How anthropology makes its object.* New York: Columbia University Press.

Fortun, K. 2001. *Advocacy After Bhopal: Environmentalism, Disaster, New Global Orders.* Chicago and London: University of Chicago Press.

Gell, A. 1997. *Art and Agency: An Anthropological Theory*. Oxford: Oxford University Press.

Gosden, C. 1999. *Anthropology and Archaeology: a Changing Relationship*. London: Routledge.

Groube, L. M. 1977. The Hazards of Anthropology. In M. Spriggs (ed.) *Archaeology and Anthropology: areas of mutual interest*, 69–91. Gloucester: BAR.

Gupta, A., and J. Ferguson. 1997. "The Field" as Site, Method and Location in Anthropology. In A. Gupta and J. Ferguson (eds.) *Anthropological Locations: Boundaries and Grounds of a Field Science*, 1–29. Berkeley: University of California Press.

Hawkes, C. 1954. Archaeological Theory and Method: Some Suggestions from the Old World. *American Anthropologist* 56, 155–68.

Henare, A., M. Holbraad, and S. Wastell. 2007. *Thinking Through Things: Theorising Artefacts Ethnographically*. London and New York: Routledge.

Hicks, D. in press. The Material Culture Turn. In D. Hicks and M. Beaudry (eds.) *The Oxford Handbook of Material Culture Studies*. Oxford: Oxford University Press.

Hodder, I. 1982a. *The Present Past: An Introduction to Anthropology for Archaeology*. London: Batsford.

Hodder, I. 1982b. *Symbols in Action*. Cambridge: Cambridge University Press.

Hodder, I. 2005. An Archaeology of the Four-Field Approach in Anthropology in the United States. In D. A. Segal and S. J. Yanagisako (eds.) *Unwrapping the Sacred Bundle: reflections on the disciplining of anthropology*, 126–140. Durham and London: Duke University Press.

Holtorf, C. 2000. Making Sense of the Past Beyond Analogy. In A. Gramsch (ed.) *Vergleichen als archäologische Methode: Analogien in den Archäologien*, 165-175. Oxford: Archaeopress.

Holtorf, C. 2002. Notes on the life history of a pot sherd. *Journal of Material Culture* 7, 49–71.

Ingold, T. 1992. Editorial. *Man* (New Series) 27, 693–696.

Ingold, T. 2000. *The Perception of the Environment: essays in livelihood, dwelling and skill.* London: Routledge.

Knappett, C. 2002. Photographs, Skeumorphs and Marionettes. Some thoughts on Mind, Agency and Object. *Journal of Material Culture* 7, 97–117.

Latour, B. 1987. *Science in Action: How to Follow Scientists and Engineers Through Society*. Cambridge, Mass.: Harvard University Press

Latour, B. 1993. *We Have Never Been Modern*. London: Harvester Wheatsheaf.

Latour, B. 1999. *Pandora's Hope: Essays on the Reality of Science Studies*. London: Harvard University Press.

Law, J. 1994. *Organizing Modernity*. Oxford: Blackwells.

Layton, R. 2008. Crisp snapshots and fuzzy trends. In D. Papagiani, R. Layton, and H. Maschner (eds.) *Time and Change: archaeological and anthropological perspectives*. Oxford: Oxbow.

Leach, E. 1973. Concluding Remarks. In C. Renfrew (ed.) *The Explanation of Culture Change: models in prehistory*, 761–771. Gloucester: Duckworth.

Lee, R. B., and I. DeVore. (eds). 1968. *Man the Hunter*. Chicago: Atherton.

Lucas, G. 2005. *The Archaeology of Time*. London and New York: Routledge.

Lucas, G. 2009. Fieldwork and Collecting. In D. Hicks and M. Beaudry (eds.) *The Oxford Handbook of Material Culture Studies*. Oxford: Oxford University Press.

Marcus, G. 1998. *Ethnography Through Thick and Thin*. Chichester: Princeton University Press.

Miller, D. 1987. *Material Culture and Mass Consumption*. Oxford: Basil Blackwell.

Miller, D. 1998. Why Some Things Matter. In D. Miller (ed.) *Material Cultures: Why Some Things Matter*, 3–21. London: University of Chicago Press.

Orme, B. 1981. *Anthropology for Archaeologists: An Introduction*. London: Gerald Duckworth.

Rabinow, P. 1986. Representations are Social Facts: Modernity and Post-Modernity in Anthropology. In J. Clifford and G. Marcus (eds.) *Writing Culture: The Poetics and Politics of Culture*, 234–262. Berkeley and Los Angeles: University of California Press.

Renfrew, C. 1973. *The Explanation of Culture Change: Models in Prehistory*. London: Duckworth.

Renfrew, C. 1984. *Approaches to Social Archaeology*. Edinburgh: Edinburgh University Press.

Rowlands, M. and J. Gledhill. 1977. The Relation between Archaeology and Anthropology. In M. Spriggs (ed.) *Archaeology and Anthropology: Areas of Mutual Interest*, 143–158. Gloucester: BAR.

Segal, D. A., and S. J. Yanagisako. 2005. Introduction. In D. A. Segal and S. J. Yanagisako (eds.) *Unwrapping the Sacred Bundle: reflections on the disciplining of anthropology*. Durham and London: Duke University Press

Shanks, M. 2007. Symmetrical Archaeology. *World Archaeology* 39, 589–596.

Spriggs, M. 1977a. *Archaeology and Anthropology: Areas of Mutual Interest.* Oxford: British Archaeological Reports

Spriggs, M. 1977b. Where the Hell are We? (Or a Young Man's Quest). In M. Spriggs (ed.) *Archaeology and Anthropology: Areas of Mutual Interest*, 3–17. Oxford: British Archaeological Reports.

Strathern, M. 1988. *The Gender of the Gift: Problems with Women and Problems with Society in Melanesia.* Berkeley, Los Angeles and London: University of California Press.

Strathern, M. 1990. Artefacts of History: Events and the Interpretation of Images. In J. Siikala (ed.) *Culture and History in the Pacific*, 25–41. Helsinki: Finland Anthropological Society.

Strathern, M. 1991. *Partial Connections.* Savage, Maryland: Rowman and Littlefield.

Taylor, W. W. 1948. *A Study of Archaeology*. Menasha: The Memoir series of the American Anthropology Association 69.

Thornton, R. 1988. The Rhetoric of Ethnographic Holism. *Cultural Anthropology* 3, 285–303.

Tilley, C. 1996. *An Ethnography of the Neolithic: Early Prehistoric Socieities in Scandanavia.* Cambridge: Cambridge University Press.

Trigger, B. 1989. *A History of Archaeological Thought.* Cambridge: Cambridge University Press.

Tyler, S. A. 1986. Post-Modern Ethnography: From Document of the Occult to Occult Document. In J. Clifford and G. Marcus (eds.) *Writing Culture: The Poetics and Politics of Ethnography*, 122–140. Berkeley and Los Angeles: University of California Press.

Van Reybrouck, D. 2000. Beyond ethnoarchaeology? A critical history on the role of ethnographic analogy in contextual and post-processual archaeology. In A. Gramsch (ed.) *Vergleichen als archäologische Methode: Analogien in den Archäologien*, 39-52. Oxford: Archaeopress.

Wagner, R. 1975. *The Invention of Culture.* Chicago and London: University of Chicago Press.

Webmore, T. 2007. What about 'one more turn after the social' in archaeological reasoning? Taking things seriously. *World Archaeology* 39, 563–578.

Witmore, C. L. 2007. Symmetrical Archaeology: excerpts of a manifesto. *World Archaeology* 39, 546–562.

Wylie, A. 1985. The Reaction Against Analogy. *Advances in Archaeological Theory and Method* 8, 63–111.

# 3

# Triangulating absence: exploring the fault lines between archaeology and anthropology

*Gavin Lucas*

## *The cracks beneath the surface: inter-disciplinary fault-lines*

Archaeology is a new discipline at the University of Iceland; when the programme was started in 2002, archaeology was placed with the Department of History in the Humanities Faculty. Recently, the university was in the process of re-structuring its academic divisions and in this re-organization, archaeology considered moving to join anthropology in the Social Sciences. I mention these events because the institutional location of archaeology raises issues of disciplinary affiliation for any university, even if other, totally unrelated reasons might weigh equally or more so in such contexts. In our discussions in Iceland, opinions varied on the intellectual kinship of archaeology, but mostly they were drawn towards three predictable options: history, anthropology/ethnology or geology/geography. In practice, the responses were strongest from the first two, one person arguing that archaeology *is* history, and another suggesting that archaeology is part of the fourfold field of anthropology. Unsurprisingly perhaps, the proponents of these extremes were not archaeologists, but a historian and anthropologist respectively.

In many ways such debates profit us little because disciplinary connections (or boundaries for that matter) are multiple and shifting; besides which, at the end of the day, most of us like to think that 'archaeology is archaeology is archaeology', in the oft-cited words of David Clarke (1973). It is always a dangerous game to define what distinguishes one discipline from the next – exceptions can always be found, and in these times of dismantling disciplinary borders, such attempts are doubly problematic. Throughout this paper I have largely chosen to keep the language of disciplinary identity but I would hope the reader will see that the issues are really about different modes of scientific operation; as a generalization, different disciplines have different modes of operation and if I use disciplinary labels as shorthand for these modes, this in part reflects the historical traditions of the disciplines. In this paper, I want to explore a few of the connections between archaeology and anthropology along a very specific path; a similar discussion could be had about archaeology's relationship to history which would raise other issues, but that is another story.

It would be difficult, even foolish to deny the extensive overlap between many of the goals and broader theoretical frameworks of archaeology and anthropology. However, I would like to suggest that such broader conceptual similarities – which indeed have a long history – conceal a troubling rift between the two disciplines at an empirical level: the differences between ethnographic and archaeological contexts. My argument here is fairly simple: by stressing the broader conceptual similarities while ignoring the empirical differences, one is faced with precisely a situation where archaeology can appear unequal or asymmetrical with respect to anthropology, simply because the archaeological record is encouraged to do work it is not up to. I have no wish to erect a barrier between archaeology and anthropology. Rather I examine the nature of the possible bridges – and blockages – that exist between the two disciplines. Yet, I would suggest that such similarities between the subjects have been forged largely in the context of abstract, over-arching perspectives (which doubtless extend beyond archaeology and anthropology to encompass all the human and social sciences) in a top-down approach. This ignores the empirical nature of each discipline and favours homogenization, even conventionalization (Murray, in Lucas 2007: 162–3). In contrast, a bottom-up approach maintains the heterogeneity of each subject while creating the possibility of empirically traceable connections; following Latour, one could also characterize this as an attempt to 'flatten' the discourse between the disciplines in order to avoid easy abstractions that paste over the empirical rifts, rather than work at suturing them (Latour 2005).

I call the differences between the archaeological and ethnographic contexts rifts or fractures because it is the discontinuities that I want to emphasize here rather than the continuities. By stressing discontinuity, it is hoped that any links can be given a more secure hold. While the sections below discuss the fractures, they equally attempt to find ways to repair them, producing a creative tension. My aim is to avoid a situation where such discontinuities are transformed into an asymmetry, by keeping my discourse as 'flat' as possible. These fractures are manifold but in order to put some kind of limits to this discussion, my focus here will be specifically on the differences between archaeology on the one hand and on the other, the branch of anthropology concerned with material culture. This is simply because this is the sub-field of anthropology which is the closest, empirically, to archaeology. Both share the same ostensible object of study, i.e. material culture – and it is the empirical differences that concern me here. Wherever I refer to the terms anthropology or ethnography in this text, I will therefore be primarily referring to an ethnography of material culture, unless otherwise stated. This latter should not necessarily be equated with the general inter-disciplinary field of material cultures studies (as centred at UCL; e.g. see Miller 1998; Buchli 2002), for in many ways the point of this paper could alternatively be defined as an exploration into the discontinuities of such a broad field as material culture studies. In the following three sections, I will examine the sites of three fractures between archaeology and ethnography as they concern material culture.

## *Missing persons: the absent subject*

One of the experiences one has when excavating a well-preserved site is the feeling of emptiness – even though you may be surrounded by fellow diggers, to work in a space with high standing walls, floors and internal features engenders an impression of being in someone else's space, where that someone is absent – that is, the people who once built and inhabited this space however many years ago. One gets the same feeling as a tourist walking around sites like Pompeii or Herculaneum or even more recent ghost towns of the 20th century like Chernobyl or Oradour. With varying degrees of effort however, the feeling can be elicited from almost any archaeological site or find, such as holding a 10,000 year old flint axe that was made by another person and is the only testament to their existence. This experience of emptiness, of lack, becomes articulated into the more dispassionate, conventional goal of archaeology: to get at 'the Indian behind the artefact' (Braidwood 1958: 734).

Perhaps the first and most apparent difference between archaeology and an ethnography of material culture is this question of the missing person. This creates something of an ostensible reversal of goals: while archaeology conventionally tries to get to people *through* things, an ethnography of material culture, superficially at least, tries to get to things *through* people.[1] This reversal of the proximate and ultimate subjects of archaeology and ethnography has a certain irony but also a certain asymmetry; for the ethnographer, both terms (people and things) are present, but for the archaeologist, the ultimate term (people) is always missing. One of the ways, in fact probably the most common way archaeologists have dealt with this absent subject is to conflate it with another, equally absent but also abstract subject where the goals of archaeology and ethnography converge: Culture, or Society (or any variation thereof such as Identity, Consumption, etc). As Kent Flannery put it, the aim of archaeology is to get at the *system* behind both the Indian and the artifact (Flannery 1967: 120). In this sense, both archaeology and ethnography are chasing abstract subjects, entities that occupy a different ontological plane to their empirical field of people and things (Figure 3.1). Whether one agrees that there is a final, shared goal where the two disciplines converge or not is not the primary issue here; rather it is the fact that for archaeologists, the absence of people is somehow rescued (and thus its relevance suppressed) by this ultimate reference, a social or cultural abstraction.

So what are the consequences of the absent subject in archaeology? In some ways, the answer to this question can be found in the history of theoretical debate in archaeology since the 1950s. Writing in 1954, Christopher Hawkes' 'ladder of inference' linked the opposition of materialism and idealism to the distinction between things and people creating an epistemological scale, where knowledge about past peoples through things was most secure at the bottom of the ladder with materialist explanations such as economy and technology and least viable when it came to understanding past ideas and beliefs (Hawkes 1954). Another way of framing this problem in North America was in

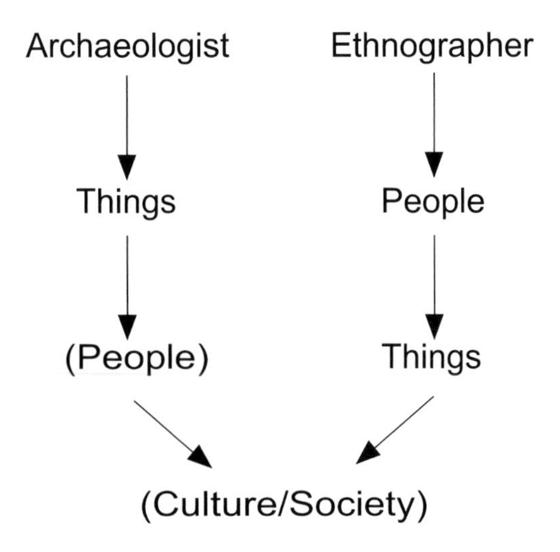


*Figure 3.1. The intentional structure of archaeology and anthropology; bracketed terms denote empirical absence.*

terms of an interpretive dilemma: archaeology performs best when it is exploring the formal and physical properties of objects through typology and material science, but this also says very little about the people who made these things. Yet as soon as one wants to go beyond this kind of 'artefact physics', one also loses any firm ground to validate interpretation (DeBoer and Lathrap 1979: 103; Wylie 1989). Despite these doubts over the limits of archaeological inference, since the 1960s archaeologists have been pushing ever wider the horizon of what things can reveal about people, scaling and ultimately discarding Hawkes' ladder. In this respect, a number of critical ideas emerged which restructured the disciplinary intentions, as depicted in Figure 3.1.

The first idea is crystallized in the work of Hodder in the 1980s with the notion of material culture as both meaningfully constituted and active. Hodder helped to develop the 'linguistic turn' within archaeology, arguing that ideologies or cosmologies can be read from material culture; he also stressed that things are not simply inert matter, reflecting the intentions and actions of people but mutually constitutive of such actions and intentions (Hodder 1982). Objects become agents. The second idea, largely coming through gender and queer theory, is almost the inverse – turning people into objects, by focusing on the embodiment of people, and how their identity and actions are inextricable from their physical form – and how the boundaries between the body and material culture are fluid and transgressive rather than stable and fixed (e.g. Meskell 1996). The third and final idea is the most recent, and comes through the development of symmetrical archaeology by Shanks, Olsen and others, influenced by Latour, where the very distinction between people and things is challenged and in its place, more hybrid collectives are proposed (see the recent collection of papers in the journal *World Archaeology* volume 39(4)). If one accepts these arguments, then clearly the articulation expressed at the beginning of this section is misleadingly simplistic; archaeologists do not aim to get at people *through* things any more than ethnographers try to get at things *through* people, since the very separation is dubious if not false. The absence of people is then, in itself, not damning – in the first place, people are present (as bodies or remnants of bodies), but more importantly, the absence of people is *potentially* no different to the absence of any thing which does not preserve, such as organic materials and so on. The fragmentary nature of the archaeological record should not overstate the absence of people over the absence of other things. Symmetry is restored – not just between people and things, but between archaeology and ethnography. Or is it?

## *From statics to dynamics: what happened in prehistory*

The notion that both people and things share agency and embodiment, that what really matters is the way in which agency is distributed within collectives or how people and things constitute each other in practice are ideas eminently suited for exploration in ethnographic contexts. The ethnographer can observe such interactions, can observe the performativity of people and things; if performance or practice is the site where people and things are constituted, then ethnographers have a front row seat. The archaeologist on the other hand, is not only not in the front row, she or he is not even in the theatre; they do not observe practice or performance, they have to infer it from the arrangement of things and bodies left lying on the stage which constitute the archaeological record. They arrive after the performance is over. There is a real difference between a skeleton and a living human being, between objects in action and objects lying inert, buried under the soil. It appears as if we have just substituted one absence for another – performance for people.

This second fracture is a traditional one for archaeologists insofar as it can be mapped onto the classic distinction of statics and dynamics articulated by Binford (1981; 1983). Binford argued that the principal problem facing archaeologists was how to infer dynamic processes from a static archaeological record; his solution, the Rosetta Stone of archaeological translation, was middle range theory which uses actualistic studies, particularly ethno-archaeology, to create bridges between dynamics and statics. However one judges the merits of middle range theory – and it has been hotly contested (e.g. Kosso 1991; Tschauner 1996) – it does not alter the basic temporal relation of the archaeologist to their data. Ethnography and even ethno-archaeology observe events in motion – observe change – while archaeologists can only infer it from spatial configurations of matter. If we want to find a way to cross the divide between the ethnographic and archaeological records, we have to deal with this problem of change.

One solution is to argue that the rate of change inferable from the archaeological record is quite different to that in ethnography, because of the different tempos – archaeology deals with slow or long-term processes often imperceptible at the level of human experience. Indeed, it has been argued that the nature of the archaeological record is such that it necessarily entails such a conclusion (Bailey 1981). Such a solution then, questions the idea that archaeologists and ethnographers are looking at the same kinds of phenomena; if they are not, then the ostensible asymmetry between archaeology and ethnography indicated in the theatrical metaphor which opens this section is open to doubt (see also Yarrow, this volume). The lateness of archaeologists to a performance is not so much an obstacle to understanding but is an advantage, insofar as it allows one to have a different temporal perspective, which is impossible for the ethnographer. For even though the ethnographer can directly observe change, this is confined to a comparatively small temporal frame; traditional ethnographies accentuated this with an emphasis on synchronic studies, but even the more diachronic or historical ethnographies which emerged in the later twentieth century are still relatively restricted in time scale, compared to archaeology.

However, even if such arguments are plausible, they do not resolve the original problem. In fact they accentuate it: archaeology, unlike ethnography, does not observe change, it only infers it, at whatever scale it happens to unfold. The first step towards a realistic resolution to this problem is to abandon the original distinction between statics and dynamics. It takes little imagination to realise that the ethnographic record is not exclusively defined by things happening – just as often as not, there is stasis. Nothing happens in a locked store room. To be sure, this is partly a question of perspective – some things happen much slower than others, often too slow to be perceived and of course periods of stasis are always temporary, even if they can last a relatively long time. But then the same applies to the archaeological record – it is never static, as Schiffer reminds us, but always undergoing transformation of some kind (Schiffer 1987). If the static-dynamic distinction is no longer helpful, especially in distinguishing the archaeological from the ethnographic context, then it opens the way for a new rapprochement between archaeology and ethnography. This comes by re-considering the nature of material collectives. Not only should we break down the distinction between people and things (as discussed in the last section), we also need to break down the distinction between objects and events.[2] This separation of object and event lies at the heart of our conventional characterization of archaeological inference, which depends on the distinction of static objects from their dynamic context. The one has survived (static object), the other has not (dynamic context). If however, one argues for the inseparability of objects and events, then the issue is not about how objects act/perform, but rather about the distribution of the *power* to act/perform within and between collectives. It is more like exploring the entropy or inertia in material organizations, the *latent* rather than manifest side of action or performance (Lucas 2008).

A room, with nobody inside and where nothing happens, is still actively charged – its material configuration gives it certain propensities for resisting or engendering change, which is not simply about the physical properties of entropy (i.e. decay or preservation) but cultural properties too. To re-align the British traffic system or electrical system to continental configurations would meet resistances of quite a different scale to re-aligning shoe or clothing sizes. These propensities are, in principle, just as observable in the archaeological record as in the ethnographic present, and reinforce symmetry between material culture in the archaeological and ethnographic records. Rather than inferring dynamic events from static things, archaeology can explore the latent forces that bind things into material assemblages or collectives.

## *Doubling the present: the archaeologist and their object*

However, while this may have removed the problem of observing events or change as a site of difference between archaeology and ethnography (or at least relocated it onto another distinction, that between latent and manifest agency), it does not remove the problem of a temporal fracture between present and past. If the last section partially sutured the rift between the temporalities of material culture in archaeological versus ethnographic contexts, in this section one faces the temporality of the relationship between the respective disciplines and their subject. Ethnographers exist contemporaneously with their object while archaeologists are always out-of-phase, existing in an anachronous rather than synchronous relationship to their object. As Edmund Leach once suggested, archaeologists are always too late (Leach 1973). To continue with the theatrical metaphor of the last section, while both an ethnographer and archaeologist can study the latent performance of an empty stage, the difference is that the ethnographer knows that someone will or might be coming on to stage any minute, whereas the archaeologist knows that everyone has already left the building. This might seem contradicted in archaeologies of the contemporary past where archaeologists study contemporary society (the classic example being Rathje's Garbage Project – see Rathje and Murphy 1992; also Buchli and Lucas 2001), but in a sense this temporal anachronism is essential to the archaeological process. Indeed, the very act of archaeological intervention guarantees this insofar as the site is put under a form of temporal quarantine. This is why such archaeologies of supermodernity work best on sites of disaster – sites which have undergone a sudden and rapid change leading to abandonment, catapulting them into a past which is yet still contemporary (Gonzalez-Ruibal 2008). But such archaeologies of the contemporary past are largely archaeologies of destruction not because destruction is a condition of supermodernity, but because such archaeologies can only effectively operate where a sudden and rapid abandonment of a site has happened. Disaster is not a characteristic of 'our time', but rather defines the possibility of an archaeology (as opposed to ethnography) of 'our time'.

The difference between material culture in an archaeological as opposed to a strictly ethnographic context, revolves around this issue of temporal fracture between researcher and their subject. However, even this is not quite so simple, for in fact an archaeologist is a contemporary of their object of study as much as the ethnographer – these remains, these artefacts exist in the archaeologist's present, otherwise the archaeologist could not study them. Binford said as much, many years ago (Binford 1983: 19). The difference lies not so much in the temporal fracture between the researcher and their object, but in the temporal fracture within the object itself in archaeology: these remains exist in the present but they are also of the past. This fracture creates something of a paradox for archaeology but also one that has obvious parallels in everyday life: memory objects (e.g. see Olivier 2008 for an interesting discussion of this theme). Souvenirs, keepsakes, mementoes – in fact almost any object – have memories attached to them: they exist in the present but are of (and hence evoke) another present, an absent present we call the past. The same is true of archaeological finds. Can archaeology be likened to an ethnography of an absent present?

Ironically, this recalls Fabian's charge against traditional ethnography and its 'denial of coevalness'; that is, a refusal to see the ethnographic subject as existing in the same time as the ethnographer (1983: 31). While ethnography may have moved on, with archaeology this separation of two presents – the archaeological present and past present – remains a fundamental premise. The troubling implications of this 'doubling of the present' are brought out when we look at the respective modes of operation for archaeology and ethnography. The two disciplines used to share a similar practice, that of collecting things. However, in the transition towards a professional and academic discipline over the late 19th and early 20th century, the two subjects diverged; ethnography became defined primarily by a mode of intervention called participant observation, while archaeology developed principles of stratigraphic excavation (Lucas 2010). Where ethnography dropped its interest in things, archaeology continued to collect, only under increasingly more rigorous and systematic conditions. What is significant is that even with the return to material culture within anthropology since the late 1980s, it has maintained its distanced position with respect to things, studying material culture through participant observation rather than collection. The reasons for this divergence in modes of intervention are complex (see Lucas 2009), but not of immediate concern; more relevant are the questions of what this difference means and how it is significant.

If one looks at collecting in the context of early ethnography, what is interesting is how conflicting value systems created tensions for the proto-ethnographer. Objects became ethnographic artefacts primarily through an act of exchange – commonly but not exclusively a commodity transaction. This set up potential conflicts of meaning around objects as they embodied multiple values according to the contexts they circulated in prior to becoming ethnographic artefacts (e.g. see Thomas 1991; Gosden and Knowles 2001). The same problematic status now attaches to archaeological objects that may have come through the (illicit) antiquities trade and there is an explicit ambivalence about how an archaeologist should respond to such artefacts. Now it may be that ethnographers simply do not need to collect objects to conduct the kind of material culture studies that thrive today, but this does not negate the fact that collecting would still be highly problematic. Issues of ownership and appropriation weigh much more heavily on objects given/received through an act of exchange, than objects found through an act of excavation. This is not to ignore the fact that even within archaeology, questions of ownership are not at stake; they clearly are, but this operates in a different sphere. Because by and large, ethnographic objects are acquired through acts of exchange while archaeological objects are acquired through acts of discovery, it sets up a very different chain of relations between people and things.

It is difficult to reconcile this difference. The only way one could do that, is to argue that the archaeologist, in the act of discovery, establishes some kind of posthumous relationship to the long dead people of the culture or society under investigation, so that discovery is in fact, a concealed or special form of exchange. In terms of the social function of archaeology, this is not so strange – even if the objects have been forgotten in an absolute sense, the archaeological operation can be viewed as a form of memory work nonetheless, a redemptive act on behalf of the dead (Tarlow 2006). But in arguing this – a not implausible case, since the issue meets concrete expression in the context of unearthing the skeletons of these same people – we are forced to re-introduce the concept of the absent subject with which we started this discussion and as a consequence, we are locked in a circle.

This circularity is reinforced theoretically when considering the nature of archaeological objects as memory objects. Any memory-object, because of its split temporality (existing *in* the present but *of* the past), is also ineluctably linked to a split subject – either the same subject as they once were and as they now are (e.g. mementos from my childhood), or different subjects such as dead ancestors and living descendants (e.g. mementos of my dead father). Now in most cases, archaeology is not an excavation into one's own past, though in principle this is perfectly feasible; so with archaeology, the artefact as a split memory-object also entails a double subject – the archaeologist in the present and the people in the past. While the one is indeed contemporary with the object of archaeology, the object itself surely implies another, missing subject; in short, an absent present entails an absent subject.

## *Triangulating absence*

In exploring the empirical differences between the archaeological and ethnographic contexts, I have pursued the sites of three fractures: the absent subject, the problem of change and anachronism. As this discussion has unfolded, these three fractures appear to be interlinked in important ways, and in fact may even be locked into a triangular relation to each other. In stepping back, these three fractures could be redefined as variations on a single theme: absence. The absent subject, the absent event and the

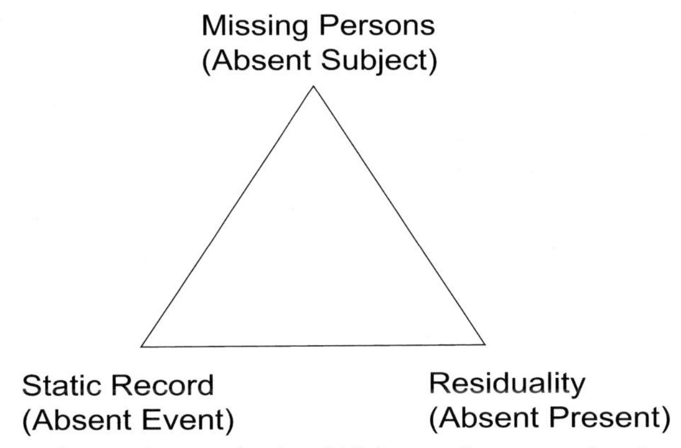


*Figure 3.2. Triangulating Absence: the threefold fracture between archaeology and anthropology.*

absent present, each term dialectically unfolding from the previous one (Figure 3.2). The absent subject referred to the missing people in archaeology and how conventionally, archaeology tries to get at the 'Indian behind the artefact'. The absent event refers to the fact that archaeologists do not observe change or things happening in time, they have to infer it – infer events from material residues of events, infer time from space. Finally, the absent present refers to the fact that the archaeologist is only partially a contemporary of the object of her study – that in fact, this object, as a residue, has a split temporality which entails an absent present, which we conventionally call 'the past'.

This absence, which lies at the heart of archaeology, is in a way what will always separate it from ethnography. But such differences should not be read as asymmetries; in a way, the problem of asymmetry emerges precisely when archaeology tries to mimic other disciplines such as anthropology as if the empirical and operational differences were unimportant. One cannot escape these absences which haunt archaeology, and rather than deny them or downplay them, archaeology needs to seriously engage with what they mean for the discipline. For they surely suggest important ontological differences between the archaeological and ethnographic records, which must impact on the sorts of narratives and interpretations the two disciplines can present. The first place to start might be to jettison the very term 'absence' which in itself conceivably adds to this perception of asymmetry. It served a useful purpose in this paper by highlighting distinctions, but new terms may come to take on more relevance, such as those of latent and manifest agency. If there is one point I would like to repeat in ending this paper, it is that for all the shared aims and ideas drawn from a broader body of social theory, each discipline has different modes of operation, which relate to the nature of their immediate subject. While the cross-disciplinary rise of material culture studies has been intellectually important, the field is not homogeneous. The practical and empirical differences between two disciplines like archaeology and ethnography should not be overlooked and in fact, in paying closer attention to them, it may be possible to build much better bridges. At the very least, it removes the possibility of asymmetry rendered as inequality, and may help to forge new and mutual forms of respect.

*Notes*

1 This is of course somewhat of a simplification – in ethnographies of material culture, both people and things are equally present to the observer and it is their relationship that is of primary concern, even if it is things which are often foregrounded as the primary subject (e.g. see Henare *et al.* 2006).

2 Here the philosophical literature is of great relevance, particularly Whitehead ([1920] 2004).

## References

Bailey, G. 1981. Concepts, Time-scales and explanations in economic prehistory. In A Sheridan and G.N. Bailey (ed.) *Economic Archaeology*, 97–118. Oxford: British Archaeological Reports.

Binford, L. 1981. Behavioural Archaeology and the Pompeii Premise. *Journal of Anthropological Research* 37 (3), 195–208.

Binford, L. 1983. *In Pursuit of the Past. Decoding the Archaeological Record.* Berkeley: University of California Press.

Braidwood, R. 1958. J. Vere Gordon Childe 1892–1957. *American Anthropologist* 60, 733–6.

Buchli, V. 2002. *The Material Culture Reader.* Oxford: Berg.

Buchli, V. and Lucas, G. (eds) 2001. *Archaeologies of the Contemporary Past.* London: Routledge.

Clarke, D. L. 1973. Archaeology: the loss of innocence. *Antiquity* 47, 6–18.

DeBoer, W. R. and Lathrap, D.W. 1979. The making and breaking of Shipibo-Conibo Ceramics. In C. Kramer (ed.) *Ethnoarchaeology: Implications of Ethnography for Archaeology*, 102–38. Columbia University Press: New York

Fabian, J. 1983. *Time and the other. How anthropology makes its object.* New York: Columbia University Press.

Flannery, K. 1967. Culture History v. Culture Process: A Debate in American Archaeology. *Scientific American* 217, 119–22.

Gonzalez-Ruibal, A. 2008. Time to destroy. An archaeology of supermodernity. *Current Anthropology* 49(2), 265–266.

Gosden, C., and Knowles, C. 2001. *Collecting Colonialism: Material Culture and Colonial Change.* Oxford: Berg.

Hawkes, C. 1954. Archaeological Theory and Method: Some Suggestions from the Old World. *American Anthropologist* 56, 155–168.

Henare, A., M. Holbraad and S. Wastell (eds.) 2006. *Thinking through things: theorising artefacts ethnographically.* London: Routledge.

Hodder, I. 1982. *Symbols in Action.* Cambridge: Cambridge University Press.

Kosso, P. 1991. Middle range theory as hermenuetics. *American Antiquity* 56(4), 621–7.

Latour, B. 2005. *Reassembling the Social.* Oxford: Oxford University Press.

Leach, E. 1973. Concluding Address. In C. Renfrew (ed.) *Explanation of cultural change: models in prehistory*, 761–771. London: Duckworth.

Lucas, G. 2007. Visions of Archaeology. An interview with Tim Murray. *Archaeological Dialogues* 14(2), 155–177.

Lucas, G. 2008. Time and the Archaeological Event. *Cambridge Archaeological Journal* 18(1), 59–64.
Lucas, G. 2010. Fieldwork and Collecting. In D. Hicks and M. Beaudry (eds.) *The Oxford Handbook of Material Culture Studies*. Oxford: Oxford University Press.
Meskell, L. 1996. The Somatization of Archaeology. Institutions, Discourses, Corporeality. *Norwegian Archaeological Review* 29(1), 1–16.
Miller, D. (ed.) 1998. *Material Cultures. Why some things matter*. London: UCL Press.
Olivier, L. 2008. *Le Sombre Abîme du temps. Mémoire et archéologie*. Paris: Seuil.
Rathje, W. and Murphy, C. 1992. *Rubbish! The Archaeology of Garbage*, New York: Harper Collins.
Schiffer, M. B. 1987. *Formation Processes of the Archaeological Record*. Salt Lake City: University of Utah Press.
Tarlow, S. 2006. Archaeological ethics and the people of the past. In C. Scarre and G. Scarre (eds.) *The Ethics of Archaeology*, 199–216. Cambridge: Cambridge University Press.
Thomas, N. 1991. *Entangled Objects. Exchange, Material Culture, and Colonialism in the Pacific*. Cambridge, MA: Harvard University Press.
Tschauner, H. 1996. Middle-range theory, behavioral archaeology, and postempiricist philosophy of science in archaeology. *Journal of Archaeological Method and Theory* 3(1), 1–30.
Whitehead, A. N. 2004 [1920]. *The Concept of Nature*. New York: Prometheus Books.
Wylie, A. 1989. The Interpretive Dilemma. In V. Pinsky and A. Wylie (eds) *Critical Traditions in Contemporary Archaeology: Essays in the Philosophy, History and socio-politics of Archaeology*, 18–27. Cambridge: Cambridge University Press.

# 4

# Spaces that were not densely occupied – questioning 'ephemeral' evidence

*Lesley McFadyen*

> The advantage of the narrow focus of the specialist is that it creates detailed perception of a problem. But it also creates blindspots, eddies of ignorance in epistemological space, which can only be perceived from another perspective. This is interesting…because it shifts the emphasis of interdisciplinarity from the purloining of other disciplines' methods in the hope that you can apply them within your own discipline, to illuminating, by the methods of one's own discipline, what those disciplines may be methodologically unable to access. This approach to knowledge also implies that it is inappropriate to attempt to reduce one area of thought to the modes of expression of another. This anti-reductionist stance – far from implying that because of an apparent incommensurability disciplines should be kept apart – instead creates the opportunity of juxtaposing them for mutual illumination (Macdonald 2007: 2).

## *Introduction*

Taking a lead from Macdonald (2007), this chapter explores how archaeology and anthropology can be juxtaposed in mutually illuminating ways, that are non-reductive of disciplinary difference. As Macdonald argues, because all disciplines lead to blind-spots and areas of ignorance, it is useful to ask what questions one discipline might ask of another. From the discipline of archaeology I want to ask: what is anthropology methodologically unable to access? This chapter is about the nature of the disciplines of archaeology and anthropology, how they concern themselves with particular kinds of evidence, and how understanding these differences creates further possibilities for what these disciplines might learn from one and other.

I want to start with a story. A few years ago, an archaeologist gave a seminar for the Cambridge University Social Anthropology Society. This seminar was slightly fraught, not least because of technical difficulties to do with the PowerPoint presentation. Put simply the computer and the data projector were not talking to one another on that day. Whilst attempts were being made to fix this problem, I overheard an anthropologist talking to the archaeologist. He commented that archaeologists are limited to the study of objects and that that is why archaeologists analyse in micro detail the matter and make-up of, say, pottery. His implication was that archaeology concerns itself with

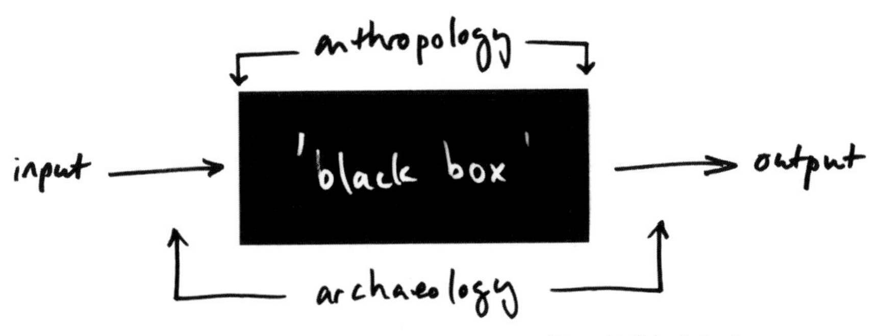


*Figure 4.1. Schematic representation of Leach's 'black box'.*

a description of objects and what they are, in order to attempt to ask how and why these objects *then* connected to people. By framing archaeology in this disconnected way, the anthropologist assumed that archaeological interpretation works in a realm of speculation. By contrast, he said that anthropologists study people, and that this gives them an advantage: for example when looking at the production of pottery, the anthropologist can talk to the potter. The anthropologist did not describe this situation in limiting or speculative terms.[1]

I was surprised by these comments for three reasons. Firstly, I have always understood archaeology to be the study of past people; in particular, the study of people's relationships with things. I have never considered archaeology to be the study of objects in their own right. Secondly, I have never thought in negative terms about the ways in which archaeologists get to know past people. Finally, I was surprised to be hearing in contemporary discussion, a view that stems from a written response to archaeologists made by Leach (1973) over a generation ago. I am not implying that all anthropologists think about archaeology in this way, but I do think there is value in exploring a sentiment that seems to reside in the discipline in quite concrete terms. It might therefore be time to re-examine Leach's position.

In his concluding address to the publication of a set of research seminar papers on archaeology and its related subjects, Leach illustrated his argument on the difference between archaeology and anthropology by drawing on the concept of a Black Box (see Figure 4.1). The Black Box represented a social system and it was inside here that the primary focus of anthropology was depicted. The interests of archaeology were shown to reside on either side of the Black Box, in the space where people met with environment, before any concern with the workings of a social system, and then in the space after, when a patterned material residue of work was left behind (Leach 1973: 766). This was not simply a statement about anthropology dealing with people and archaeology dealing with objects. The model depicted a situation in which the anthropologist was positioned inside and a part of the workings of humanity, whilst the archaeologist was seen to be outside of these.

*Figure 4.2. Schematic representation of archaeologists' relationship with those they study.*

If both positions are as Leach has drawn them then archaeology will never get anywhere, because it can never reach its subject. Leach describes a situation in which the workings of humanity that the archaeologist is interested in are unavailable. And by viewing the material as a 'residue', essentially exterior to the people who produced it, he assumes that this material does not embody enough of the substance of life for the archaeologist to gain access in that direction either. Because the material is being measured by what can or cannot remain, Leach overlooks the reality of the relationship of the past to the evidence (as is argued by Barrett 2006: 196).

I would draw the position of the archaeologist, in relation to the people that they want to get to know, in a different way (see Figure 4.2). In this drawing the archaeologist is not on the outside, nor completely on the inside. The drawing conveys a shared context, but on complex terms. It might therefore be time to examine this position too, and to discuss in a different way the limits of archaeology.

As I have said, as an archaeologist, I have never felt frustrated that there are some things that I will never know about past people simply because I do not exist face to face with them in the exact same time-space. For example, I can never ask them a question about their world, I can only get to know them through the relationship they had with the evidence that I study. But I learn from this conditional situation, and this is how I learn to be an archaeologist. I understand that not knowing some things has implications for what and how I do know (see Lucas this volume). Archaeology focuses on knowing people through their relationship with things. This is a limited kind of knowledge but in no sense do I mean this to be negative. Archaeology involves a particular kind of knowing, and to change it would be to do a different kind of study. I want to be clear here: past people had a relationship with the material that the archaeologist studies, and this relationship is based on presence; otherwise there would be no material to study. However, because the archaeological engagement is always through a partly shared context with another's world, an archaeological account of what it is to perceive something will fail if it accounts only for our perception of presences.

I want to extend a little this idea that not knowing some things can have positive implications (see also Yarrow, this volume). I want to suggest that, perhaps, it is the condition of the unknown in animated archaeological accounts that draws people to the kinds of history that it writes. This idea draws from Byatt's discussion of historians who write fiction and fiction writers who write history, in which she foregrounds the specific relevance of the 'unknown':

> The writer of fiction is at liberty to invent – as the historian and the biographer are not. Simon Schama's fiction, mixed with documentary, in 'Dead Certainties' lacks the dramatic power and imaginative grasp of his history, as the postmodern dialogues between biographer and subject that Peter Ackroyd inserted into his Dickens biography seemed trivial and false beside the mystery of the known facts and the unknown nature of the life being told (2001: 54–55).

Resonating with Macdonald's understanding of disciplinary difference elucidated above, Byatt is saying that it is inappropriate to attempt to reduce one area of thought to the modes of expression of another. But in pointing out instances when this has happened, she also shows up that which is unique to each mode of writing. Anthropology, like fiction, has limitless narrative possibilities; it has to struggle with the problem that there are potentially infinite things to know. By contrast archaeology, like history, is restricted. I want to suggest that is precisely why it is exciting, particularly when it attends to how this is the case.

Archaeology focuses on knowing people through their relationship with things. This is a limited kind of knowledge, and it is important to note that it is not one that is based on self-imposed restrictions. The relationship between present and past, and between the archaeologist and the people that they encounter, is one created through a *partly* shared context (Figure 4.2). By this I mean that other people's lives have created the material and historical conditions that archaeologists engage with. In these contexts I (as an archaeologist) am not at home in their world nor in my own. I am engaged with a negotiation of past and present conditions, in which neither my own subjectivity nor those of the people I attempt to understand can be neatly delimited.

In this situation it is not the job of archaeologists to try make amends for what is 'missing'. Rather I suggest that archaeologists should make the effort to understand humanity in the different way that these limits permit. Byatt writes of the dramatic power and imaginative grasp of history, and of the mystery of the known facts and the unknown nature of the life being told. This does not entail uncontrolled speculation, nor does it define history in terms of absence. Rather she talks of a particular and conditional presence.

If we go back to the comments of the anthropologist cited at the start of this chapter, these seem to assume that anthropologists and their subjects are physically present together. Was the implication that anthropology involves the study of people that are living and the here and now, and archaeology involves the study of the dead and the distant past? If so this is problematic because archaeologists do study contexts of the living, where humanity is very much present. People had a relationship with the evidence that the archaeologist studies, and as a result the archaeologist does share part of the same context. I hope to demonstrate in this chapter that archaeologists engage in a study of an occupied space, where both of our subjectivities are decentred, but there is a material presence of those others and of *their* relationship with the evidence (after Barrett 2006). Through this it becomes evident that time does not necessarily create a distancing effect (contra Fabian 2002), but is a key condition of the kind of knowledge of humanities that archaeology constructs.

## *Mesolithic evidence and time*

I have stated that in archaeology, the archaeologist and the people who they study are not physically present together in the way that they are in anthropology. However, there exists in some quarters of the discipline a discourse which passes judgement on different kinds of archaeological evidence. This would seem to be an attempt to get as close to the anthropological situation as possible. For example, of early prehistoric sites, Gamble has written:

> In order to construct and confirm arguments we move from the precision of *mint-fresh* artefacts, so-called flagship sites, to the coarse palimpsest of heavily rolled stone tools, dredgers by comparison, found in river terraces (Gamble 1999: 68, my emphasis).

Similarly, Milner and Woodman have commented on how one or two sites, due to the quality of preservation, are expected to set the scene for the Mesolithic period:

> An analogy with the famous television series 'Little House on the Prairie' is quite appropriate here in that some key sites have been expected to provide us with *the setting for virtually a complete story* (Milner and Woodman 2005: 5, my emphasis).

This judgement also apparently extends to different kinds of material. For example, Rowley-Conwy has argued: 'animal bones are usually the best, and frequently the only, method of establishing the seasonality of a site. They also form one of the *clearest sources of evidence* about the purpose of the site', and he concludes by stating that, in comparison to worked flint, animal bone is, '... often more capable of answering the relevant questions than other classes of material does raise one final bone of contention, namely the value of excavating sites with no organic preservation' (Rowley-Conwy 1987: 74 and 80, my emphasis).

It is as if some archaeologists think that there are particular contexts and things which almost defy time and which very nearly take the archaeologist into a space where (s)he and those that they study are physically present together at the same time.

In different ways these approaches aim to put the archaeologist back inside the Black Box of Leach's anthropology.

By contrast I argue that archaeology is never completely on the inside of the workings of humanity. In this chapter I am going to discuss contexts *within* time, rather than of the same time, in order to deal directly with the materiality of time and all that that entails. This understanding of the Mesolithic does not come about through flagship sites, and is not based on the animal bone that Rowley-Conwy describes as the clearest source of evidence.

The Mesolithic evidence that I will describe comprises contexts/things not in their 'original' or existing state. I openly refer to this evidence as 'fragments from antiquity' (after Barrett 1994): it does not offer easy access to others' lives, and does not enable a 'complete story' to be told. In terms of evidence, I am deliberately choosing material constituted from the most extreme conditions, and which sits at the opposite end of the spectrum to that set out in the above. Nonetheless, this evidence for Mesolithic people's lives is defined by its presence, and it is precisely this point that makes it so exciting. Even within these extreme conditions there is something to engage with; something that is to do with past people's lives.

I will refer to a series of Mesolithic[2] 'sites'. In this case, by 'sites', I mean assemblages or concentrations of worked flint objects that have been found in the ground. Most of this material has come from surface scatters of worked flint that have been picked up during small-scale field-walking projects in Wiltshire. Geographically, this space is created from evidence on and above a scarp-foot bench in northern Wiltshire. Historically, this space is created from evidence for people's lives from the eighth millennium BC onwards. Information on the total number of pieces, and a breakdown of each assemblage in terms of tool types, has been stored on the Wiltshire Sites and Monuments Record (SMR) database of Mesolithic sites. From their national grid references I can plot the physical location of each site. My work then takes as its focus the potential of the assemblage, and raw material availability, in order to get at process in the past. For example, information on the total number of pieces, and a breakdown of the assemblage in terms of tool-types, is generated in order to define the character of the flint scatters (see Mellars 1976, Foley 1981). This information is used to infer different types of activity, such as whether people were predominantly working hides or working wood. In addition, the relative size of each assemblage is used to make interpretations as to whether it was created over a short time scale or as a result of multiple events. For example, auroch and beaver bone were found at Cherhill. Alongside these, a small number of microliths, scrapers, burins and flakes were a part of the worked flint found at this site and these types of tools are often connected with tasks such as the butchery of animals for their meat, bone and hides. All the worked flint in this assemblage was Mesolithic. This would suggest that the bone and lithics are co-associated, that these materials were caught up in task-specific activities that occurred over a short time scale, and that these tasks were carried out by a small group of people. In contrast at Summerlands Farm, scrapers, flakes, blades and awls were found. These kinds of tool-type can be connected to the processing of plants or animals, and probably hide working. In terms of the size of the assemblage, and the character of tool-types which make up this assemblage of worked flint, I infer that it is evidence for multi-tasking activities. In this case, there was either a larger group of people carrying out various tasks together, or a series of tasks were undertaken through time by smaller groups.

There are differing scales, rhythms and tempos caught up in these assemblages of worked flint. Archaeological evidence exists as a medium of activity: by which I mean we cannot assume that at each location where worked flint has been found that people carried out a task from start to finish. These groups of lithics do not exist as a mirror record of past activity, and they do not hold a static contemporaneity for the archaeologist to analyse. As Barrett states, we cannot think of archaeological sites as a record of 'something', because to do so would be to think that time had stopped in the Mesolithic: that actions had been completed *then* and subsequently frozen and that *now* we can simply read off their original meaning (Barrett 1994: 5). Archaeology is not a discipline that is about the material and historical conditions of other people's lives, it is a subject that is a part of those conditions. Within the medium of action, rather than being outside of the context and looking back at a record, archaeological evidence remains open. Time is ongoing and still at work. There being no guarantee that actions were frozen after they had been carried out in a distant past means that the archaeologist has to be actively open to an engagement whereby there is a distinct possibility that some activities were started whilst others were completed, and where some actions were abandoned whilst others held the possibility of return. This is an example of how not knowing some things has important implications for what and how archaeologists *do* know.

Furthermore, by comparing and contrasting the assemblages (in terms of the frequencies of major tool-types), I get an idea of the extent of inter-assemblage variability. This is where the various processes that connected to the making, using and discarding of worked flint had dimensional qualities that existed on their own terms. They did not stay fixed at the level of the area of the site but extended elsewhere. They dealt with breaks in occupation as much as with measuring its duration. Rather than focusing on how to characterise an assemblage at the level of the site, I focus on inter-site variability, examining how sites connect up through various tasks. It is in this way that networks of practice are traced through the landscape. These concentrations of worked flint can be thought of as assemblages of effects (after Conneller 2004). Assemblages of worked flint are evidence for past practice (such as working flint, hunting animals, the butchery of animals, the processing of plants, cutting wood, the preparation of food). These assemblages are therefore about process and they connect to other things: animals (through microliths, scrapers, burins, awls, flakes), trees (axes, scrapers), plants (microliths, serrated blades, flakes). Assemblages of worked flint are evidence for tasks, and the ways in which these actions connected to, or interlocked with, other activities created an extended network of structured action (McFadyen 2006).

If I select out one kind of practice – the manufacture of microliths[3] – then attention focuses on four places in the landscape, Cherhill, Cocklebury, Cow Down and Peckingell. From the relative proportion of artefact types in the assemblage (after Mellars 1976, Foley 1981), and from refitting exercises (the piecing back together of waste flakes and tools to reconstruct the original flint nodule and thus determine which missing pieces had been removed from site), it is possible to infer that microliths were made at these sites but that several of the tools are missing. Conversely, there are other sites in the landscape where microliths have been recovered but there is no evidence for them having been manufactured *in situ*. It is in this way that we can surmise that the manufacture of microliths connected to future activities at other sites; microliths were taken elsewhere in order to butcher further animals and gather other plants. Each task, because of the way in which it interlocked with previous and future activities, and also how it connected to other materials (moving from flint to bone, or flint to plants), would have made material the presence of other people and other things elsewhere in the landscape. Not only different spatial scales but also various temporal dimensions were caught up in these assemblages of worked flint. Practices of making extended out to other materials and activities elsewhere. The concept of futurity, and not historical or past time, is a key condition here. Space materialised through the ways in which people connected activities together, from the manner in which they shared tasks, and through their openness to the future (cf. Grosz 2001: 12).

## *Anthropological evidence and time*

I want now to return to a discussion of anthropology and time in order to deal specifically with this question of the materiality of time. In recent anthropological studies of the relationship between people and things, scholars have emphasised that the processes of materialisation are more significant than materiality itself. The implication is that the ways in which the anthropologist gets to understand human action, and/or different frames of reference that are co-opted in its interpretation, are important (Buchli 2002; Henare, Holbraad and Wastell 2007).[4]

In the story that I started this chapter with, the idea that the anthropologist and the potter were physically present together carried with it the assumption that the anthropologist was part of the context s/he studies. The fact that the anthropologist could talk to the potter was emphasised. However, as I would see it, there are nevertheless still many problems to overcome. Does being able to talk to someone actually make you more physically present in the context of their world? Is talk being treated here as if it is an original, or the purest, form of contact? Is this physical presence enough to guarantee that both are *completely* within the same context, or is the anthropologist a part of a shared context in a particular way? Is this medium any less complicated than the medium of activity that archaeological evidence is a part of?

Drawing on work by the archaeologist Barrett, I would suggest not. Barrett has written that: 'The meaning of any form of communication is always situated within a time-frame extending from the intentions behind the 'saying' or 'doing' through its execution to its interpretation' (Barrett 1994: 75). The condition of time now, rather than time then, is not a key to opening up this situation more directly.

Remember that archaeological evidence remains open, and time is ongoing and still at work. An engagement with Mesolithic evidence demonstrates that there is no guarantee actions were frozen after they had been carried out in a distant past. This means that the archaeologist has to be actively open to an engagement whereby there is a distinct possibility that some activities were started whilst others were completed, and where some actions were abandoned whilst others held the possibility of return. Is this not also the case within anthropology? The anthropologist and the potter do not stick to each other, track by track, in a continuous present whereby actions run their course one after the other. As the philosopher Arendt has pointed out, no one could perceive of their life in those terms:

> Seen from the viewpoint of man, who always lives in the interval between past and future, time is not a continuum, a flow of uninterrupted succession; it is broken in the middle, at the point where 'he' stands; and 'his' standpoint is not the present as we usually understand it but rather a gap in time which 'his' constant fighting, 'his' making a stand against past and future, keeps in existence (Arendt 1961: 10–11).

Arendt argues that we all live our lives in an interval between past and future, and it is through our own interventions that we always come to know how to deal with and understand the past and future. But the archaeologist engages with a shared context where the *only* way they can come to know another is through evidence of past people's relationships with things. The omission of the past person in terms of their physical living bodies, and the subsequent insertion of the archaeologist's body into a partly shared context, means that archaeology is attentive to things 'not quite here but yet at hand' (after Arendt 1961).

It is interesting to note that when thinking through things, this movement back and forth in time is also to be found in anthropology. For example, in Moutu's description of an exhibition that that the Iatmul people of Papua New Guinea produced after the tsunami in 1998, time is a key condition in an appreciation of these people's knowledge practices. In his discussion of collecting, Moutu writes:

> one can see how collection interrupts the sequential flow of temporality, impregnates this interruption with loss, and then prompts people to reconfigure themselves in the midst of both despair and hope so that such a process of reconfiguration is itself an aspect of collection (Moutu 2007: 97).

For the Iatmul, time did not stop after the tsunami and so there is no representation of an original meaning to an event that can be read off in the exhibition. Instead time is ongoing and still at work particularly through the concept of futurity. The bringing together and juxtaposition of things in the exhibition, reconstitutes the tsunami in a unique way; Moutu describes this as a way of being.

## *The materiality of time and archaeology*

In her work on Mesolithic sites in North Yorkshire, Conneller has drawn attention to the nonlinear trajectories and complicated relationships between space, things, animals, and people, and has demonstrated how further connections were continuously being made (Conneller 2000 and 2004). The site of Seamer D was successively a site where raw materials were cached, and then a place where tools were used (Conneller and Schadla-Hall 2003). She points out that flint material was not fixed as a fossilized object within a place (as a trace or as the remains of what had existed or happened), but was still active in the sense that there was the potential for it to be returned to and reused (Conneller 2000). The activities of caching nodules of flint, and then using lithics, seem more to do with maintaining the medium of space rather than closing it down. On the southern edge of the Mesolithic shoreline of Lake Flixton, an assemblage of flints had been brought together that represented the different stages involved in the biography of a flint object. Old flint nodules (which had weathered but never been made into anything), were next to partly knapped blades (where work had started but then had stopped), which were next to finished tools that had been used many times. Different items were assembled together from different temporal stages of working, creating points of contact between seemingly disparate things. I would like us to focus on the whole composition of the assemblage, and how it contains both the brand new and the old in the same frame or context. People lived surrounded by objects from different times. This is at its most acute or noticeable in the juxtaposition of the various objects – for example the patina that has developed on the old nodules of flint next to the freshness of partly knapped blades. The spaces that were occupied during the Mesolithic were made up of the past and present and these cannot be easily separated out into static layers or surfaces. They existed as a series of dynamic and historical relationships. Whereas some things remain, we can be sure other things have been covered up or removed.

## *Archaeological anthropology*

I want now to return to my 'ephemeral' evidence, the specific relevance of the 'unknown' in archaeology, and the particular and conditional presence of the Mesolithic lives that are the subject of my study. Through all of the activities that I have described so far runs an ambiguous and elusive element: these animated accounts can never be grounded in certain terms. For example, although accounts of the Mesolithic are worked through embodied occupation, they remain enigmatic in that they cannot be defined in terms of a particular individual's actions. Similarly, I have argued that archaeological evidence is a medium for practice, but this is a shared practice where it is not possible to differentiate between one person's actions and another's. This kind of archaeology does not deal with the specifics of dividing out who did what in the past, or of putting names to people and what they did. Instead it deals with the specifics of material and historical conditions, and in doing so enables a unique understanding of how time is a key condition of knowledge of humanities.

Equally, I suggest that archaeologists should not be afraid to think through issues of 'ephemerality' in archaeological histories. There is no need for a desperate search for flagship sites in order to defy time and we do not require more material evidence. What I am leading up to, is the suggestion that at times our evidence for Mesolithic life may actually be *ephemeral,* that is, transitory in nature and defined through movement. The gaps in time that exist between different kinds of evidence for occupation and the nonlinear trajectories between space, things and people signify that past people were not present in one place all of the time. This does not mean that Mesolithic people had a marginal presence in the areas of Wiltshire that I have drawn on. Rather I mean that because these people made space and lived spatially in different ways, we need to consider what these conditions might be saying about the mobility of their lives. We do not need to give an essence to that presence in order to make the evidence less ephemeral. Instead, by engaging with the specificity of the material and historical conditions of past people's lives, we can consider how spaces were less densely occupied. These were spaces that were transitory, whilst remaining dynamic, mobile and ever-changing.

I want to go back to the quote by Macdonald that prefaces this chapter. He has written of interdisciplinary work that it creates the opportunity of juxtaposing disciplines for mutual illumination. I hope that I have achieved something of this in my own discussion. What shape should an archaeological anthropology take? What I hope is clear is that there is little mileage in simply purloining another discipline's methods in the hope that you can apply them within your own. Instead the archaeologist can point out to the anthropologist that a partly shared context with another's world, through material and historical conditions, is something to be embraced; if anthropologists do not recognise this, it is not a blind spot in the evidence but a blind spot in anthropology's methods. There is a lot to learn from understanding humanity through a particular and conditional presence.

## Acknowledgements

Special thanks to Thomas Yarrow and Mark Knight for helping me to think about spaces that were not densely occupied. I would like to thank the Wiltshire Sites and Monuments Record for access to their database of Mesolithic sites. I would also like to thank Chantal Conneller for helping me think about worked flint. Jen Baird, Duncan Garrow, Mark Gillings, Thomas Yarrow and the two anonymous reviewers of this chapter, have to be thanked for their important comments and suggested changes.

### Notes

1 The anthropologist cited Leach's (1973) comments on an unequal difference between archaeology and anthropology approvingly. In 1973, Leach had noted how several archaeologists took a functionalist approach in their archaeology whilst anthropology was within a structuralist paradigm. Leach used this distinction to define archaeology as limited to the study of objects whilst anthropology was opened up through its access to language. But it was more than this. Leach understood the objects that the archaeologist studied to be residues. These then become objects defined through an absence of a connection to people, through what they have lost, rather than through presence. On these terms anything that the archaeologists says about the relationship of objects to people has to stand outside of a human dynamic and so will be considered as add on or speculative.

2 In Britain, the Mesolithic (or Middle Stone Age) lasts between c. 8000 and 4000 BC. Generally, the period is characterised by hunter-gatherer-fisher subsistence practices (with a particular emphasis on coastal/riverine locations) and seemingly mobile rather than permanent settlement practices.

3 Microliths are a small worked flint, the manufacture of which was directed toward production of a generalised design pattern, and they were a standardised component of composite tools.

4 Some of the approach that Henare, Holbraad and Wastell set out in their introduction is quite problematic from the perspective of the archaeologist. If things are literally taken to be their meanings, *sui generis*, then this all seems to depend on being able to talk to people. Meaning (for all they say about collapsing dichotomies) ultimately has its reference in discourse and in what people say.

## References

Arendt, H. 1961. *Between past and future: six exercises in political thought*. London: Faber.

Barrett, J.C. 1994. *Fragments from antiquity: an archaeology of social life in Britain 2900–1200BC*. Oxford: Blackwell.

Barrett, J.C. 2006. Archaeology as the Investigation of the Contexts of Humanity. In D. Papaconstantinou (ed.) *Deconstructing Context. A Critical Approach to Archaeological Practice*, 194–211. Oxford: Oxbow Books.

Buchli, V. 2002. Introduction. In V. Buchli (ed.) *The Material Culture Reader*, 1–22. Oxford and New York: Berg.

Byatt, A.S. 2001. *On Histories and Stories. Selected Essays*. London: Vintage.

Candea, M. 2007. Arbitrary locations: In defence of the bounded field-site. *Journal of the Royal Anthropological Institute* 13, 167–184.

Conneller, C. J. 2000. Fragmented Space? Hunter-Gatherer Landscapes of the Vale of Pickering. *Archaeological Review from Cambridge* 17(1), 139–50.

Conneller, C. J. 2004. Becoming Deer: Corporeal Transformations at Star Carr. *Archaeological Dialogues* 10(2), 37–56.

Conneller, C. J. and T. Schadla-Hall. 2003. Beyond Star Carr: the Vale of Pickering in the 10th Millennium BP. *Proceedings of the Prehistoric Society* 69, 85–106.

Fabian, J. 2002. *Time and the other. How anthropology makes its object.* New York: Columbia University Press.

Foley, R. 1981. Off-site archaeology: an alternative approach for the short-sited. In G. Isaac, I. Hodder, and N. Hammond (eds.) *Pattern of the Past*, 157–183. Cambridge: Cambridge University Press.

Gamble, C. 1999. *The Palaeolithic Societies of Europe.* Cambridge: Cambridge University Press.

Grosz, E. 2001. *Architecture from the Outside. Essays on Virtual and Real Space.* Cambridge, MA, and London: MIT Press.

Henare, A. Holbraad, M. and Wastell, S. 2007. Introduction: thinking through things. In Henare, A. Holbraad, M. and Wastell, S. (eds.) *Thinking through things. Theorising artefacts ethnographically*, 1–31. London and New York: Routledge.

Leach, E. 1973. Concluding comments. In C. Renfrew (ed.) *The explanation of culture change: models in prehistory: proceedings of a meeting of the Research Seminar in Archaeology and Related Subjects held at the University of Sheffield*, 761–71. London: Duckworth.

Macdonald, M. 2007. *A Note on Interdisciplinarity.* Paper given at the AHRC-funded Learning is Understanding in Practice project, University of Aberdeen.

McFadyen, L. 2006. Landscape. In C. Conneller and G. Warren (eds) *Mesolithic Britain and Ireland. New Approaches*, 121–38. Stroud: Tempus.

Mellars, P. A. 1976. Settlement Patterns and Industrial Variability in the British Mesolithic. In G. Sieveking, I. H. Longworth and K. E. Wilson (eds) *Problems in Economic and Social Archaeology*, 375–99. London: Duckworth.

Milner, N. and Woodman, P. 2005. Looking into the canon's mouth: Mesolithic studies in the 21st century. In N. Milner and P. Woodman (eds.) *Mesolithic Studies at the Beginning of the 21st Century*, 1–13. Oxford: Oxbow Books.

Moutu, A. 2007. Collection as a way of being. In A. Henare, M. Holbraad, and S. Wastell (eds.) *Thinking through things. Theorising artefacts ethnographically*, 93–112. London and New York: Routledge.

Rowley-Conwy, P. 1987. Animal Bones in Mesolithic Studies: Recent Progress and Hopes for the Future. In P. Rowley-Conwy, M Zvelebil, and H.P. Blankholm, (eds.) *Mesolithic Northwest Europe: Recent Trends*, 74–81. Sheffield: Department of Archaeology and Prehistory.

# 5

# On the boundary: new perspectives from ethnography of archaeology

*Matt Edgeworth*

## *Introduction*

There are multiple and overlapping boundaries in any area of human perception and experience. This paper attempts to envisage the many and shifting ways in which the disciplinary boundary between archaeology and anthropology is seen, constructed and experienced. It will focus not so much on the crossing of theories or ideas from one side to the other, but rather on the more practical interactions, collaborations, tensions and occasional conflicts between ethnographers and archaeologists that are occurring out on site in the emerging field of 'ethnographies of archaeology'. This is an area of research which situates and defines itself in relation to a supposed disciplinary boundary zone – at once dismantling and reifying the boundary in the process of crossing it. By looking at instances of archaeologists taking up ethnographic perspectives on their own practices, and conversely at ethnographers becoming participant-observers on archaeological sites, the chapter will move beyond discussions of the nature of the boundary to consider some of the implications of this work for the development of an archaeological anthropology.

## *Where ethnographies of archaeological practice come from*

Ethnographies of archaeological practice have developed in association with an increasing concern with reflexivity in archaeological theory and practice (Hodder 1997, 2000; Chadwick 2003). Each discipline has its own understanding of reflexivity, which takes a slightly different form in archaeology than it does in anthropology (Salzman 2002; Robertson 2002). Archaeological reflexivity might be defined in the following way. The cultural backgrounds of archaeologists, and the particular social and material practices through which we 'do' archaeology, clearly influence the way evidence is interpreted and how the past is understood. Therefore, in addition to fixing our gaze on cultural activity in the distant past, it is also important to turn attention to our own cultural activities in the present through which that view of the past is made possible. As well as studying material artefacts from the past, it is also important to be reflexively aware of the artefacts of archaeological practice through which material evidence is shaped and fashioned by archaeologists in the present.

But how are we to build into our understanding of the past a sense of our own role in constituting it? It is difficult to apprehend one's own cultural background and embodied skills, one's own cultural standpoint *from* that standpoint. This is the central problem that ethnographies of archaeology grapple with. Reflexive methods and techniques (such as the keeping of diaries by excavators – see Roveland 2006; Wilmore 2006) help up to a point, but it is important to acknowledge the very real limits of reflexivity. Much knowledge is in the form of embodied habit and expertise that cannot be articulated in the form of verbal propositions; it consists of 'ways of doing' that can be demonstrated but not explicitly formulated in words or thoughts. Such tacit knowledge (Polanyi 1966) is by definition not readily accessible to conscious reflection. To view the things and activities that are tacitly held or taken for granted it may be necessary to go beyond reflexivity as it has been understood within archaeological discussions, to shift standpoint beyond the boundaries of conventional disciplinary thinking.

In order to escape the inevitable circularities of reflexivity, it could be argued, one would have to look at the familiar world to some extent from outside – rather as anthropologists have traditionally looked at distant and 'exotic' tribes. This idea of taking up an ethnographic point of view on archaeological practice lies at the heart of the cluster of new studies that are in different ways situated at the intersections of anthropology and archaeology. Whilst recognising considerable heterogeneity in terms of their theories and aims I collectively refer to these as ethnographies of archaeological practice (Edgeworth 1991, 2003; Bartu 2000; Hamilton 2000; Holtorf 2002; Yarrow 2003; the various authors in Edgeworth 2006).

At first glance this work might seem superficially similar to a number of other more established areas of research which also make use of the ethnographic method. To avoid confusion, then, a distinction should be made at the outset between ethnographies of archaeological practice and the rather similar-sounding fields of ethnoarchaeology (David and Kramer 2001) or archaeological ethnography (Meskell 2005). Both the latter use the ethnographic method to augment conventional archaeological work in understanding *other cultures.* Ethnographies of archaeological practice, by way of contrast, use ethnographic methods to try to understand the *cultural practices of archaeology* itself. It might reasonably be argued, following Bourdieu (1977), that we cannot explain other cultures without also attempting to understand our own culture of explanation: to produce viable knowledge about the past we must also at least partially understand the cultural and material processes through which that knowledge is produced. In this important sense ethnography of archaeology does not seek to undermine archaeological knowledge. Although it is certainly true that explicating the cultural foundations of scientific knowledge can be taken by some as an attack on its essential 'truth', the overriding goal of such approaches is to augment and enrich archaeological practice by illuminating crucial and up to now neglected dimensions to it.

Much closer to ethnography of archaeology, then, might be 'ethnography of ethnography' (Van Maanen 1995) or 'archaeology of archaeology' (Lucas 2001: 200–204; Roveland 2006: 59, 66). Both these approaches are reflexive, in the sense that they involve a recognition that the practices of ethnography and/or archaeology are forms of cultural production in their own right, accessible to study by their own methods of inquiry. Ethnography of archaeology is similar, except that there is some dissonance between the method of observation and the method observed. Through taking up a method and set of perspectives different from its own, (ethnography of) archaeology can escape from some of the circularities of existing approaches and move beyond the reflecting mirrors that reflexivity can otherwise entail.

## *Envisaging fields and boundaries*

Ethnographies of archaeological practice set up movements between archaeology and anthropology – transpositions of perspectives and points of view – in both directions. First of all practising archaeologists have taken-up ethnographic stances as a means of gaining new perspectives on archaeological practices that seem impervious to mere reflection (Edgeworth 1991, 2003; Gero 1996; Yarrow 2003; Holtorf 2006). Second, there is the movement of ethnographers into the world of archaeology, as participant-observers of archaeological practice. Interestingly, this has usually happened at the request of archaeologists themselves. At Çatalhöyük in Turkey, for example, Ian Hodder brought in Carolyn Hamilton (2000), Ayfer Bartu (2000) and other social anthropologists to observe the processes of production of archaeological knowledge (Hodder 2000). At the site of Leskernick on Bodmin Moor, Chris Tilley, Sue Hamilton and Barbara Bender invited sociologists to help study an archaeological landscape that, unusually and innovatively, was taken to be inclusive of archaeologists themselves and their activities (Wilmore 2006, Bender et al 2007). Sometimes, as in the case of Van Reybrouck and Jacobs' work at Maaskant in the Netherlands, there is a shifting back and forth between the perspectives of archaeologist as ethnographer on the one hand and sociologist/ethnographer as archaeologist on the other hand, both working in tandem (Van Reybrouk and Jacobs 2006). Whichever way it happens, the impetus for this kind of trans-disciplinary work seems to have come mainly from the archaeological 'side'.

Ethnographies of archaeological practice, then, should not be envisaged in conventional fashion as a 'field' of study, in the sense that this might imply a bounded area undivided by internal boundaries. Rather these constitute a cluster of studies that span the very boundary of archaeology and anthropology, and depend upon the dissonances between these as a source of creativity and insight. Indeed, it could be suggested that people from each discipline invoke the other as a way of creating distinctions and boundaries in the context of discourses, theories and practices that are largely internal to both 'sides' of this divide. If neither archaeology nor anthropology are internally coherent 'fields', then it follows that the forms that these inter-disciplinary boundaries take are also multiple and variable.

Problems arise when we try to envisage what these boundaries look like. Are they merely abstract lines, drawn in cognitive space between different sets of ideas or subject matters? Or do they take the more material form of a notice on the door at the end of a university corridor, signifying the division between one academic department and another? Sometimes the existence of the boundary can be detected by the *absence* of certain things, such as the lack of citation of specific texts in bibliographies, relative to the *presence* of references to other kinds of texts. Like any boundaries, the ones which exist between archaeology and anthropology have both material and cognitive dimensions. They are as much 'out there' in the world as they are 'in here' in the mind. But their exact geographical locations, their precise material forms, are hard to pin down.

One way of configuring the disciplinary boundary is to examine what happens when people cross the boundary from one side to the other. Ethnographies of archaeological practice are good places to look in this sense because they clearly consist of movement from archaeology into anthropology and vice-versa – movement that might well be taken as transgression by some scholars on both sides (of which more will be said below). Here the changing relationships between the two disciplines take the form of actual encounters and interactions that occur in the material setting of archaeological sites. Focusing on these has the great advantage of shifting many otherwise intractable theoretical issues into a less abstract and more practical sphere.

## *The archaeological site as the site of ethnography*

A good example of the archaeological site as the site of ethnography is the excavation of Arroyo Seco in the pampas of Argentina. It was here in 1992 that archaeologist Joan Gero carried out her study of gendered encounters with fieldwork data (Gero 1996), which has become so well known in archaeological circles. Not so well known is that working alongside Gero on the same site that year was the linguistic anthropologist Charles Goodwin. Using video as a primary means of recording, he was interested in the embodied actions and the mundane linguistic exchanges that are embedded in archaeological work. He later went on to work as an ethnographer on several other archaeological sites and field schools. His encounter with archaeology is worth exploring in some detail, since it manifestly had a considerable effect on the development of his ideas over the next decade or so, and continues to influence his work today. In trying to envisage new forms of relationship between archaeology and anthropology, we would do well to look at those anthropologies, like Goodwin's, that already draw from archaeology in a significant way.

Goodwin is a linguistic anthropologist who specializes in the ethnographic study of work practices. In his seminal paper, *Professional Vision* (1994), he juxtaposes modes of vision employed by archaeologists at Arroyo Seco and other excavations, with those of attorneys in the trial of the policemen who beat up Rodney King. How do experts in different fields make significant patterns stand out? Goodwin compares the case of an archaeologist trowelling a feature with the case of a defence lawyer highlighting details in video evidence. Such juxtapositions illuminate both ways. They shed light on the everyday routines of archaeology as embodied skills central to the organisation of the profession. At the same time they demonstrate that ethnographic observations of archaeologists at work can increase our understanding of other quite different areas of cultural activity, and thereby of human action and perception generally.

Subsequent papers by Goodwin (2000, 2003) develop this form of comparative analysis further. He compares the use of Munsell colour charts by archaeologists with the totally different social context of two Latina girls playing in a hopscotch grid. Both kinds of grid, he argues, are 'semiotic fields' – providing material frameworks for orientating action, language, gesture and perception (Goodwin 2000). He goes on to develop a sophisticated and comprehensive theory of human action in which (highly unusual in the context of linguistic anthropology) a crucial and dynamic part is played by material objects and artefacts, and the material environment generally (Goodwin 2003).

Goodwin himself acknowledges the contribution of these encounters with archaeological practice to his work. He argues that linguistic anthropologists and archaeologists take two radically different views of the human condition. For the former, it is language which above all else defines human beings and makes cultural development possible. For the latter it is the human ability to make and use artefacts and to shape the material environment. Drawing from his work on archaeological sites, Goodwin's thinking encompasses and combines both, not just on the macro level of cultural theory but also on the micro level of situated human action in particular work contexts. A crucial factor shaping this approach, according to Goodwin, was his encounter with archaeological practice through conducting ethnographic investigations on excavations: as he himself explains, 'sustained exposure to the work and presentations of archaeologists, and to workplace settings, led me to see that in my own research I had drawn an invisible analytical boundary at the skin of the speaking, embodied actors I was investigating, so that material structure in the environment was effectively ignored' (Goodwin 2006: 48).

In relating how his work on excavations led him to redress this imbalance, Goodwin credits his encounters with archaeological practice with a profound shift in the development of his ideas. These, he goes on to suggest, led him to treat language and the material structure of the environment as entangled together in unfolding human experience, rather than as separate compartments unrelated to each other (Goodwin 2006).

Interestingly, Goodwin's account provides an instructive example of how the inter-disciplinary exchanges characteristic of ethnographies of archaeological practice do not simply represent exchanges of ideas, but also lead to new understandings of the routine and often unthinking assumptions that underpin disciplinary orientations to the world. In other words such an approach leads to increased mutual intelligibility of the means by which disciplines generate and use ideas. Rather than merely drawing from archaeological ideas, Goodwin also draws from his experience of the archaeological site and the physical, embodied nature of much archaeological work. As he puts it, 'the work practices of archaeologists ... during field excavations and in the laboratory, has provided a perspicuous site to investigate the consequential organization of embodied action that encompasses both language and structure in the environment' (Goodwin 2006: 48). Hence, although Goodwin's explicit substantive focus is on the disciplinary practices of archaeology, his account also brings to light a reflexive understanding of his own practices as an anthropologist.

Perhaps the important point to make here is that such encounters to some extent constitute a counterpoint to the often 'asymmetric' theoretical exchanges that have taken place between archaeologists and anthropologists (Gosden 1999, Tilley 1996, see also Garrow and Yarrow, this volume). The ethnography of archaeological practice is productive partly because it reveals archaeological practice from the perspective of anthropological theories, and hence in a new light. In the process, however, Goodwin's paper reveals how it leads to a re-orientation of those theories, demonstrating how anthropologists can be inspired and influenced on a profound level by an encounter with archaeologists.

The nature of that inspiration, in this case at least, is surprising. What is it about archaeology that we expect to be of use to anthropology? It is often imagined that archaeological contributions to wider intellectual currents inhere in the capacity for archaeologists to understand the distant past or long-term social processes. By contrast the insight that emerges from Goodwin and other ethnographic studies of archaeological practice is that archaeological fieldwork is underpinned by distinct forms of relationship and practice, that constitute a profoundly material orientation towards the world. It is this material orientation that is itself of great potential value to other social scientists.

## *Archaeology as a special form of encounter*

If, as I have suggested above, the ethnographic study of archaeology sheds light on the ideas, assumptions and practices that underpin anthropological work, then it does so partly in its revelation of a specifically archaeological orientation to the world. What is it that makes archaeological practice different compared to other kinds of knowledge production?

Shapin points out that "science is undeniably made in specific sites, and it discernibly carries the marks of those sites of production, whether sites be conceived as the personal cognitive space of creativity, the relatively private space of the research laboratory, the physical constraints posed by natural or built geography for conditions of visibility and access, the local social spaces of municipality, region, or nation, or the 'topical contextures' of practice, equipment, and phenomenal fields" (Shapin 1995: 306). Archaeological practice is underpinned by a series of conventions, many of which may be broadly characterised as 'scientific', and makes use of some of the sites of production of science (such as the laboratory) that Shapin refers to. But at the same time archaeological sites are very different; they have their own physical constraints, modes of creativity, social and personal spaces, topical contextures and fields of phenomena. In directing attention to such sites, ethnographies of archaeological practice can significantly add to insights obtained from ethnographies of laboratory work and other kinds of scientific practice.

The laboratory is a highly artefactual environment, characterized by complex arrays of apparatus which mediate transactions between scientists and the materials being worked upon. As Knorr-Cetina put it in an early study of scentific knowledge (SSK) work, noting the absence of any truly raw material in the laboratory:

> It is clear that measurement instruments are the products of human effort, as are articles, books, and the graphs and print-outs produced. But the source materials with which scientists work are also preconstructed … 'Raw' materials which enter the laboratory are carefully selected and 'prepared' before they are subjected to 'scientific' tests (Knorr-Cetina 1983: 119).

There is little direct contact between scientist and material. Transactions between persons and object tend to be mediated by layer upon layer of complex instrumentation.

By contrast to the laboratory practices that have been the focus of many science and technology studies, archaeological sites form part of the landscape itself. It is the setting in which archaeologists work and the surface on which they stand. In many cases archaeologists construct their work spaces (for example, by excavating trenches or large features) so that they themselves are positioned *inside* of and are *surrounded by* this material field. Parts of the material field have been worked and constituted as evidence but there is also always a vast presence of as yet unworked raw material that is still to be made sense of as it emerges or unfolds from the ground 'under the moving blade of the trowel' (Edgeworth 1991) or 'at the trowel's edge' (Hodder 1997). The actions of archaeologists upon the material field, instead of being highly mediated by an intervening advanced technology, are direct and physical. They are embodied actions, making great use of the sense of touch and other senses alongside vision. The degree of instrumentation is correspondingly small, including relatively simple technologies such as spades, trowels, wheelbarrows and other hand-held tools being substituted for the more complex array of instruments in a laboratory.

Archaeological excavations present opportunities for ethnographers of science that laboratories do not. It is more than just the embodied aspects of archaeological work;

such aspects are present in most scientific activity (Latour 1986, Hutchins 1995). In all these settings investigators are probing and exploring materials. Whether using a trowel to explore an archaeological feature or a carbon nanotube cantilever to manipulate and measure atomic particles, there is a complex interaction going on between humans and materials, persons and things, leading to the production of knowledge about the world. The incredible amount of instrumentation which makes interactions with particles on a nano-scale possible, however, also makes those same interactions (which take place at the cantilever tip, thousands of times smaller than the point of a needle) extremely difficult for the ethnographer to observe; in many cases the ethnographer has to rely on the measurements and observations made by scientists themselves.

An archaeological site is different. Here the transitions of material from a 'raw' to a meaningfully-constituted state (and the processes through which this transition is brought about) are fully open to view. The relationships between persons and things are not so highly mediated by intervening technology. An ethnographer can study the whole practical process of 'making sense' of evidence in the context of human-material and associated social interactions which take place on a human scale. Social and political relations can be clearly seen to be grounded in manifestly material processes of knowledge production.

There is no dependence upon the observational apparatus or methodologies of the investigators whose activities are being studied. The ethnographer can literally jump in to archaeological features where archaeologists are working, touch the unfolding evidence with his or her own hands, watch features and other patterns take shape under the moving blade of the trowel, pick up and use the tools of the trade directly on the emerging material, join workers in the physical task of bringing further evidence to light. There is the opportunity not only to study the shaping of emerging evidence through the application of material and cognitive tools, but also the ways in which raw material might resist, constrain or change knowledge that is constructed and applied. In short, human-material interactions are much more accessible to the ethnographer on an archaeological site than on many other sites of the production of scientific knowledge.

## *Native informants*

Many ethnographic texts go unchallenged by those who have been the objects of ethnography simply because the latter do not have access to the academic world of journals and the language of western intellectual discourse. While it is true that ethnographies of western knowledge practices have dealt at length with these issues, it is rare to find a field of study that is at once so close to anthropology and yet at the same time set apart from it, in quite the same way as archaeology is. Ethnographies of archaeological practice, then, are different. Archaeologists who are the ethnographic informants often live and work in the same academic structures, broadly speaking, as the ethnographer; they are both 'native'. In some cases the professional status of informants is partly created and reproduced through publications of archaeological material in the very journals or other texts that the ethnographer will publish the ethnographic report in. This means that they are likely to be concerned with how they are represented in the report: they may also have power to respond to the way in which they are portrayed. And this is unusual. Subjects of conventional ethnographies do not normally have this power. The implicit superiority of point of view of the explainer over the explained, or the privileged standpoint of the observer over the observed – though subject to internal critique – remains largely unquestioned and unchallenged by the people who are the objects of conventional ethnographies.

In contrast, when Gero (1996) published the results of her ethnography of the influence of gender on the production of archaeological data, the director of the excavation responded by publishing a counter-argument (Politis 2001). This was essentially a critique of the cultural standpoint of the ethnographer that gave rise to her interpretation in the first instance. The details of the exchange are not relevant here. The point is that such feedback changes the nature of ethnography itself, forcing it into a re-evaluation of its own conditions of production.

Ethnographers of archaeological practice using material from excavators' diaries (e.g. Wilmore 2006) may encounter related issues. Who has authorship and copyright on these diary entries? Is it the ethnographer, the archaeological site directors, or the archaeological workers themselves? And to what extent should the latter be consulted in publishing selected comments drawn from the diaries? Normally such questions would simply not arise, not because they are not relevant or important, but rather because the rights of ethnographic informants are rarely asserted, at least not by informants themselves. While there has been extensive anthropological debate on the politics and ethics of representation (e.g. contributions in Clifford and Marcus 1986), with anthropologists changing their practices to fit the new guiding principles, here is a domain where informants themselves will raise the relevant issues of their own accord, forcing anthropologists to take appropriate measures, irrespective of top-down representational and ethical considerations.

Ethnographies of archaeological practice represent an area of study, then, of both cultural affinity and difference (precisely because archaeology is a part of anthropology on the one hand and yet quite separate from it on the other hand). There is proximity and distance, familiarity and unfamiliarity. In this interstitial space, ethnographies are necessarily built less on the overlaying of one point of view on another and more on an interleaving of points of view between observer and observed. Through being brought to bear upon such a paradoxically close-to-home yet far-away area of human practice, the ethnographic method itself is challenged and transformed.

## *Policing boundaries*

With both Gero (an archaeologist) and Goodwin (a linguistic anthropologist) simultaneously carrying out ethnographies of archaeological practice at the site of Arroyo Seco, it might be supposed that an intersection of sorts between the two disciplines has taken place. But there is also a sense in which each of these authors are embedded in forms of disciplinary practice which act to reproduce the very boundaries that their work seeks to challenge.

Consider, for example, the fields of discourse the two authors situate themselves in and the audiences addressed by the respective papers that resulted from their work on the site. These can be assessed by making use of citations listed for each publication in Google Scholar. At the time of writing the final draft of this chapter (April 2009), Google Scholar lists 614 publications which cite Goodwin's 1994 *Professional Vision* paper. Almost all of these come from linguistic anthropology, cognitive anthropology, ethnography of work and similar fields. It is hard to find an archaeological publication which cites this particular article, or indeed any of the other numerous papers Goodwin has written which include analyses of archaeological practice. Similarly, Google Scholar lists 43 publications which cite Gero's 1996 *Gendered Encounters* paper. Almost all the publications listed come from theoretical archaeology, feminist archaeology and similar fields, with few anthropological texts citing the paper.

This striking divergence gives a strong indication that the written world of books, journals and bibliographies constitutes one of the principal areas in which disciplinary boundaries are manifested and reproduced. While various kinds of interaction take place between archaeologists and anthropologists in their multiple intersecting and overlapping fields, these are not necessarily reflected in what happens to written accounts of their work. Indeed, citation and other rhetorical practices often seem to rebuild boundaries, recreate divergences and reinstate divisions. Even work which presents radical challenges to the ways disciplinary boundaries are organized quickly gets subsumed into a system of knowledge partition which reproduces those very structural divisions.

The absence of reference to Goodwin's work in archaeological texts, or for that matter to Gero's work in anthropological texts, raises the wider issue of the visibility of innovative inter-disciplinary approaches, and whether the existence of other such work might be hidden by citational practices. An archaeological anthropology, it would seem, will only develop if relevant texts can find their way through the 'well-policed boundaries of anthropology' (Gupta and Ferguson 1997: 29), and the different, though equally well policed boundaries of archaeology.

Boundaries are also reproduced and 'policed' in terms of entrenched methodological and theoretical differences of orientation. It has been argued in this paper that the very act of conducting ethnography of archaeology involves a crossing of disciplinary boundaries between archaeology and anthropology, often in both directions simultaneously. Both archaeologists and anthropologists on either side of the border, however, may regard the opening up of a new interdisciplinary space and the consequent incursion into their territory as an act of transgression. Such boundary crossings, then, can meet with considerable resistance. Indeed, the encountering of resistance is a good indication that a significant boundary is being crossed.

One way that resistance manifests itself is in the belief that archaeologists should not do ethnography and ethnographers should not do archaeology. As Hollowell and Nicholas (2008: 85) state, 'Most agree that an archaeological project that has an ethnographic component should work with a trained or experienced ethnographer'. Major sites such as Çatalhöyük (Hodder 2000) and Leskernick (Bender et al 2007) followed this rule, bringing in anthropologists to carry out ethnographic components of archaeological work – thereby reproducing one manifestation of the disciplinary boundary.

The idea that only trained persons should take on the role of ethnographers is set out by Forsythe (1999) in relation to the use of ethnography by researchers working in the design of computer software.[1] Forsythe's characterization of non-anthropological ethnographies as relatively crude and superficial, removed from the intellectual roots and traditions of the discipline – whatever its basis in reality – has the effect of excluding those studies from core anthropological discourse. In her account of learning to be an ethnographer on archaeological sites in Mexico, the anthropologist Lisa Breglia – herself an ethnographer of archaeology – concurs with Forsythe (Breglia 2006c). But the division of the world into anthropologists and non-anthropologists, trained and non-trained, is far too simplistic (yet another manifestation of the disciplinary boundary). Partly as a product of the status of archaeology as a sub-discipline of anthropology in the USA, the development of ethnoarchaeology and archaeological ethnography, and the proliferation of academic departments worldwide teaching combined degrees, there are many archaeologists/anthropologists who are effectively hybrid investigators. These belong wholly neither to one field nor the other but rather identify themselves with the area of overlap, being equipped with some measure of expertise in both ethnographic and archaeological techniques. Most ethnographers of archaeology come from such inter-disciplinary spaces.

Archaeologists as well as ethnographers may be protective of what they perceive as their territory. Finding themselves in the unaccustomed position of being constituted as part of the objective field of ethnographic study, archaeologists sometimes object to the intrusion of the ethnographer into their space. There is no doubt that archaeological sites can be difficult places to do ethnographic fieldwork in this respect. As Shahina Farid, the director of excavations at Çatalhöyük, explains, 'Initially, and much to our shame, the anthropologist ... was treated with considerable caution and distance. The field team's reaction was that here was yet another kind of scrutiny, probing, questioning of motives...The tension of being on view by a different medium yet again and having our thought processes dissected was inhibiting and unnerving' (Farid 2000: 26). Farid goes on to explain that these initial difficulties were overcome, but her comments serve to illustrate the level of friction that can exist on the boundary between two disciplines, in the context of practical interactions.

Wherever there are different points of view there may be tension and conflict – characterised as 'faultlines' in the construction of archaeological knowledge by Hamilton (2000). Tension is there in this case partly because archaeologists are not used to being constituted as the object of the anthropological gaze, or to turning that gaze back onto their own activities. But tensions can be creative, leading to an interchange of stances and perspectives. An ethnographer working as a participant-observer on an excavation becomes through participation to some extent an archaeologist, acquiring aspects of associated embodied skills and competencies (e.g. learning to recognize and excavate the different types of features) and the language of archaeological practice (e.g. what the features are called). It is also the case that an archaeologist can become to some extent an ethnographer, by virtue of adopting a particular kind of perspective, method and approach towards archaeological practice – thereby constituting it as the object of study. These points of view are not mutually exclusive, and the boundaries between them are fluid and shifting. In this sense it is perhaps wrong to envisage the boundary as having a fixed location in space which has to be 'crossed' at all.

## *Towards an archaeological anthropology*

What distinguishes ethnographies of archaeology from other kinds of ethnography is the way that social, political and cultural aspects of practices are seen to be grounded in the sheer materiality of archaeological sites. An emphasis on artefacts, soils, surfaces, layers, features, and other material entities has always marked archaeology out as different from other social sciences (see also Gosden, this volume). This emphasis is retained in ethnographic studies of archaeological practice, and ties in with recent work in Actor Network Theory (ANT) and non anthropocentric approaches towards material agency (Latour 2005, Knappett and Malafouris 2008).

Until recently, the materiality of archaeological sites did not fall within the rubric of the 'social' or the 'cultural' and therefore fell outside the scope of ethnography. Artefacts, monuments and other such things were considered to belong to the past, not the present; their study was accordingly regarded as the province of archaeologists, not anthropologists. Yet now archaeologists and the cultural practices of archaeology are gradually coming into the range of the ethnographic gaze. The archaeological site, recognized as an important site of social production, is increasingly becoming the site and focus of ethnography too. There is a collision and convergence of archaeological and ethnographic points of view. As some archaeologists experiment with ethnography and a growing number of ethnographers conduct anthropological fieldwork on archaeological sites, a new point of entry is opening up through which archaeology is having an impact on anthropology (Castañeda 1995; Breglia 2006a, 2006b).

It is of course the case that archaeological sites as 'historically produced social spaces' and 'active, dynamic, contingent spaces of the production of social relations' (Breglia 2006b: 7) should have figured in the anthropological landscape all along. Archaeological sites are not any less social or cultural for having a strong material basis and setting in the landscape. The fact that ethnographers never ventured onto them or included them within the bounds of the ethnographic field site was simply yet another of the many concrete manifestations of disciplinary boundaries, now being crossed in both directions.

But even when archaeological sites are brought within the range of the anthropological field of vision, the tendency is still to detach the social and the political from the material. Thus Lisa Breglia offers an approach which 'releases heritage from its own confines of monumental materiality' so that heritage is understood 'first and foremost as a particular kind of social relationship between all kinds of users of a heritage site – for example between local populations and state agencies or between archaeologists and site labourers' (Breglia 2006b: 14). This is fine, highlighting the important aspect of heritage as a set of practices in the present rather than just as a group of monuments or assemblage of artefacts from the past. But in separating the inextricably inter-connected material and social aspects, it follows ancient lines drawn between the respective roles of archaeologists (with their principal focus on the material) and anthropologists (with their overriding emphasis on the social and political) – thereby reproducing disciplinary boundaries that in other respects are being broken down (see also Ingold, this volume). Just as there is resistance in archaeology to the view of itself as a set of cultural as well as material practices, so there is a subtle resistance within anthropology to the idea of rooting an understanding of socio-political life in the material domain, or to allowing material artefacts to intrude too much into a cultural sphere that is essentially regarded as non-material in character. This resistance is associated with a rigidity of boundaries when it comes to allowing archaeological versions of anthropology to reach core areas of the discipline.

The convergence of archaeological site and the site of ethnography is actually bringing together two very different points of view, with all the friction and conflict that this entails. In my opinion it is a field of creative rather than destructive conflict, where both archaeologists and anthropologists can draw elements from the other's approach and perspective without compromising the integrity of their own distinctive disciplinary standpoints. The challenge for ethnographers is to subsume the materiality of archaeological sites and the broader landscape into their accounts of the social, the cultural, the linguistic and the political – thereby incorporating also the material presence of the past into their view of the present. The challenge for archaeologists is to come to terms with the social and political character of the material practices of archaeology through which knowledge of the past is produced and reproduced. Archaeological anthropology is a field of tremendous potential that will develop out of the convergence and interweaving of social and material dimensions in the study of past and present human activity.

*Note*

1 See Radin (1970: 5–6) and Gupta and Ferguson (1997: 22–24) for an alternative view.

## References

Bartu, A. 2000. Where is Çatalhöyük? Multiple sites in the construction of an archaeological site. In I.Hodder (ed.) *Towards reflexive method in archaeology: the example at Çatalhöyük*, 101–09. Cambridge: McDonald Institute Monographs.

Bender, B., S. Hamilton and C. Tilley 2007. *Stone Worlds: Narrative and Reflexivity in Landscape Archaeology*. Walnut Creek: Left Coast Press

Bourdieu, P. 1977. *Outline of a theory of practice*. [Trans. R. Nice]. Cambridge: Cambridge University Press.

Breglia, L. 2006a. Complicit agendas: ethnography of archaeology as ethical research practice. In M. Edgeworth (ed.) *Ethnographies of archaeological practice: cultural encounters, material transformations*, 173–184. Lanham, MD: Altamira Press.

Breglia, L. 2006b. *Monumental ambivalence: the politics of heritage*. Austin: University of Texas Press.

Breglia, L. 2006c. Uncommon sense troubling the 'work' of ethnographic fieldwork (available on-line: www.socsci.uci.edu/~ethnog/Turns/Breglia.pdf).

Castañeda, Q. 1995. *In the museum of Maya culture: touring Chichén Itzá*. Minneapolis: University of Minnesota Press.

Chadwick, A. 2003. Post-processualism, professionalization and archaeological methodologies: towards reflective and radical practice. In *Archaeological Dialogues* 10(1), 97–117.

Clifford, J. and G. Marcus. 1986. *Writing culture: the poetics and politics of ethnography*. Berkeley: University of California Press.

Edgeworth, M. 1991, *The act of discovery: an ethnography of the subject-object relation in archaeological practice*. Ph.D thesis, University of Durham.

Edgeworth, M. 2003. *Acts of discovery: an ethnography of archaeological practice*. Oxford: Archaeopress.

Edgeworth, M. (ed). 2006. *Ethnographies of archaeological practice: cultural encounters, material transformations*. Lanham, MD: Altamira Press.

David, N and C. Kramer. 2001. *Ethnoarchaeology in action*. Cambridge: Cambridge University Press.

Farid, S. 2000. The excavation process at Çatalhöyük. In I. Hodder (ed.) *Towards reflexive method in archaeology: the example at Çatalhöyük*, 19–29. Cambridge: McDonald Institute Monographs.

Forsythe, D. 1999. It's just a matter of common sense: ethnography as invisible work. *Journal of Computer Supported Cooperative Work* 8, 127–145.

Gero, J. 1996. Archaeological practice and gendered encounters with field data. In J. Gero and M. Conkey (eds.) Engendering archaeology: women and prehistory, 251–80. Philadelphia: University of Pennsylvania Press

Goodwin, C. 1994. Professional vision. *American Anthropologist* 96(3), 606–633.

Goodwin, C. 2000. Action and embodiment within situated human interaction. *Journal of Pragmatics* 32, 1489–1522.

Goodwin, C. 2003. Pointing as situated practice. In S. Kito (ed.) *Pointing: where language, culture and cognition meet*. Mahwah, New Jersey: Lawrence Erlbaum Associates.

Goodwin, C. 2006. A linguistic anthropologist's interest in archaeological practice. In M.

Edgeworth (ed.) *Ethnographies of archaeological practice: cultural encounters, material transformations*, 45–55. Lanham, MD: Altamira Press.

Gosden, C. 1999. *Anthropology and Archaeology: a Changing Relationship*.London: Routledge.

Gupta, A. and J. Ferguson. 1997. Discipline and practice: 'the field' as site, method and location in anthropology. In A. Gupta and J. Ferguson (eds.) *Anthropological locations: boundaries and grounds of a field science,* 1–46. Berkeley: University of California Press.

Hamilton, C. 2000. Faultlines: the construction of archaeological knowledge at Çatalhöyük. In . I.Hodder (ed.) *Towards reflexive method in archaeology: the example at Çatalhöyük,* 119–27. Cambridge: McDonald Institute Monographs.

Hodder, I. 1997. Always momentary, fluid and flexible: towards a self-reflexive excavation methodology. *Antiquity* 71, 691–700.

Hodder, I. (ed.) 2000. *Towards reflexive method in archaeology: the example at Çatalhöyük*. Cambridge. McDonald Institute Monographs.

Hollowell, J. and Nicholas, G. 2008. A critical assessment of ethnography in archaeology. In Q. Castañeda (ed.) *Ethnographic archaeologies: reflections on stakeholders and archaeological practices.* Lanham, MD: Altamira Press.

Holtorf, C. 2002. Notes on the life history of a pot sherd. *Journal of Material Culture* 7:1, 49–71.

Holtorf, C. 2006. Studying archaeological fieldwork in the field: views from Monte Polizzo. In M. Edgeworth (ed.) *Ethnographies of archaeological practice: cultural encounters, material transformations*, 81–94. Lanham, MD: Altamira Press.

Hutchins, E. 1995. *Cognition in the wild.* Cambridge, MA: MIT Press.

Knappett, C. and L. Malafouris. 2008. *Material agency: towards a non-anthropentric approach.* New York: Springer.

Knorr-Cetina, K. 1983. The ethnographic study of scientific work: towards a constructivist interpretation of science. In K. Knorr-Cetina and M. Mulkay (eds.) *Science observed: perspectives on the social study of science*, 115–140. London: Sage.

Latour, B. 1986. Visualization and cognition: thinking with eyes and hands. In H. Kuklick and E. Long (eds.). *Knowledge and Society. Studies in the sociology of culture past and present* 6, 1–40.

Latour, B. 1987. *Science in action: how to follow scientists and engineers through society.* Cambridge, MA: Harvard University Press.

Latour, B. and Woolgar, S. 1979. *Laboratory life: the construction of scientific facts.* Beverly Hills: Sage Publications.

Latour, B. 2005. *Reassembling the social: an introduction to actor-network-theory.* Oxford: Oxford University Press.

Lucas, G. 2001. *Critical approaches to fieldwork: contemporary and historical archaeological practice.* London: Routledge.

Meskell, L. 2005. Archaeological ethnography: conversations around Kruger National Park. *Archaeologies* 1(1), 81–100.

Polanyi, M. 1966. *The tacit dimension.* New York: Doubleday.

Politis, G. 2001. On archaeological praxis, gender bias and indigenous peoples of South America. *Journal of Social Archaeology* 1(1), 90–107.

Radin, P. 1970. *The Italians of San Francisco: their adjustment and acculturation.* San Francisco: R and E Research Associates.

Robertson, J. 2002. Reflexivity redux: a pithy polemic on 'positionality'. *Anthropological Quarterly* 75(4), 785–93.

Roveland, B. 2006. Reflecting upon archaeological practice: multiple visions of a Late Palaeolithic site in Germany. In M. Edgeworth (ed.) *Ethnographies of archaeological practice: cultural encounters, material transformations*, 56–67. Lanham, MD: Altamira Press.

Salzman, P. 2002. On reflexivity. *American Anthropologist* 104(3), 805–13.

Shapin, S. 1995. Here and everywhere: sociology of scientific knowledge. *Annual Review of Sociology* 21, 289–321.

Tilley, C. 1996. *An Ethnography of the Neolithic: Early Prehistoric Socieities inScandanavia.* Cambridge: Cambridge University Press.

Van Maanen, J. 1995. An end to innocence: the ethnography of ethnography. In J. Van Maanen (ed.) *Representation in ethnography*, 1–35. London: Sage.

Van Reybrouck, D. and Jacobs, D. 2006. The mutual constitution of natural and social identities during archaeological fieldwork. In M. Edgeworth (ed.) *Ethnographies of archaeological practice: cultural encounters, material transformations*, 33–44. Lanham, MD: Altamira Press.

Wilmore, M. 2006. Landscapes of disciplinary power: an ethnography of excavation and survey at Leskernick. In M. Edgeworth (ed.) *Ethnographies of archaeological practice: cultural encounters, material transformations* (ed.), 114–125. Lanham, MD: Altamira Press.

Witmore, C. 2004. On multiple fields. Between the material world and media: two cases from the Peloponnesus, Greece. *Archaeological Dialogues* 11, 133–164.

Yarrow, T. 2003. Artefactual persons: the relational capacities of persons and things in the practice of excavation. *Norwegian Archaeological Review* 36(1), 65–73.

# 6

# Archaeology and the anthropology of memory: takes on the recent past

*Paola Filippucci*

*Archaeologists are at work in a wood in Northern France: they are excavating the remains of a trench dug by Allied soldiers some time during 1915.*[1] *There's not much to find except for rusty debris, hard to identify: the trench must have been cleared before being backfilled at the end of the war. It's a sunny day, it's pleasant under the shade and the people at work in the trench are chatting, exchanging jokes. Towards the bottom of the trench, one of them hits a lens of more compacted soil, preserving some evidence of the trench's occupation: the ubiquitous tins of corned beef, remains of a gas mask, and then a thin, flat, moist scrap: after examining it, and deciphering traces of writing on it, the finder says 'it's a cigarette pack'. All come to have a look. 'You can just see him, sitting there having a fag, having a minute to himself'. For a minute, all are silent. The find has suddenly revealed an 'absent present' (Buchli and Lucas 2001: 12): emotion is triggered as 'he' seems very close, almost one of us (cf. Brown 2007; Filippucci in press a.).*

*

*I am in the Argonne, a region of Eastern France that was one of the main battlefields of the Great War. The war devastated the area, its inhabitants were refugees between 1914–18 and returned to find a lunar landscape, a sea of mud and debris. 88 years after the end of the war, I am there to ask questions about what is remembered locally of the Great War, of the civilian experience in particular. 'You have come too late', I am told again and again: 'they have all died now, those who remembered the wartime'. 'You should have come ten years ago'. The tone is of polite regret, and the war, the wartime seems very distant, beyond retrieval.*

These two vignettes are drawn from my experience of research in the former battlefields of Northern France: in the first case as an archaeologist, in the second case as an ethnographer. Each time, I was looking at the same past: the Great War, 1914–18, but the 'distance' between now and then, the relationship between past and present felt rather different in each case: close, almost touching in the first case; remote and disconnected in the second case. This may appear paradoxical: archaeology, relying on mere traces and fragments of the past, is conventionally held to work at a remove from its object of study, past social and cultural reality, and to have to contend with absences and gaps. The anthropologist, by contrast, can 'speak to the people', and so access social reality 'up close' and in its fullness. However when looking at 'how societies remember' (Connerton 1989), anthropologists may also be confronted by gaps and absences as my example suggests. Even in the case of a past that is relatively recent, as in my case, 'the past' may seem irretrievably distant and out of reach. As I will argue, anthropology faces a gap between past and present also from a theoretical point of view: current conceptualisations of 'social memory' put the past firmly beyond the compass of the present, casting 'social memory' as a construct in, of and for the present. This way of conceptualising memory overlooks the intrinsic temporality of social practices, including those associated with remembering. Archaeology, with an epistemology centred on 'traces' of the past, offers a different vantage point on how the past features in the 'ethnographic present'. In particular around the notion of traces archaeology develops a concept of the past as something encountered 'in' and by the present as well as posited retrospectively from it, and posits time as recursive, illuminating the manifold temporality of the 'present'. This is helpful in formulating an understanding of social memory that is more sensitive to the 'diachronic sweep' of social life (Hirsch and Stewart 2005: 268; cf. Shaw 2002).

## *Gaps*

In my opening vignettes, the perceived distance between past and present shifts depending on which discipline, archaeology or anthropology, one is looking from: 'where' the past is in relation to the present depends on the respective epistemology of each discipline. In each case the 'gap' between past and present is defined relationally to the kind of 'data' being considered: inanimate traces, as with archaeology; or animate beings, as with anthropology. Each of these has an intrinsic temporality, a certain 'lifespan' against which 'distance' is defined.

So, in my ethnographic example, the war past is 'distant' in relation to the idea that the people who lived and narrated it are dead. From the anthropological point of view (shared by the anthropologist's subjects), 'the past' takes first and foremost the form of lived experiences and narratives of it. In an enquiry that gathers its primary data from living people, as in anthropology, it is people's lifespan that determines 'where' a certain past is in relation to the present: when people die, the past they have lived dies away with them, becoming irretrievably lost or at least distant because it is accessible only in a mediated way, through second-hand accounts or material documents and traces. This is so at least according to indigenous epistemology that, in the case of modern Western Europe, sees 'memory' primarily as an individual faculty, imperfectly transmissible. Anthropology's notion of 'social memory', centred on the transmission and sharing of memories beyond the individual, ostensibly moves beyond this native assumption; however as I shall consider below, it does not do so sufficiently to breach the gap between past and present posited in this basic model.

In my archaeological example the war past seems 'close' in relation to the 'life-span' of inanimate traces of past lives. Archaeologists uncover and construct their knowledge of the past primarily through those material remains that outlive the living beings with which they were once associated (or they were part of, as with bones), in this case people who lived the Great War. The war past, 'distant' because the people who lived it have died, can feel closer when contemplating the traces they have left behind. How close the past feels arguably depends on how close are its remains to their original state. On the Western Front, the cigarette packet, a flimsy paper construction, is still recognizable, writing on it still readable; corned beef tins still have remains of meat in it, emanating a very discernible, nasty smell; ordnance can still explode. Both give the impression of, and indeed literally embody, a past that is still partly 'alive', active, not quite finished (cf. De Silvey 2006; Saunders 2001). As Buchli and Lucas (2001) have noted, this unfinished, imperfectly decayed state tends to trigger affective reactions. One may experience a sense of uncanny immediacy, breaching the boundary set between 'past' and 'present' by chronology or indeed by cultural assumptions such as that already mentioned, that a past exits from a present with the demise of the people who lived it. Even if the remains are partial, their materiality has the potential to bring the past 'into' the present. By contrast anthropologists rely primarily on narrative as evidence of 'the past' in the ethnographic record: they thus tend to consider 'the past' as a representation that as such is always inevitably at a remove from the past in the sense of 'what happened'.

## *Anthropology and 'social memory'*

Anthropologists have long recognised that 'the past' is an important object of discourse and practice in society. In line with the discipline's focus on the ethnographic present, anthropologists tend to consider the past from the point of view of the present, in terms of 'how societies remember' (Connerton 1989). The concept of 'social memory' was first formulated in the early 20th century by Durkheimian sociologist Maurice Halbwachs (1980, 1992) whose ideas remain the main basis for anthropological theorisations to this day. Influenced by Durkheim's theory of the social origin of knowledge, Halbwachs theorised that remembering, while always inevitably individual, is always mediated by social categories and occurs in social relations; moreover, by remembering the past people sustain and reinforce social relations and groups (Halbwachs 1980). The main part of Halbwachs' argument which has influenced anthropology is that what is remembered is selective and driven by concerns and interests of and in the present, echoing Malinowski's point that accounts of the past can be charters for present arrangements. This approach has been very valuable in showing how discourse concerning the past is a central political and symbolic resource in and for the present (Appadurai 1981: 202; Watson 1985; Gillis 1994). Another strength of the concept of 'social memory' is that it allows for a non-linear relationship between past and present: by positing that people tell the past with the present and future in mind, anthropologists envisage a 'shuttling' motion that defies chronological order (see Portelli 1991: 65).

In practice, however, this potential is denied by a tendency in conceptions of social memory to flatten 'the past' into the present (Shaw 2002: 9): because the past is remembered selectively in response to present concerns, these shape and determine 'the past in the present' at any point in time. As Peel has noted (1984), the 'well-grounded methodological warning' not to take accounts of the past as accurate reflections of 'what happened' has lead to 'the logical absurdity of unhinging the present from the past completely' (1984: 112). The past tends to be characterised as 'boundless resource' for the present, functionally related to contemporary needs and desires that determine what is and is not remembered (see Appadurai 1981: 201; Shaw 2002: 12). This is even more pronounced in models of memory formulated in anthropology and the social sciences more broadly in response to poststructuralism and the post-modern conception of history as narrative discourse (e.g. White 1987). So for instance Frow (2007) proposes a model of memory 'predicated on the non-existence of the past', whose relation to the past 'is not that of truth but of desire', in which 'meaning and truth are constituted retroactively and repeatedly' and 'alternative stories are always possible' (2007: 153–7). This account has echoes of Halbwachs' functionalism, insofar as Frow presents social memory as self-contained within a single time, the present: 'a dynamic but closed system, where all moments of the system are co-present, and the end is given at the same time as the beginning' (Frow 2007: 154). Although Frow is not an anthropologist, a similar approach colours recent anthropological discussions of memory (e.g. Forty and Kuchler 2001; Hirsch 1997). For Hirsch and Stewart, anthropologists continue to be mostly interested in the 'present present or the past present' as once noted by Evans-Pritchard (2005: 268). In spite of the fact that a key part of the post-structuralist critique in anthropology has been to problematise the 'ethnographic present' and adopt a more historical outlook on culture and society (e.g. Marcus and Fisher 1986: 34), recent work on social memory has tended to imply a self-contained, self-referential present.

Anthropology's take on social memory therefore tends to disconnect past and present, positing 'social memory' as fully contained within the latter. Shaw (2002) explains the continuing presentism and functionalism of current theories of social memory by the analytic privileging of rupture and instability and focus on discourse and representation under the influence of postmodernism (2002: 9). Current notions of representation drawing on post-structuralism posit an irreducible gap between it and its object, between signifier and signified (e.g. Wallace 2006: 14). Accordingly by focusing on representation anthropology posits what may be called a 'metaphorical' relationship between present and past: insofar as representation can only ever allude to the world beyond it, 'the past' narrated and referred to in social memory is always inevitably 'not there', disconnected from the present. This is problematic because it downplays a central feature of memory as an individual or social human faculty: its intrinsically temporal nature, 'between' past and present insofar as it evinces the human ability to think and act in a 'past-present-future' nexus (Hirsch and Stewart 2005: 262). In downplaying this aspect, current studies consider social memory as just 'another form of expressive culture' (Hirsch and Stewart 2005: 268) and detract from the concept's analytical effectiveness: its semantic range is now so wide that it 'may become indistinguishable from either identity or culture' (Fabian 1999: 51 cit. in Berliner 2005: 198). In a bid to restore to social memory some of its distinctiveness, we may turn to archaeology, a discipline whose epistemology is centred on traces, parts of (lost) 'wholes' that link past and present, so to speak, metonymically.

## *Archaeology and the past*

Hauser (2007) identifies the core of what she calls 'the archaeological imagination' in the assumption that the past 'exceeds our capacity to record or represent it' (2007: 281). She attributes this assumption to a particular incarnation of this 'imagination', found among writers and artists as well as archaeologists in inter-war Britain that she links with Romantic conceptions of history. Archaeology has moved on theoretically since the inter-war period, embracing the social scientific idea that all accounts of the past, including its own, are speculative, partial, and reflect the concerns of later times (see e.g. Hodder *et al.* 1995). By the 21st century, archaeology has become 'interpretive and self-reflexive' and many archaeologists acknowledge that what they uncover is not 'the past' but an artefact of their own making (Hodder 1999: 5, 15–16). Indeed some have also proposed that archaeology might not have to be about 'the past' at all (Buchli and Lucas 2001). To this extent today's archaeologists, like anthropologists, disengage past and present.

However this assumption is tempered by two factors. Firstly, mainstream disciplinary practice remains firmly committed to analysing a material 'record' held to have been deposited in the past and to have a causal relationship with it. Secondly all but the most reflexive archaeologists grant 'the past' some autonomy from 'the present' represented by the archaeologist's gaze. Minimally it is assumed that there are traces of 'the past' to be found and that, as traces, they can potentially operate as clues to past realities, as witnessed by the continuing commitment to excavation. In addition, though these traces are always interpreted through present-day eyes, through 'pre-understandings' and 'pre-judgements', both scientific and social/cultural, it is argued that they have the potential to challenge and interrogate present certainties, to 'assert their own independence' (Hodder 1999: 32–3).

Hodder (1999) posits a recursive relationship between theory and data, mutually constituted in the ongoing process of archaeological interpretation both within an individual excavation and over time as new excavation takes place. He describes the archaeologist as a 'mediator', 'neither simply describing data nor simply translating it into "our" terms' (Hodder 1999: 63). For Hodder, 'the past is not objective or subjective. It is both. By this I mean that archaeological evidence has an "objective" materiality which limits and confronts what can be said about it, and which contributes to the experiences of "subjective" observers. At the same time, the "subjective" interpreter of the evidence constructs "objective" data from a particular perspective' (1999: 200). Archaeological knowledge is produced in and through a dialectic between traces from/of the past and ideas and concerns from/of the present (see also Lucas, and McFadyen, this volume).

Traces may be incomplete, fragmentary in relation to the fullness of past life that must be reconstructed through scientific reasoning but also imagination (Hodder 1999: 71 ffw.; cf. Schnapp 1993: 13). However an epistemological paradigm centred on the idea of 'traces' posits a less arbitrary link between past and present than a paradigm such as that of anthropology, centred on narrative and representation. This is because traces are held to have an intrinsic link with the past reality that made or left them: they are a part of the past, metonymically related to it (cf. Ginzburg 1986: 158). Even with Hodder's cautions that archaeologists 'construct' the trace through their methodologies (1999: 15 ffw.), archaeologists still envisage that there are traces to be found 'of' and 'from' the past. In other words by their very epistemology archaeologists posit that the past is not fully contained within the present: it produces traces that linger and traverse time, and thereby shape and partially determine later representations of the past in which they originated. These representations are therefore not solely driven and shaped by contemporary concerns, as in anthropological renderings of social memory, but also by the engagement and encounter with what is understood to be a residue of earlier times, incomplete but, ultimately, causally related with past realities.

The idea that the past has an autonomous existence, that there is 'a real past that challenges the present' (Fasolt, cit. in Hirsch and Stewart 2005: 264) and can be potentially reconstructed via its traces causally related to it, is central to the historicist paradigm (Hirsch and Stewart 2005: 264). One problem with historicism is that in positing the past as utterly past it naturalises linear chronology, instead of considering it as a culturally and historically specific construct (Hirsch and Stewart 2005: 264–65, following Fasolt). Linear chronology overlooks the fact that from the point of view of social actors and social action time is not linear, and past, present and future interpenetrate in complex ways (cf. Hirsch and Stewart 2005). In spite of its historicist roots, archaeology can escape this limitation because of its focus on material traces. Such traces can be fully interpreted within a linear chronology and indeed can be the basis for it in archaeological contexts (when dated, classified typologically, etc.). However, as already considered, many archaeologists today posit that traces are partly constructed and interpreted in and by the present. In addition, in their materiality traces have the potential to challenge linear chronological understandings of time. At least from a subjective, phenomenological point of view, material remains can bring the past 'into the present' (and/or the present 'into' the past) in an immediate way, cross-cutting and unsettling the idea of temporal sequence and succession (see Buchli and Lucas 2001).

By associating the past with material traces, archaeology thus represents the past as at once *other* than the present and *in* the present: rather than entirely *of* the present, traces are neither totally past nor totally present. This has the implication that each 'present' is manifold temporally, less self-referential, self-contained and synchronic than is allowed by anthropologists' prevailing conception of social memory. Thinking about the ethnographic present in this way can enrich the anthropological understanding of 'how societies remember'. I demonstrate this by turning to an ethnographic example from the former Great War battlefields of Eastern France.

## *Villages détruits*

In September 2005 I attended a ceremony commemorating the destruction of a village near Verdun in 1916, remembered on the feast of the village's patron saint. Some fifty people were present, including the mayor and some other local authorities and representatives of veterans' associations. While this scenario does not sound unusual in today's France, in this case the village in question, Bezonvaux, had not existed for 89 years (in 2005). Bezonvaux is one of thirteen villages in the vicinity of Verdun that were destroyed so severely and completely at the Great War that they were never reconstructed and have remained part of the 'Red Zone' [*Zone Rouge*], land that could not be reclaimed for habitation.[2] Most of the villages still hold annual commemorations at chapels and/or monuments erected on the former sites during the 1920s and early 1930s. The ceremonies are officiated by a mayor and a municipal council, instituted by prefectoral law on 22 April 1922 in order to ensure the 'symbolic survival' of the municipalities, as monuments and memorials to the destruction and 'heroism' of the villages (each of which was also awarded a *Croix de Guerre*) (Villages Détruits n.d.: 7, 15). After the war, the initiative of public authorities was matched and supported by the activism of former villagers, permanently evacuated to other localities but from the early post-war years busy collecting funds for monuments and chapels, most of which were inaugurated by the early 1930s and became then the focus of an annual ceremony/pilgrimage.

The interesting point for my purposes is that the villages still mobilise public interest in the early 21st century, almost a century after their disappearance. What has kept and keeps alive the memory of their brutal, violent destruction? A central role, as mentioned, is played by administrative procedure, providing for the periodic nomination by the prefect of a mayor and members of the communal council. These posts have until recently been occupied by former villagers. As time has gone by, those born in the pre-war village (that is, before evacuation that in all cases occurred between 1914 and 1915) have become too elderly or passed away, and the posts have been taken on either by their direct descendants or also (as in the case of the current mayor of Bezonvaux) by friends of descendants who do not have family in the village but have an amateur historical interest in Great War matters. Descendants, however, remain centrally involved in keeping the memory alive: so the other principal means by which the memory of the villages endures, the annual or biannual commemorative ceremony, is still attended by several direct or indirect descendants of the pre-1914 villagers. For instance, at Bezonvaux in 2005, as proudly stated during the ceremony, some thirty *descendants* (as they call each other) were present, including the last living pre-1914 villager, a woman born in 1913 and evacuated from the village at 18 months old; and more were expected the following year, marking the 90th anniversary of the destruction.[3]

After the formal ceremony, the authorities, *descendants* and their guests attend a convivial meal where, by their own account, whether or not they have ever met before, they catch up with each others' news and also 'reminisce' about the village, drawing on received memories, photographs and old documents to retrace former connections of kinship, friendship or neighbourhood. Even during the ceremony I witnessed several instances of *descendants* discovering that others among those present were distant relatives, friends or neighbours named by parents or grandparents in their recollections of the village, in a latter-day, ghostly recreation of 'village' networks. In recent years, with the gradual disappearance of the original villagers, *descendants* have been increasingly aided in this activity by the gathering of material vestiges of various kinds. In the immediate post-war period the remains of the villages, very fragmentary and mixed up with the lethal debris of combat, were buried and planted over with trees. However since the late 1990s the ruins of some of the villages have been cleared of vegetation by volunteers and the remains of buildings and artefacts have been conserved and used to create *sentiers de mémoire* [memory trails] for visitors. This has partly occurred with the financial support of departmental authorities in the context of their '*politique de mémoire*' ['memory policy'] begun with the commemorations for the 80th anniversary of the Great War.[4] However the impulse and much of the work has come from descendants, who have also built picnic areas aimed partly at tourists but also explicitly said to be for family and 'village' gatherings.

In Bezonvaux the 'memory trail' was completed in 2001. This includes displays of old postcards and photographs of the pre-war village and villagers, graphic reconstructions of village landmarks and cadastral maps from 1914 identifying the position and owner of various houses, making it possible to put family names and/or pre-war function to some of the ruins still visible (the bakery, the mill and so on). Along the path are also displays of material debris retrieved from the ruins: fragments of kitchenware, of furniture, the mangled remains of agricultural implements on the surface of which, as some pointed out, 'you can see the force of the shelling'. After the ceremony, all of those present process from the monument to chapel via the 'memory trail', some pausing in silence at the site (or supposed site) of their family's former house. Photographs and documentation about the village have been donated by former villagers and, lately, *descendants* of the original inhabitants. Images of the village have also been found in archives by the current Mayor, a keen amateur historian, who has collected them in big albums that he takes to the annual ceremony. Here, by his account, they are avidly perused by those present. In other villages, some of these mementoes have been collected in published books (e.g. Fisnot and Chavrelle 1999).

In 2005 the *descendants* and others involved in activities around the *villages détruits* [ruined villages, lit. 'destroyed villages'] as they are known, lamented the demise of the last original villagers and worried that the memory might die out as 'the young' don't want to get involved. In this sense their understanding was underpinned by a view of memory more broadly indigenous to Euro-American societies, and shared by anthropologists. In this view 'memory' is essentially an individual, interior faculty that tends to 'die out' with the person holding it, unless an effort is made by those who have it to transmit it to others who in their turn can pass it on and so that it is carried forward into later times. However several *descendants* by their own account had themselves been rather uninterested when young, and only began to attend commemorations and/or collect mementoes of the village when their parents or elder relatives could no longer attend, through death or illness or old age. For instance one woman had begun to attend in 2000, to accompany her mother who was becoming increasingly frail (so that by 2005 she could no longer make it to the ceremony); in turn her mother had begun to attend when the chapel was first inaugurated in 1932 because her parents had originated from the village. She had, however, never seen the village because she was born in 1917 in the village to where they had evacuated from Bezonvaux in 1915. In other words, people take the baton of commemoration from their elders, particularly parents or grandparents, when they can no longer do it. This was the case even for the current Mayor of Bezonvaux. Although not a *descendant*, he became Mayor because he had been studying the history of the village and in the process had become a friend of the previous mayor (a *descendant*). Nevertheless he attributed his own willingness to take up the post to the fact that his parents had lived at the site of one of the other *villages détruits* in the Verdun area,[5] when they had come to work at the post-war clearance of the battlefield in the 1920s.

Following a conventional interpretation, the 'social memory' of the *villages détruits* can be seen to be perpetuated by 'present concerns': first and foremost the public *politique de mémoire*, formulated to promote tourism to the Meuse Department of which the Verdun area is part, in turn part of regional policy to promote economic development in a relatively depressed area. More broadly interest in the Great War is arguably driven by a contemporary fascination for the world wars, partly fuelled by present-day geopolitical concerns about European unification as well as by the ethical and political issues raised by wars on a global arena (e.g. Prost and Winter 2005; Winter 2006).

On another level, however, remembrance of such a brutal and unsettling past is perpetuated by social structures and structures of sentiment 'from the past'. Firstly in this case there are institutional mechanisms and rituals dating from the post-war period which were explicitly aimed at ensuring that future generations attended to these sites and the events they are associated with. Secondly, people today become interested in 'remembering' the destroyed village through kin and friends and, arguably, 'for' them, in their name or memory. In other words they remember to fulfil personal moral obligations and in a web of moral relations, such as those of kinship, that have a fundamental temporal dimension (cf. Carsten 2000).

As Lambek has noted, memory is a profoundly moral practice, moved by our commitments, relationships and loyalties (1996). This is nowhere more explicit than in relation to the World Wars. Post-war commemoration in the Great War was centred around the idea of a 'debt' with the war dead, who had 'suffered' and 'sacrificed' their lives 'so that we may live', to use a phrase common at the time (see e.g. Winter 2006). This sentiment was dominant in post-war commemoration and also materialised on and by monuments and memorials whose mood and purpose was mainly funerary and voiced an ethical 'duty to remember' (Prost 2002: 19; King 2001: 152). The monuments and the surrounding rhetoric not only mediated a reflection on the past but also an appeal to the future: we should not forget so that such horror may never happen again. In France this was the core mission of Associations such as the *Anciens Combattants* [War Veterans' Association] and *Souvenir Français* [French Remembrance] both still centrally involved in war commemoration today (see e.g. Prost 2002). As Dyer has acutely observed, the Great War was lived *as if it was already past and in danger of being forgotten*, something he finds reflected in memoirs and literature written during the war as well as in monuments and memorials (Dyer 1994: 18 and *passim*).

More broadly, therefore, at the time of the war people set about memorialising it by building monuments, formulating discourses and creating social and moral networks and practices that were not purely synchronic. Instead they both responded to the past and looked to the future with the aim of interpellating it by ensuring that a certain past was carried forward into time, remembered by posterity. In other words, people constructed 'social memory' of this event with a keen consciousness of temporality and a keen sense of their own historicity: seeing themselves in a diachronic chain stretching between the past and present into the future and seeking to transmit something from the past to the future. The same consciousness of temporality, of being part of a diachronic chain of transmission underpins today's bid to remember 'for' kin and friends. Here the purpose of reconstruction is not to suit present concerns but instead to encounter the war past *as past,* as something that 'really happened'. This particular phrase was used by many people I have met on the Western Front, to explain the value of uncovering, exploring and conserving the material vestiges of the conflict (see Filippucci in press a and b). This includes residents, visitors and my archaeologist colleagues, one of whom said in a recent radio broadcast (BBC 2008) that these remains show the war in its 'raw' state; or, as many of my informants put it, 'the war as it really was'. In the words of one of them, 'reading books about the war one forgets the emotional side, one thinks of it only as a technical fact – but going on to the places where it happened, one realises once again that it really happened'. To put it in another way, the material remains give us access to the past as 'an absent present' (Buchli and Lucas 2001: 12): they unsettle and disturb the sense of our present as present, revealing that which is normally invisible, the consciousness of our own present as, in future, a past (2001: 11).

This material suggests a quest for retrieving the emotion of the war past. Arguably this is undertaken in order to let that past unsettle us and, in the process, regain a sense of our own being in history. How can this be explained? Once again, 'present concerns' may be invoked: for instance, it may be a reaction to the increasing presentism and 'unreality' of our lives dominated by the time and space of virtuality (Huyssen 1995; Augé 2004). However, as in the case of the 'destroyed villages', this urge to expose the material remains of the Great War seems to have intensified in recent years, just as the last *descendants*, immediate survivors of the wartime, have passed away. Arguably, the material remains respond to a need to be back in touch (somewhat literally) with those who were in the war, substituting for the living presence of 'those who have lived the war', so that we may fulfil our sense of duty and commitment towards them: both that owed publicly to 'the Fallen' and also perhaps primarily, that which we more privately owe to our kin.

## *Memory traces: towards an 'archaeological' model of social memory*

One problem with the presentism in anthropological theorisations of social memory, as Shaw has noted (2002), is that it cannot account for the fact that societies remember unsettling, unwelcome or troubling past events. In Eastern France, for instance, the Great War, though beyond living memory and linking the place with unimaginable violence and tragic loss, is insistently evoked in local discourse and practice today as I have shown above, even if this past is at the very least saddening or depressing, and so unlikely to serve contemporary interests or desires.

In explaining the lingering presence of negative or damaging pasts, some draw on the psychoanalytic concept of 'trauma', but its applicability in a social context is debatable (see Antze and Lambek 1996; Feuchtwang n.d.). This is because by definition trauma is inaccessible through words and ordinary discourse (for Freud), or even 'the very thing about which nothing can be said' (for Lacan) (Wallace 2006: 3; cf. Bowie 1991: 103); and identified with involuntary recollection driven by the individual unconscious rather than social and cultural mechanisms of signification (see e.g. Whitehead 2007). Hirsch (1997), writing about the children of Holocaust survivors, suggests that trauma is transmissible through its very incommunicability: in the sense that the silence of parents about their experiences creates a void that descendants' imagination seeks to fill, prompting or indeed forcing a vicarious relationship with the traumatic past (see Young

2000: 2). This is 'postmemory', when later generations must bear as theirs a past known only indirectly through the memories of those 'shaped by traumatic events that can be neither understood nor recreated' (1997: 22; cf. Young 2000: 3). This is a powerful argument that I find very valuable in interpreting my material (see e.g. Filippucci in press b). However once again it posits that the motor for remembrance is the needs of the present: those of a younger generation beset by a gap in their knowledge of 'where they've come from' (see Carsten 2000; cf. Hirsch and Spitzer 2002).

In the case I have presented, this last point is undoubtedly a factor. However, in addition, I have suggested that other sentiments are at work, such as filial obligation and affection, or ethical commitment towards the dead. These compel descendants to want to know about the village, even when they have never lived in it; these compel us to want to remember a war we have never lived. In other words in trying to account for the lingering presence of a negative past, I put the focus on practices and sentiments that more or less consciously exist and unfold between past and present, seeking to bridge time. In formulating my analysis I was assisted by an 'archaeological' model of the past: as capable of leaving traces that endure into later times, caused by the differing temporalities of what makes up each moment.

Just as different substances have different lifespans, some more enduring than others and able to take the past 'into' later times where they operate as traces, so there are social practices and discourses with different lifespans, some ephemeral, consciously 'of the present', and some consciously aimed at enduring and interpellating later times: in my case, formal rituals and commemorations (see Connerton 1989) but also the informal practices and discourses of kinship and kinship sentiment: story-telling, ideas of filial obligation and duty, the whole make up of parent-child affection, and of friendship (cf. Winter 1995; Feuchtwang n.d.).

These aspects remind us that the 'social' is intrinsically temporal and diachronic: obligation, affection, hope, debt, expectation, fear and the 'social structures' and relations constructed around and through them project individuals and societies across time, from pasts into futures (cf. e.g. Greenhouse 1996; Hirsch and Stewart 2005). One of the potential strengths of the anthropological concept of social memory is precisely to chart a non-linear temporality, in which past and present are not discrete entities. As they remember, people 'shuttle' between past and present: so they tread a terrain in which the past is not totally past and by implication, the present not totally present. This aspect is played down in current anthropological theorizations that emphasise the constructed nature of the past in the present and thereby separate the two. A comparison with the archaeological rendering of the past through material traces helps us focus back on that terrain between past and present, wherein we may locate a theory of social memory that is more sensitive to the diachronic nature of social life.

## *Acknowledgements*

The author would like to gratefully acknowledge the financial support of an Eileen and Phyllis Gibbs Travelling Fellowship from Newnham College, Cambridge, for the ethnographic fieldwork on which this paper is partly based.

*Notes*

1 My work with Great War archaeologists has been partly moved and also made possible by my own background in archaeology, in which I have an undergraduate degree and field experience through participating in excavations for a number of years. Although I moved to anthropology for graduate study, archaeology has remained an abiding interest.

2 See e.g. http://www.cheminsdememoire.gouv.fr/page/affichelieu.php?idLang=en&idLieu=2911; Connaissance de la Meuse 2001; cf. Clout (1996: 25 ffw).

3 A participant reported that recent annual ceremonies have been attended by some 200 people, an impressive number given that in 1914 the village only had 170 inhabitants.

4 See www. http://www.cg55.fr/culture/user_memoire_politique.htm (cf. Becker and Audoin-Rouzeau 2001).

5 Where he had also served as a Municipal councillor for some years.

## *References*

Antze, P. and Lambek, M. (eds.) 1996. *Tense past: cultural essays in trauma and memory*. London: Routledge.

Appadurai, A. 1981. The past as a scarce resource. *Man (N.S.)* 16, 201–19.

BBC 2008. 'Art in the trenches', conducted by Dan Snow, BBC Radio 4, broadcast on 24-2-2008

Augé, M. 2004. *Rovine e macerie*. Torino: Bollati Boringhieri.

Becker, A. and Audoin-Rouzeau, S. 2000. 1914–1918: *Understanding the Great War*. London: Profile Books.

Berliner, D. 2005. The abuses of memory: reflections on the memory boom in anthropology. *Anthropological Quarterly* 78 (1), 197–211.

Bowie, M. 1991. *Lacan*. London: Fontana Press.

Brown, M. 2007. The Fallen, the front, and the finding: archaeology, human remains, and the Great War. *Archaeological Review from Cambridge* 22 (2), 53–68

Buchli, V. and Lucas, G. 2001. *Archaeologies of the contemporary past*. London and New York: Routledge.

Carsten, J. 2000. "Knowing where you've come from": ruptures and continuities of time and kinship in narratives of adoption reunions. *Journal of the Royal Anthropological Institute* 6 (4), 687–703

Clout, H. 1996. *After the ruins: restoring the countryside of Northern France after the Great War*. Exeter: Exeter University Press.

Connaissance de la Meuse n.d. Villages détruits, villages reconstruits. Zone Rouge de Verdun et Pays d'Étain. Pont-à-Mousson: Presses de l'Imprimerie Moderne.

Connerton, P. 1989. *How societies remember*. Cambridge: Cambridge University Press.

DeSilvey, C. 2006. Observed decay: telling stories with mutable things. *Journal of Material Culture* 11 (1/2), 318–38.

Dyer, G. 1994. *The missing of the Somme.* London: Phoenix.

Feuchtwang, S. n.d. Two or three times: an essay on temporality and trauma. Paper given at EASA Biennial Conference, Bristol, 20 September 2006.

Filippucci, P. in press a. Archaeology and memory on the Western Front. In D. Boric (ed.) *Archaeology and memory*, Oxford: Oxbow Books.

Filippucci, P. in press b. In a ruined country: place and the memory of war destruction in Argonne (France). In N. Argenti and K. Schramm (eds.) *Remembering violence: anthropological perspectives on intergenerational transmission.* Oxford: Berghahn Books.

Fisnot, A. and Chavrelle, J. 1999. *Haumont-près-Samogneux: Un ouvrage de souvenirs.* Verdun: Association de sauvegarde de la mémoire de Haumont.

Forty, A. and Kuchler, S. 2001. *The art of forgetting.* Oxford: Berg.

Frow, J. 2007. From Toute la mémoire du monde: repetition and forgetting. In M. Rossington and A. Whitehead (eds.) *Theories of memory: a reader,* 150–56., Edinburgh: Edinburgh University Press.

Gillis, J.R. 1994. *Commemorations: The politics of national identity.* Princeton: Princeton University Press.

Ginzburg, C. 1986. *Miti, emblemi, spie.* Torino: Einaudi.

Greenhouse, C.J. 1996. *A moment's notice: time politics across cultures.* Ithaca, N.Y. and London: Cornell University Press.

Halbwachs, M. 1980 [1950]. *The collective memory.* New York and London: Harper and Row.

Halbwachs, M. 1992 [1942]. *On collective memory.* Chicago: The University of Chicago Press.

Hauser, K. 2007. *Shadow sites: photography, archaeology and the British landscape 1927–1955.* Oxford: Oxford University Press.

Hirsch, E. and Stewart, C. 2005. Introduction: ethnographies of historicity. *History and Anthropology* 16, 261–74.

Hirsch, M. 1997. *Family frames: photography, narrative and postmemory.* Cambridge, MA.: Harvard University Press.

Hirsch, M. and Spitzer, L. 2002. "We Would Not Have Come Without You": Generations of Nostalgia. *American Imago* 59 (3), 253–276.

Hodder, I. 1999. *The archaeological process: an introduction.* Oxford: Blackwell.

Hodder, I., Shanks, M., Alexandri, A., Buchli, V., Carman, J., Last, J. and Lucas, G. (eds.) 1995 *Interpreting archaeology: finding meaning in the past.* London and New York: Routledge.

Huyssen, A. 1995. *Twilight memories: marking time in a culture of amnesia.* New York and London: Routledge.

King, A. 2001. Remembering and forgetting in public memorials of the Great War. In A. Forty and S. Kuchler (eds.) *The art of forgetting.* Oxford: Berg, 147–169.

Lambek, M. 1996. The past imperfect: remembering as moral practice. In P. Antze and M. Lambek (eds.) *Tense past: cultural essays in trauma and memory*, 235–54. London: Routledge.

Marcus, G. and Fischer, M.M.J. 1986. *Anthropology as cultural critique: an experimental moment in the social sciences.* Chicago and London: The University of Chicago Press.

Peel, J. 1984. Making history: the past in the Ijesha present. *Man* (N.S.), 111–32.

Portelli, A. 1991. *The death of Luigi Trastulli and other stories: form and meaning in oral history.* New York: State University of New York Press.

Prost, A. 2002. *Republican identities in war and peace: representations of France in the 19th and 20th centuries.* Oxford: Berg.

Prost, A. and Winter, J. (eds.) 2005. *The Great War in history: debates and controversies, 1914 to the present.* Cambridge: Cambridge University Press.

Shaw, R. 2002. *Memories of the slave trade: ritual and the historical imagination in Sierra Leone.* Chicago and London: The University of Chicago Press.

Saunders, N. J. 2001. Matter and memory in the landscapes of conflict: the Western Front 1914–1999. In B. Bender and M. Winer (eds.) *Contested landscapes: movement, exile and place*, 37–53. Oxford: Berg.

Schapp, A. 1993. *The discovery of the past*. London: British Museum Press.

Villages Détruits n.d. Verdun 14–18: les villages détruits. Paris: Sécretariat d'État à la Défense.

Wallace, I. 2006. Trauma as representation: a meditation on Manet and Johns. In L. Saltzman and E. Rosenberg (eds.) *Trauma and visuality in modernity*. Hanover and London: University Press of New England.

Watson, R. 1985. *Memory, history and opposition under state Socialism*. Santa Fe: School of American Research Press.

White, H. 1987. *The content of the form: Narrative discourse and historical representation*. Baltimore and London: The Johns Hopkins University Press.

Whitehead, A. 2007. Trauma: Introduction. In M. Rossington and A. Whitehead (eds.) *Theories of memory: a reader*, 186–191 , Edinburgh: Edinburgh University Press.

Winter, J. 1995. *Sites of memory, sites of mourning: the Great War in European cultural history*. Cambridge: Cambridge University Press

Winter, J. 2006. *Remembering War: the Great War between memory and history in the twentieth century*. New Haven and London: Yale University Press.

Young, J. 2000. *At memory's edge: after-images of the Holocaust in contemporary art and architecture*. New Haven and London: Yale University Press.

# 7

# Resolving archaeological and ethnographic tensions: a case study from South-Central California

*David Robinson*

Hidden behind rocks in a narrow crevice inside a cave, organic materials can be seen secreted away at the site of Cache Cave in the remote backcountry of South-Central California (Figure 7.1). Arrow shafts, basketry rim fragments, a large raptor claw, and carved 'witch-sticks' are just some of the *in-situ* materials cached in the confines of this recently discovered site. Such finds are now very uncommon: when found, they would invariably be considered remains of the prehistoric Chumash who lived in these hills and towards the Pacific Coast long before European contact (Figure 7.2). The Chumash are famous for their often spectacular and beguiling multi-coloured prehistoric rock paintings. Located in the sandstone rock-art zone of the Chumash, prehistorians would be greatly interested in analyzing these materials, seen as survivors of organics of a deep indigenous past. However, on closer inspection, it can be seen that some of the carved and modified pieces show work with metal tools; more significantly, cattle bones on the surface of the cave floor confirm this site to be historical since cattle were not introduced to California until the Spanish Mission system was established in the late AD 1700s. To put it in Americanist terms, the remains of Cache Cave are not in a secure indigenous provenience. That provenience is a modern temporality, not a premodern one.

Many historical archaeologists, while finding the artefacts intriguing, may question that provenience. The artefacts are *essentially* prehistoric: vestigial extensions of the premodern, their value would be seen as forms of resistance to colonialism and modernity, proof of localized attempts of cultural revitalization, and ultimately, the brevity of the short but tumultuous pause between the establishment of Franciscan missions (AD1769) and the ultimate floodtide of capitalistic modernity in the AD1849 Gold Rush and the birth of California as an American state. They would, in Lucas' (2004) terminology, be indicative of the *ontology* of prehistory even though they do not fall within its strict temporality. Modification with metal tools would not make them modern.

The artefacts at Cache Cave represent what Chakrabarty (2000) calls *time-knots* – 'ironic disjunctures' uneasily joining together non-modern and modern pasts. Even so, Chakrabarty suggests that these knots can be 'straightened out' since the very fact that they are knotted means that, however problematic the knot may be, they share

*Figure 7.1. Cached in situ artifacts in crevice at Cache Cave, South-Central California.*

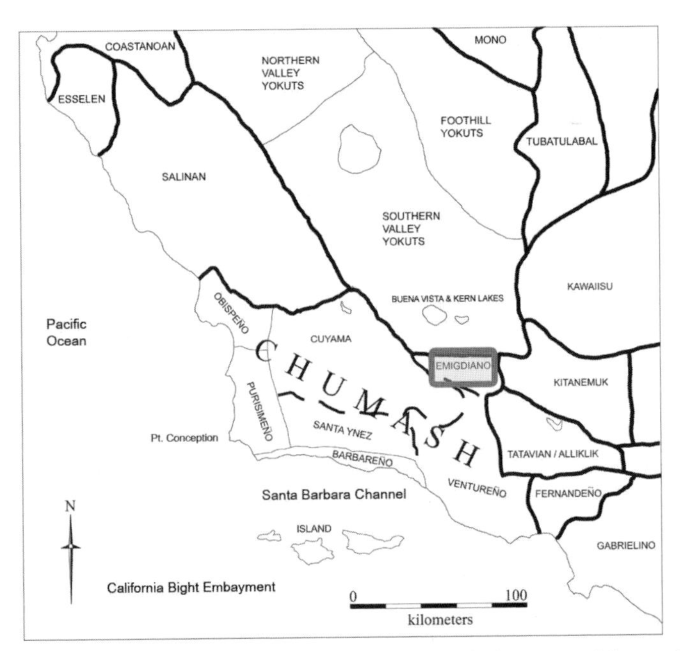


*Figure 7.2. Linguistic areas of South-Central California as documented by anthropologists. The Emigdiano area in the centre forms the focus of much of this paper.*

the same temporal moment. Chakrabarty derives this term from his own Bengali language, stating that:

> It is because we live in time-knots that we can undertake the exercise of straightening out, as it were, some part of the knot (which is how we might think of chronology). Time, as the expression goes in my language, situates us within the structure of a *granthi*; hence the Bengali word *shomoy-granthi*, *shomoy* meaning "time" and *granthi* referring to joints of various kinds, from the complex formation of knuckles on our fingers to the joints on a bamboo stick (2000: 112).

While Chakrabarty discusses time-knots in relation to the Santal, a group that resisted colonial British and elite Indian rule in early 19th century India, his concept has wider application in looking at other indigenous pasts within colonial and post-colonial contexts. Chakrabarty further argues that time-knots bind together non-modern and modern pasts in 'a shared and constant "now"' but are woven from the different ontological strands of coloniser and colonised' (2000: 112). As 'ironic disjunctures' time-knots tie together modern and indigenous temporalities: they share the same space, but do so in an uneasy, convoluted sense because of their fundamental differences and alternate historical trajectories.

Here, I argue that like the artefacts found in Cache Cave, the written records of indigenous people in California are entangled within historical knots in a similar vein to Chakrabarty's time-knots. Texts such as mission registers, military documents, but particularly ethnological studies by early 20th century anthropologists that resulted in the ethnographic record left to us today emerged through complex historical trajectories that nevertheless occurred in a specific shared moment of time. These ethnographies were documented in post-Mission and post-Gold Rush times by a group of 'salvage' anthropologists from Berkeley and the Smithsonian who worked not to document that moment in time so much as to record a 'vanishing' way of life. This form of anthropology was not participant observation, but the documentation of 'memory culture' involving interviews with indigenous elders about their childhood and past generations of their relatives (see Lightfoot 2005: 32–33; Lightfoot and Parrish 2009: 77–96).

In essence, this memory anthropology attempted to document indigenous lifeways that were a vestige of the past *predating* that documentation. Kroeber, the founder of Californian anthropology, described his work as an attempt to 'reconstruct and present the scheme within which [Native Californians] in *ancient* and more recent times lived their lives' (1925: v, emphasis added). Other sources survive from the 16th through to the early 19th centuries as Spanish mission and later colonial Euro-American powers took control of California. Prehistorians point out that this ethnographic record is 'tainted' by Euro-American influence, calling into question any interpretation of 'indigenous' practice through its colonial, and therefore temporal, alteration. Conversely, some historical archaeologists relegate ethnographic documentation into the realm of the pre-modern, or, at best, see it standing as an exemplar of what once was, a contrasting foil to show the essential difference between the West and the Indigenous, the Modern and the pre-Modern. As Lightfoot (1995) points out, post contact 'native remains' fall into a 'fuzzy domain', in part, because of the 'artificial division' between prehistoric and historical archaeology in North America. Ethnographic sources also fall into this 'fuzzy domain', therefore playing an ambiguous role in archaeological research. Even so, they have structured archaeological work in California since the early 20th century, and have most directly influenced current interpretation of California rock-art. As Whitley and Clottes have shown, the history of rock-art research in the North American Far West may be 'characterised as a tension between purely ethnographic versus exclusively archaeological approaches' (2005: 175). Like Chakrabarty's time-knots, and reflective of colonial and post-colonial histories, the trajectory of anthropological work that created the ethnographic record is woven into a complex relationship with archaeological research in California.

In this paper, I will point out that this tension does not only exist in the history of rock-art research, but also in the interpretations derived from these two separate yet entwined discursive strands – archaeology and ethnography. I will set out to resolve this tension by disentangling these knotted strands of research that focuses on the indigenous Californian past. In looking at the interpretations derived from Californian ethnographic and archaeological approaches, there are apparent contradictions which serve to highlight that, as a discipline, archaeology is not entirely separate from anthropology: even as it only partially articulates with anthropology, it does so inextricably and irrevocably. In this contribution, I am proposing that if we wish to interpret the indigenous past, we need to examine the relationship between ethnography and archaeology and disentangle the knotted relationship between them. To do this, I will focus upon the problematic nature of this relationship as seen in rock-art research in California. As I will argue, ultimately this requires looking beyond the unhelpful artificial division that separates prehistory and history within archaeological practice itself.

## *Archaeology as defined by anthropology*

Californian archaeology has from the beginning been intimately conjoined to anthropology. For most current Californian archaeologists, archaeology is simply a subfield within anthropology, as are its siblings – linguistics, physical anthropology and cultural anthropology. As one of the 'four fields', archaeology is typically found within anthropology departments, and is thought of as being the anthropological study of the human past, particularly through physical or material remains. Because this is essentially a 'matter of fact' relationship between archaeology and anthropology, it has rarely been considered in depth in either the histories of the disciplines or even within critical theories. This is in part attributable to a surprising lack of Californian archaeological historiography. This is problematic because even though archaeologists define themselves as anthropologists most would maintain a very different identity from the other fields in terms of their methodology, theoretical approaches, and ironically their willingness to incorporate other anthropological views into their archaeological perspectives. These methods, theories and relationships to the other fields have shifted in complex ways since the beginnings of archaeological and anthropological research starting in the 1900s.

By the 1920s, anthropological and archaeological research in California was primarily sponsored by University of California anthropology headed by Alfred L. Kroeber at Berkeley. Anthropology looked at the 'surviving' indigenous culture while archaeological research logically studied its past before colonisation and Euro-American influence. However, Kroeber purposefully set archaeological research to the side as a major focus in California in favour of an ethnological 'push' to document as much of the remaining indigenous culture from living California native informants. This has been termed 'salvage anthropology' and resulted in an explosion of ethnological studies and the consequent ethnographic publications, making California one of the best documented indigenous areas in the world. Kroeber simply 'decided that the archaeology could safely wait in the ground and that the task of recording the ethnology before the last survivors died was more urgent' (Heizer 1978a: 12). This meant that for the decades of the mid-20th century, the majority of anthropological resources were dedicated to ethnographic rather than archaeological fieldwork, resulting in rich accounts of Native Californians living during the early to mid 20th century but poorer archaeological understandings of their deeper past.

Archaeological research did not have a solid foundation in the state until the establishment of the University of California Archaeological Survey in 1946. As A.L. Kroeber's wife and biographer Theodora Kroeber stated, the creation of the Archaeological Survey was 'one of Kroeber's last administrative tasks for the university, [the archaeological survey] becoming official… on the first day of his emeritus status' (T. Kroeber 1970: 145). This period of archaeological research took on the 'Classificatory-Historical' approach as defined by Willey and Sabloff (1980) before Seward's theory of multi-lineal evolution and the New Archaeologist's theories of adaptation came to be the predominant approach within California archaeology (see Yarrow, this volume for an explanation of 'New Archaeology'). Occurring after the heyday of ethnographic research these later theories and methods began to more firmly divide archaeology from the other fields. This trend has been noted by Whitley and Clottes (2005) in their recent discussion of the historiography of rock-art research.

Outlining the changing approaches to California and Far Western rock-art, Whitley and Clottes point out that the relation between archaeologists and their view of ethnographic information derived from 'salvage' anthropological research has been at the heart of both the marginalization of rock-art research in the mid-20th century and its more recent re-emergence within mainstream research. They argue that rock-art marginalization occurred 'because American archaeologists perceived it as an ethnological, not archaeological, topic for study' (2005: 167) during the post salvage years when archaeologists distanced themselves from the other three fields of anthropology. A re-appreciation of those ethnographies by rock-art researchers has been ongoing since the 1980s – this is at the heart of the re-emergence of rock-art interpretation into mainstream Californian academic discourse. A small group of researchers turned to information from the works of anthropologists such as A.L. Kreober, Anna Gayton, Harold Driver, and J.P. Harrington amongst others, putting forth shamanism as a pan-North American Indian religion underlying the making of rock-art. The use of ethnography (combined with the neuropsychological model) rather than archaeology was behind what could be called the 'shamanic turn' in rock-art interpretation. Current interpretations of rock-art remain primarily a direct result of reading the ethnographic texts of those early anthropologists.

## *The place of rock-art: ethnography 'versus' archaeology*

Again, it is important to realise that there are no firmly etched disciplinary lines that place a California researcher into a category of anthropologist or archaeologist or even ethnohistorian (e.g. researcher of ethnographic and other historical documents such as mission records, explorer's accounts, historical maps, etc.). Most researchers who focus on the indigenous past routinely move between the various forms of data that are available: this is a strong aspect of California research, but can be problematic in the sheer complexity of the different forms of data. As Chakrabarty's idea of time-knots suggest, tensions do arise from these tangled complexities. Rock-art is an ideal subject to explore the knotted and tensioned relationship between archaeology and ethnography because of its prominence in each sub-discipline. In some regions across the globe, rock-art is tens of thousands of years old and was of obvious great significance to prehistoric communities; in other areas, it remains equally important within recent and even contemporary indigenous communities (Figure 7.3). The study of rock-art in many places across the globe therefore incorporates either, or both, archaeological and anthropological approaches.

Taçon and Chippindale (1998) identified this divide in rock-art research, and famously proposed that rock-art research falls between two methodologies: that of 'informed' research in which accounts from native informants give information about the rock-art of a region (i.e. ethnographic); the second they termed 'formal' in applying archaeological techniques such as survey, mapping, or excavation in situations without the benefit of indigenous oral information. In ideal circumstances, both methodologies can be 'cabled' together (e.g. Wylie 1989) to build the strongest possible inferences. Where ethnographic and archaeological research are practiced in tandem, combining both informed and formal approaches, the result should twine together stronger interpretations of rock-art. However, what if the two strands do not twine together

*Figure 7.3. Indian Henry, a Tubatulabal informant, touching a red pictograph (photo by Tomas T. Waterman, June 1916. By kind permission of the Phoebe Hurst Museum).*

neatly? What happens when, rather than wrapping together to build stronger inferences, these two approaches appear to work against the other, each fraying in a tug-of-war of apparently divergent tensions?

When considering where rock-art is found in the landscape setting of South-Central California, just such a tensioned 'tug-of-war' exists between ethnographically documented indigenous perceptions of place and the archaeological correlate of that perception. Researchers in California have long noted the frequent close association of pictographs,[1] rock-shelters, and water sources (Grant 1965: 74; Whitley 1996, 2000). Ethnographic accounts clearly show that rock-shelters and small bodies of water such as ponds or springs were considered to be inherently 'dangerous' (Blackburn 1975: 38; Gayton 1948a: 279; 1948b: 277; Mayfield 1993: 113; Voegelin 1938: 60–62; Zigmond 1977: 71–75). For the coastal Chumash, these places were to be avoided (Blackburn 1975: 38). Likewise, in the far interior, the Tubatulabal thought that, 'in every spring, pool, river there dwells spirit who owns that particular body of water'(Vogelin 1938: 61). Ambivalent or ever malicious entities dwelt there, and could choose to send sickness if one approached improperly. For societies where almost all illnesses were considered the result of intentional action by sentient beings – human or otherwise – and transmitted supernaturally through a causative agent, we can see how dwelling

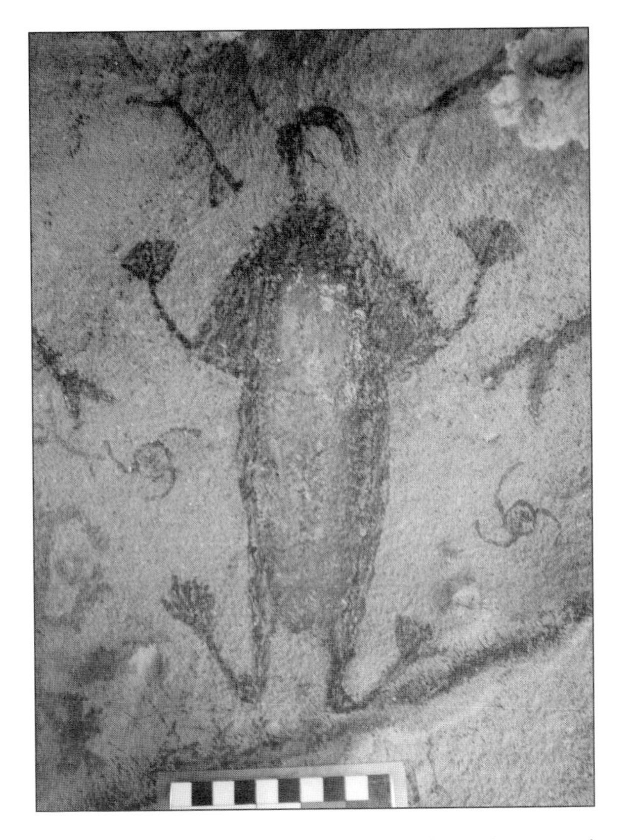

*Figure 7.4. Pictographs at the Emigdiano Chumash site of Three Springs; the shelter overlooks a riparian area with three springs.*

at springs or ponds would have been considered a hazardous undertaking. Zigmond (1977: 71–75) documents how the interior Kawaiisu were indeed afraid to go to springs, or scared off at such places by sightings of supernatural beings.

In many cases, the pictographs found at some of these springs were regarded with similar mistrust to the water itself (Figure 7.4) (Gayton 1948a:113; Whitley 2000:82): The famous Chumash site of Painted Cave near Santa Barbara was supposed to be avoided because its rock-art depictions of death could bring death to the beholder (Walker and Hudson 1993: 37) – for the Kawaiisu it is said that pictographs were 'out of bounds' and that touching them will 'quickly lead to disaster', or even to death (Zigmond 1977: 71). Some of the rock-art probably drew upon the sentient powers of the locality while pigment was often ascribed supernatural power (Robinson 2004). Thus the presence of pigment itself would only magnify the potentially inimical potency of the locale – 'dangerous signs at dangerous places' (Robinson 2006).

This information has logically led rock-art researchers to view pictographs and the places where the art is found as places of exclusion (Grant 1965; Whitley 2000). Drawing further upon ethnographic sources, some rock-art researchers argue that most rock-art was made by shamans, depicting their trance experiences, and in some instances relating to the supernatural entities residing in nearby water and rock formations: thus rock-art sites are often interpreted as having been owned by individual shamans and avoided by the general populace (for instance, see Whitley 2000: 54). This ethnographically informed perspective would lead us to expect that the art, the formations it was placed upon, and associated dangerous water bodies would be separated from the larger populace, either found in remote locations in the landscape or only at the margins of inhabited places.

In his investigation of rock-art sites of the Chumash, Grant (1965: 89) long ago noted that the 'paintings are almost always confined to the mountains' and that Chumash rock-art shelters 'were in no sense living quarters'. Whitley (2000: 54) more recently observed that pictographs were found at 'the edge or within a few hundred meters of a habitation site' so that the 'positioning of the paintings would not usually promote ready viewing, or suggest a use in public rituals' (*ibid.*). Certainly these archaeological observations are consistent with our expectations derived from the ethnography. Despite this, archaeological survey in Chumash areas has quietly but repeatedly associated South-Central Californian rock-art with nearby archaeological features and deposits suggesting some kind of occupational activity near rock-art (Horne 1976; Horne and Glassow 1974; Hyder 1989; Hudson and Lee 1984; Whitley 1987). This archaeological approach was particularly a focus of the research that took place before the shamanistic interpretation became the dominant strand in the 1990s. With the bulk of these investigations primarily focused on Chumash rock-art, they found that the pictographs were typically found near to 'camps, gathering areas, or other [areas with] evidence of day-to-day human activities' (Hyder 1989: 34).

Since the archaeology indicated that people must have spent considerable time in the vicinity of pictographs, this early formal archaeological research did not emphasize the idea that rock-art was separated from the general populace (see Hudson and Lee 1984). Rather than neatly cabling together as Wylie might suggest, the two methodologies of informed ethnography and formal archaeology appear to be in tension, pulling in opposite directions in a tightening time-knot. If rock-art locales are dangerous places to be avoided as the ethnography clearly states, then why does so much archaeological evidence nearby imply that people spent much time and effort near them? How can these two contradictory views – one (ethnographically derived) that springs and rock-art sites were assiduously avoided; the other (archaeologically derived) that they were consistently inhabited – be reconciled?

## *Presencing rock-art*

In order to address these tensions, we need to understand more accurately how rock-art was visibly positioned in the lives of past people. While the archaeological studies mentioned above suggest people in the past undertook activities in the vicinity of pictographs, we have no detailed understanding of whether or not pictographs exerted

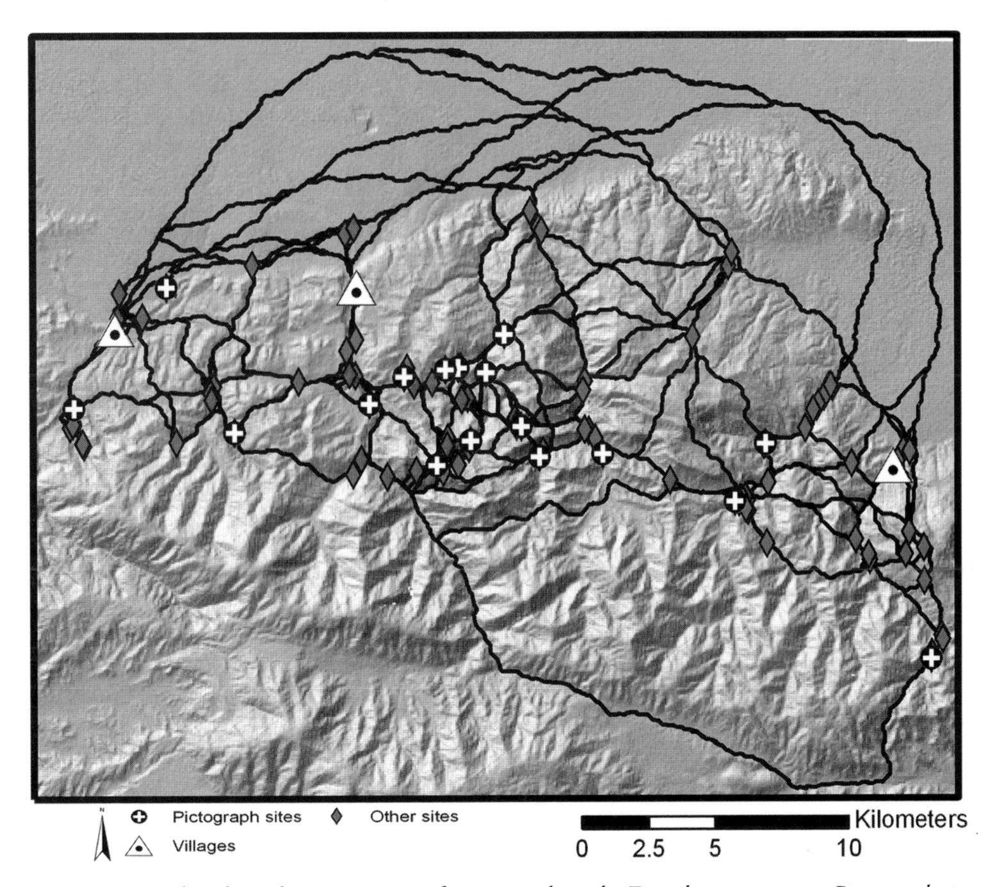


*Figure 7.5. Archaeological sites on cost-surface network in the Emigdiano territory. Pictograph sites (cross within circle) are firmly situated within this network.*

any significant visual presence where people actually dwelled. To examine this question, I undertook fieldwork focusing on some of the most elaborate pictograph sites in South-Central California by looking at a territory formally occupied by the indigenous group known as the Emigdiano Chumash, found within the interior epicentre of South-Central California.[2] In analyzing the location of pictographs painted on sandstone formations within Chumash Emigdiano territory, I found that they were not normally isolated in the mountains (*contra* Grant 1965) but firmly within the foothill orbit of internal prehistoric movement patterns. I ran a suite of cost-surface analyses[3] which demonstrated that the polychrome paintings of the Emigdiano were positioned within well utilized trails and that rock-art sites were therefore firmly within the land-use patterns (Figure 7.5). This meant that pictograph sites would have been encountered by the inhabitants in their seasonal movements to take advantage of different biomes and collect different resources as they dispersed from village sites into the landscape (see Robinson 2006).

Found in the San Emigdio Hills at the southern extent of the San Joaquin valley, the Emigdiano landscape lies at the interface between the different linguistic groups known as the Chumash and Yokuts. This semi-arid region relies on north flowing drainages that spill from the San Emigdio Hills into what used to be large fresh water lakes along which large Yokuts villages clustered. Drained by modern agriculture, these once well populated villages could be seen by the smaller Emigdiano villages found at the mouths of canyons, major apertures into the foothills of this uplifted terrain. Further up into the hills, along these watersheds, sandstone formations intermingle with oak groves, providing the richest biotic areas within Emigdiano territory. It is here, either along the wooded margins or within the oak zone, that most of the pictographs can be found.

Intriguingly, 15 out of the 17 pictograph sites identified within Emigdiano lands are closely associated with just the type of water bodies that ethnographic accounts state would be avoided – springs, ponds, wetlands, and/or perennial creeks. However, in contrast to the ethnographic accounts, archaeological evidence at the majority of these sites suggests they do not appear to have been avoided: 11 of those 15 pictograph sites have high concentrations of a ubiquitous archaeological phenomenon in California called bedrock mortars – conical depressions intentionally carved into bedrock formations that were used for pounding acorns and other foods. Additionally, most of these Emigdiano rock-art sites had other archaeological deposits such as midden material and stone-working debitage seen in association with the bedrock mortars.

This evidence suggests that not only did people routinely visit these pictograph sites with their attendant water sources, but that they must have inhabited them for extended stretches of time while investing significant labour in the production of food and other activities such as working lithics. Such complex bedrock mortar and midden sites are well known in other places in South-Central California and have come to be known as K-locales (from Jackson 1984: 199–203). These K-locales are multi-component occupation sites that seem to be primarily places for processing acorns into edible and storable food. They are also undoubtedly places where multiple family groups came together to pound acorns for long periods and 'were situated to accommodate systematic annual movements across the landscape to collect and process, primarily, the acorn resource'. Archaeologist T.L. Jackson (*ibid.*: 312) further argues that, 'These food processing sites represent the creation by women of fixed production facilities on the landscape which are related directly to the organization of women's labour and production' (Figure 7.6). Rather than being avoided, rock-art sites appear to have been at the heart of complex indigenous movements through the landscape, tethered to seasonal fluctuations in the food supply, and were specifically sites from which people, especially women, could gather food to return and process it.

*Figure 7.6. Three Mono women prepare acorns on a bedrock mortar station (photograph by Nellie T. McGraw Hedgpeth, 1904-1905. By kind permission of the Phoebe Hurst Museum).*

## Natural architecture

But what of on-site visibility? Did people actually see the rock-art and those sandstone formations it was painted on? To investigate this relationship between pictographs and nearby activity, I reconsidered rock-art locales as places of natural architectural rather than simply being the backdrop for painting. This allowed me to consider pictographs as visual components within a suite of other physical components, with the archaeology indicative of past human activity. I wished to consider if the art, like the walled away artefacts in Cache Cave, was placed in such a way as to be hidden from view. If this were the case, then the ethnographic and archaeological tension could be resolved. But if the art was visible, I wanted to know in what circumstances would people have been able to see the art? This kind of detail requires understanding how archaeological components fit spatially together. This point is crucial: archaeological components such as lithic scatters, substantial middens, or modified bedrock such as mortars tell us precisely where people spent portions of their lives performing repetitive tasks.

To analyse the relationships between the Emigdiano and their rock-art, I digitally mapped a series of eight different rock-art locales (see Robinson 2006). Using archaeological survey data, three-dimensional models of the rock-art sites were made. Once completed, the activities people engaged in and the manner they may have dwelt can be considered. Importantly, digital analysis of 'viewsheds' (the part of the landscape that can be seen from a particular archaeological site or locale) also allowed the visual

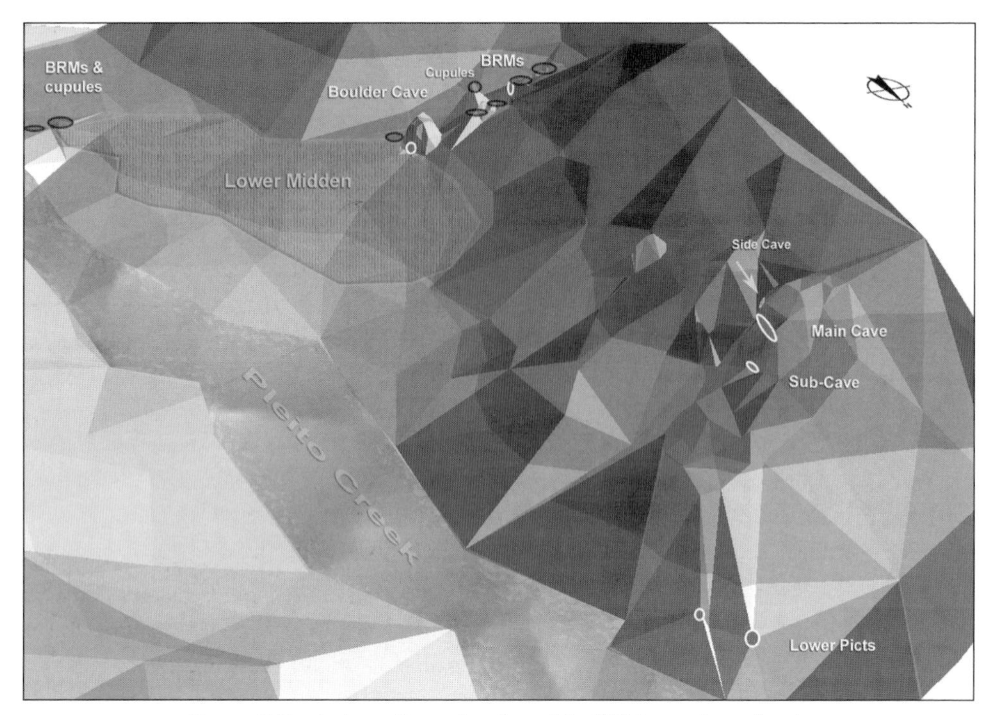


*Figure 7.7. A three-dimensional model of Pleito rock-art locale.*

relationships between rock-art, rock-formations, topography, and archaeological features/deposits, to be explored. Each rock-art locale is comprised of a complex mix of natural and archaeological components (Figure 7.7). The manner in which people occupied, inhabited and related to each location varies, but there is a certain repertoire of attributes that each site is comprised of: rock outcrops; relatively level terrace landforms; a spring, pond, or riverine habitat; often, nearby oak stands. In each instance, people integrated themselves into the locales in a similar manner: they placed their rock-art on rock outcrops, both on vertical surfaces and within shelters; they made mortars on low lying bedrocks; they occupied level terraces, leaving lithic scatters and other midden material; they moved about the site, particularly between water source and where they used the bedrock mortars. These examples show that rock-art sites were far more than just locales for the art: they were places with a variety of important attributes, where people adjusted their repertoire of actions to best match the attributes of the particular locale.

But what about the placement of the art within the locales? There is no evidence that the art was placed so as not to be seen or that people modified their behaviour to avoid seeing it. In some cases, the art is encountered at the boundaries of the sites. Even when the art is contained within shelters and not easily seen because of shadow, the apertures and the rock-formations themselves are the major visual and physical components of the locales. In all cases, the art is found within the very core of the site, with midden and bedrock mortars closely, even intimately associated. As all of the digital models show, the art interfingers within habitation areas, forming a strong presence on site and was easily viewable and integrated rather than hidden and separated.

As I have discussed elsewhere (Robinson 2006, 2007), the occupation of these complexes likely occurred during acorn autumnal harvesting, and probably lasted for weeks if not a couple months. The bedrock mortars testify to the labour intensive processing of acorns. This was the primary staple of late prehistoric and historical indigenous California (Fagan 2003). All healthy members of society were involved in the actual gathering of this crucial resource, and the midden evidence indicates that the entire community likely dwelled temporally on site.

## *Reconsidering ethnography*

Far from 'cabling together' (e.g. Wylie 1989) archaeological and ethnographic views, this analysis of rock-art sites reiterates and further emphasizes the tensions between the two divergent interpretations. It is clear that the ethnographic view (that rock-art sites were assiduously avoided) is directly contradicted by the archaeology.

Rather than simply jettison one, or give primacy to one over the other, a reconsideration of the use of ethnography is necessary. In particular I suggest that the ethnographically derived view of rock-art location is based upon a rather fragmentary way of extracting information from ethnographic texts. Thus this problem is not of ethnographic information *per se*, but of the way in which research draws upon it. Yes, ethnography is a fragmentary form of documentation which in itself is problematic. However, I wish to stress here the very difficult problem of working with ethnographic texts. Specifically, when delving into the vast ethnographic information on indigenous California in order to address a specific question, one must necessarily hone in on specific references having to do with that question. For instance, anthropologists rarely asked their informants specifically about rock-art, so that many quotes related to rock-art are found in larger narratives or select sections on mythology, paint, or cache sites. Each quote is a node or knuckle linking multiple aspects of indigenous culture. In extracting quotes, information can become decontextualised from the very complex cultural situation within which that information emerged. In regarding information about places where rock-art is found, the specific written accounts can be seen as nodes in the ethnographic text, woven into multistranded narratives covering a variety of topics. This methodological approach of searching out only those nodes that are of interest has the effect of particularising and isolating the cultural element being looked at rather than seeing how it may be a strand within the larger cultural system.

In the case of California, the rich ethnographic record fortunately contains much broader views of indigenous society that allow us to revisit the cultural context for particular informant statements. In ideal circumstances, methodologies that integrate several forms of data mitigate against the limiting effects of isolating a narrow range of statements. For instance, Johnson (1988) has combined ethnography compiled from the unpublished work of J.P. Harrington with Mission Period documents to reconstruct indigenous marriage patterns, which in turn inform polity dynamics of Chumash village leaders. Lightfoot and Parrish (2009: 78–80) have recently pointed out how the work of Johnson and others has shown how Kroeber underestimated the complexity of Native Californian socio-political organisation. These more recent reassessments of ethnographic data often stress the integrative nature of indigenous social systems. Blackburn has also drawn upon Harrington's work to point out the overall integrated nature of Chumash society in their ceremonial, economic, and political system (1976). Throughout her career, Gayton collated her own ethnographic information in a series of papers examining the intersections of different elements that make up Yokuts society (1945, 1976). In all of these cases, aspects of the ethnographic record are only understandable by looking at its relation to other aspects of the ethnographic record. In the remainder of this paper, I use a similar approach, revisiting the ethnographic record in light of the archaeological evidence. My aim is to see if these can be made to work together rather than against each other.

Since we can see that symbolic visual media were integrated with subsistence and economic activities at places ascribed supernatural potency where the entire community congregated at K-locales, I wish to look first at evidence for the integrated nature of indigenous society in a broader South-Central California context, in its politics and ideology. For the Chumash, political and religious organisation was interwoven in an elite society called the *antap* institution, with chiefs (known as *wots*) and other officials involved in directing community ceremony: at special moments in the year, these rituals involved the exchange of material culture, the display of symbolic media, and the use of pigment in performance. This interplay between political institutions, economy, and ceremony is seen in other portions of South-Central California. As mentioned previously, the Emigdiano were a group of the Chumash linguistic family, with their territory lying at the immediate border with Yokuts populations. Ana Gayton's ethnological research into the Yokuts is particularly relevant. Gayton found similar integrations, with the *tiya* as their counterpart to the Chumash *wot*:

> The administrative powers of the chief [*tiya*] covered the salient features of Yokuts life: he held directive control of the great mourning ceremony, an intertribal affair of extensive proportions, authorized the movements of families on seed-gathering and trading expeditions, sanctioned reprisal killings of asocial persons (1945: 417).

The *tiya* did not operate as an autonomous political power: typically allied with other chiefs, his messenger, the *winatum*, acted to maintain political links externally and bolster the *tiya's* authority internally. Importantly, the justification for these two complementary political offices was grounded in mythology and passed down through moiety lineages – the *tiya* in Yokuts society was 'an institution of prehistoric antiquity who in human times held his position as successor to Eagle himself' (Gayton 1930: 371, 412–413).

Political power was not maintained exclusively through allusion to myth: the *winatum* could act as 'henchmen', carrying a cane ornamented with red paint to signify their authority: to say to someone, 'You're going to get a red cane' was a portent of death since the *winatum* used the cane when making such announcements (Gayton 1930: 398). Inter-and intra-group competition sometimes prompted *tiyas* to employ the use of 'doctors' or 'poisoners' against an enemy (Gayton 1930). Even though the 'chiefs, with their winatums as manipulating instruments, constituted the sole legal authority in the political system' (*ibid.*: 408), Gayton shows that the alliance between *tiyas* and shamans – the doctors and poisoners who were professionals in engaging with the supernatural – was fundamental to society, with the threat of supernatural reprisal a mechanism of control (*ibid.*: 413–414). In short, this political system promulgated an indigenous ideology, affirming and reproducing the structure of society through allusions to the past and the potency of the supernatural.

The employment of rock-art similarly was 'ocular evidence' of power put at specific places. Rather than seeing the potency of rock-art as prohibiting the use of sites – a view that is archaeologically unsustainable – it is better to see rock-art's potency as fitting within an indigenous ideology that displays that potency. It may be that some of the rock-art was a visual display of the ability of individuals to mitigate the sentient powers dwelling at springs, so that the people themselves could dwell there and engage in activities – most notably processing acorns. The presence of art at so many backcountry sites abundant in bedrock mortars suggests that some of it was very likely related to acorn-harvest festivals (Gayton 1945: 416). *Tiyas* also had responsibilities in authorising seed gathering expeditions and granted permission to outsiders' use of the land: as Gayton put it the *tiya* 'effected the control of the acorn crop' (Gayton 1945: 417). Gayton's (1948a: 11) detailed information on the Yokuts show that oak groves were owned by a tribe, specific trees claimed by individual women, marked by stakes, and passed down to their daughters – the same was true of bedrock mortar stations[4] (Jackson 1991: 319).

In looking at this much wider ethnographic information, the accounts of the dangerous attribute of rock-art, rock formations, and springs can be best explained. The cultural belief that ambivalent or inimical beings resided at springs was ideologically prudent: as the most important economic places in the landscape, it was sensible that they were ascribed an elevated supernatural importance. These attitudes towards springs made it no easy proposition for people to visit them at will: they needed both specialists who could facilitate being there, as well as the permission from authority to do so. Controlling such sites would effectively enable the control of acorn production. For the Emigdiano, it is clear that acorn production was a primary staple in lands abundant in oaks but lacking in other necessities such as shell for beads or lithics for tools: pictograph sites are one and the same with sites producing an exportable resource. It is highly probable that these acorns would have been traded to the Lake Yokuts to the immediate north, in their oak-poor lacustrine environment: it appears acorns were not available to either the Buena Vista or Tulare Lake Yokuts except through trade (Beals and Hester 1974: 4, 9). The abundance of Yokuts Temblor chert found in Emigdiano territory indicates that they must have traded with the Lake Yokuts for lithic material: acorn production can be seen as the raw material constituting the basis for the wealth of not only the chiefs, but also all of the Emigdiano population.

Acorn harvesting was not straightforward: different trees and different groves produced acorns differentially in alternate years (Basgall 1987: 24). Storage was an important strategy in building-up food for lean years, for conspicuous consumption, and for trade. Rock-shelters at these locales would have been ideal for the caching of acorns: some of the same statements in ethnographic narratives that associated rock-art with danger specifically reference cache sites (see Gayton 1948a, 1948b). Steps carved onto some of the sandstone formations at rock-art sites suggest that hands needed to be free: perhaps this aided transport of goods for storage. Harrington documents several ethnographic accounts where food is stored in caves (in Hudson and Blackburn 1983: 84): 'JJO says that in former times when they had a fiesta they would go to a cave and take out great quantities of stored away food to use in feeding the people'. Another account states that acorns and *chia* were good for two years when stored in a cave blocked off with stones and leaves (1983: 84). Stone walling found at other Emgidiano and more distant rock-art shelters having rock-art (Robinson 2006) may have been blocking to store away acorns processed at that K-locale, indicating that rock-art sites, similar to cache caves, were places for storage. Large 'granary storage baskets' have been found at a number of cache caves in the rock-art zone (see Gollar 1996): like special split sticks called "spirit-sticks" found in these cache caves[5] (1996: 51), the presence of rock-art may have discouraged trespass in the absence of the group maintaining rights-of-access. Pictographs certainly would have been powerful indicators of ownership of K-locales, signifying the authority of those who made or sponsored the making of the art: their display at these sites also may have given rights to share the product of the women's labour. Over-painting, or the adding of new layers of paint over the top of older pictographs (Figure 7.8), may have reiterated or even articulated competition for such rights. Certainly it becomes clear that rock-art sites and cache sites were far more than simply places for the exclusive use of shamans: they performed a variety of functions with rock-art as only one of its constituent components.

So far, I have stressed how the inimical potential of the supernatural played an ideological role in the form of pictographs at K-locales: it is indeed curious that people could engage in so many activities, including food preparation and eating, directly in view of pictographs and shelter apertures. To do so means that people on-site must

*Figure 7.8. Pictographs from Pleito showing extensive overpainting.*

have been comfortable with the presence of pictographs: it is likely that those who made the pictographs were not foreigners from distant lands, but members of the local community who used the site. If springs were considered dangerous, then this may further imply that rock-art helped people to properly occupy spring sites, meaning that pictographs were beneficial for everyone within the group.

As with the archaeological record, the ethnographic record is comprised of sometimes fragmented and disparate accounts. In broadening the scope of inquiry of ethnography, a more holistic account can tie together and resolve interpretive tensions that arise from focusing only on a small suite of specific accounts. By looking at those accounts – in this instance the accounts attributing a view of exclusion when it comes to rock-art, rock formation, and water bodies – in a wider context, we can see those fragments as part of a larger whole. We also appreciate ethnography as a complex body of literature that offers something that is rather different than a straightforward, literal interpretation of factual accounts. In the light of this wider view derived from ethnography, it is also important to take another look at archaeology, and rethink the placement of rock-art and my own archaeological methods to examine it.

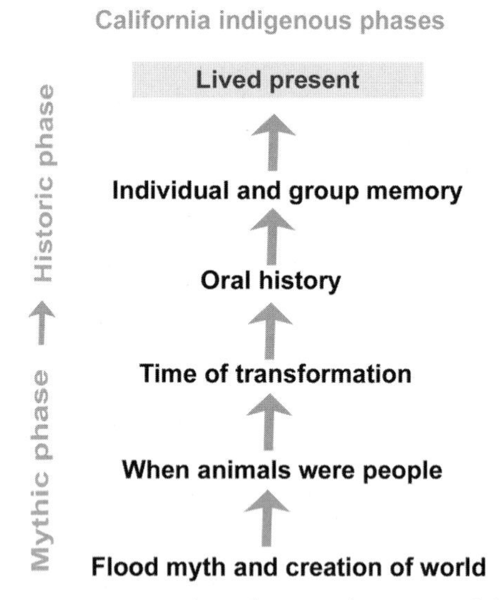


*Figure 7.9. Schematic representation of South-Central Native Californian notions of time.*

## *Rethinking archaeology: indigenous temporalities*

We need to examine ethnography and archaeology: as our ideas of each change, it then influences how we view the other. In the process of rethinking ethnography, we should also rethink archaeology. It is useful here to stress Chakrabarty's temporal emphasis in his concept of colonial 'time-knots'; that the chronology of subaltern or indigenous people cannot simply be considered from the researcher's view of linear, sequential time, but is bound within indigenous beliefs of time and their own past. A crucial strand within the 'time-knot' is the indigenous view of the past and their own perceptions of history. Californian ethnography does contain indigenous people's perspective on their own historical trajectory, and equally documents Native Californians' perceptions of time. In this respect, we are offered the opportunity to follow one strand within the historical knot from an indigenously informed point of view. Just as archaeologists have their own concepts of deep time, the mythological stories collected by ethnographers contain information regarding native Californians' ideas of the past. These ideas were grounded in the topography and geological matrix of the landscape. The physical environment of rock-art sites was ascribed potency that is understandable within indigenous ontology as told in mythic narratives concerning their own conceptualizations of the past.

In rethinking my own work, I was not only investigating the past as defined by strictly archaeological notions of time-periods and western chronometric notions, but was doing fieldwork in a landscape inhabited and perceived in a fundamentally differently temporal framework. The mapping programme that produced the digital models presented above was not exclusively the mapping of a western Cartesian defined space, but the mapping of the indigenous mythological landscape where ideological statements referencing the past were placed. Here, in following the indigenous strand concerning time, some of the apparent tensions in the knot may be released.

As demonstrated in South-Central California oral narratives (Blackburn 1975; Gayton 1935; Gayton and Newman 1940; Gifford 1923; Heizer 1978b: 655–656; Kroeber 1907; Latta 1936; Zigmond 1977) there was a distinct myth-time when animals were people in a separate in-the-distant-past (Figure 7.9). During this time, the landscape was altered. Distinctively shaped formations were often explained as animals turned to stone or formed by them through supernatural feats. Regarding the Chumash, Harrington says:

> The country in Indian times was literally populated with "petrified" "first people," who lived at the beginning of the world and were transformed to stone for one reason or another, as special legends tell. There is a rocky pinnacle on a hilltop which used to be a person and evidently still has some life in it (1927: 235).

Abundant information has been collected on widespread beliefs concerning rock formations across South-Central California (see Latta 1936; 1977; Gayton and Newman 1940:97; Weinberger 1983). As I pointed out above, just such rock formations dominate the locales that I mapped. These same formations are where the pigment making up the rock-art was applied. The application of imagery smeared onto the bare rock surface associated with mythic contexts would have been an act performed on a stone canvas redolent with the past. These would have been formations with narratives already attached: pigment may have been smeared onto the petrified bodies of mythological beings who retained a sense of enduring power. Contacting it put indigenous people in touch with their own conceptualization of their own past. However, the application was made by people in a living present. The surviving imagery was more than a reference to the surface it occupied: it was a reformulation of that surface by adding a new layer of indigenous history to the place. By the time that ethnographic work was undertaken, many rock-art sites were specifically mentioned as places where mythic beings had been turned to stone, dormant but still present (Cummins 1992; Lee and Horne 1978; Zigmond 1977).

As places where the mythological past was encountered, K-locales and their attendant rock-art were sometimes recorded as places of gathering and fiestas. This is particularly well documented in the case of the Kawaiisu, a group neighbouring the Emigdiano Chumash. Zigmond (1977: 76) recorded that 'in mythological times the animal-people held celebrations' at the rock-art site of *Tomo Kahni*. The Kawaiisu site of Horse Canyon is said to be associated with fiestas in mythic times with particular reference to the bedrock mortars:

> The mortar holes and pictographs ... were made by different kings of animal-humans. Each one made his on paha'zi (mortar hole) and his own painting. That is why each pictograph is different (Guthrie 1950: 7).

In reconsidering both the ethnography and the archaeology, we can see that each documents the mythological landscape and the elevated importance of sites redolent with the past. It is through indigenous notions of time, seen in ethnographic information that is comfortably in accord with the archaeological record, that we ease one tensioned strand within the colonial 'time-knot'. As a form of archaeology, pictographs illustrate the importance of certain rock formations, just as do oral histories, recorded in ethnographic accounts. Moreover, archaeology clearly shows that rock-art is not found in isolation. It is clear that ethnographic accounts of rock-art and the places it occupies as redolent with potency are not in error, but that its interpretation is not straightforward. The ascription of supernatural potency to rock-art and the features it occupies was a logical extension of using the mythological past as a source of ideology at places of the greatest social value, economically, ceremonially, mythologically, and politically. Paintings should be seen as a means of engaging with the inherent potency of these places in relation to the entire community who worked and dwelt there rather than as a form of social exclusion. The dislocation of the indigenous community from rock-art sites was not a traditional practice, but most likely the result of 18th to 19th century colonial processes; ethnographic accounts were gathered after this dislocation took place.

By understanding indigenous notions of time, ethnohistory and archaeology intertwines history with prehistory, not only helping to resolve tensions between conflicting interpretations, but alleviating apparent dichotomous tensions and 'false' fields. Here we can see how reconsidering the archaeological mapping of sites as a mapping of mythology brings the archaeologist into contact with an indigenous mythological landscape. This is a very different temporal relationship than standard archaeological chronology. By rethinking ethnography within the archaeological framework, I have followed a strand where disciplinary notions of prehistory or history are irrelevant. By *doing* the archaeology of an indigenous landscape, I operated at a node linking two different temporal views. This presented the possibility of 'straightening out' the ethnographic/archaeological knot and alleviating some of the tensions inherent in rock-art interpretations.

## *Conclusion*

This case study from California underlines the very complex relationships out of which ethnographic work has emerged. As archaeologists often employ cross cultural ethnographic analogy, drawing upon ethnographic records from around the globe to interpret their 'patch' so to speak, this is all the more important when realizing that I use only the ethnographic information from the very groups who lived in the same landscapes where that archaeology is found. Others have pointed out the pitfalls of using the ethnographic present (e.g. Trigger 1981) in any 'direct historical sense' (i.e. extrapolating backwards directly from known historical periods to interpret prehistory);

Wobst (1978), for instance, warned of the 'tyranny' of the ethnographic record in the interpretation of the archaeology of hunter/gatherers. This should be a cautionary tale for archaeologists who employ cross-cultural ethnographic analogy, using ethnography from one area to interpret the archaeology of another area. While Gosden (1999: 9) questions the morality of such transported cross cultural interpretations, I would say that in cases such as California, the ethnographic record is an indigenous testimony that we are obligated to pay close attention to. The archaeological record is equally an indigenous testimony. However, we must keep in mind the fragmentary nature of both ethnography and archaeology, and continue to employ sophisticated and in-depth critiques of the textual sources and their relationship to the archaeological record.

Of course, in focusing upon the interplay of ethnography and archaeology, I have only just begun to examine the colonial condition from which specific ethnographies arise. To delve into the dynamics of colonial encounters and more fully understand the ethnographic accounts they are drawing upon, researchers must address indigenous 'systems of value' (Gosden 2004) as well as those of the colonialists. As seen in South-Central California, indigenous 'systems of value' can intersect at specific K-locales, where subsistence, economy, ceremony, and ideology were all enmeshed at specific places. The special quality of rock-art elaborated those places, reiterating, adding, and increasing its value (Robinson 2007). Some rock-art sites continued to be places for the display of ideological statements seen in graffiti by Euro-Americans at rock-art sites. The interplay of both indigenous and colonial systems of value are reflected at such sites, further illustrating how they became entangled throughout later colonial times, into the 1800s. During this time, the rock-art zone became marginalized, encompassed by large Mexican and American cattle grants where indigenous communities had been greatly reduced or entirely displaced while incoming settlers were sparse. By the time ethnographic work was undertaken, indigenous land-use had become disassociated – the isolation of rock-art sites documented by ethnographers was not due to indigenous ontology; rather rock-art sites became separated from living populations as a result of the flow of events instigated by colonial encounters.

However, there is no neat divide before and after colonial contact; no line between prehistory and history. The fields of archaeology and anthropology are strands in Chakrabarty's time-knot. As historical artefacts found at pictograph sites in the backcountry 'rock-art' zone reflect, the site of Cache Cave represents an indigenous reinvestment within these very important places in the midst of colonial California. Just as rock-art sites were embroiled within colonial discourse, the gathering of ethnography occurred within the living memory of the colonial moment. As Gosden (1999: 10) points out, the 'mass of observations' comprising the ethnographic record are the product of colonialism. However, he also reminds us that the changes brought about by colonialism are impossible to understand without the longer time perspective offered by archaeology. In order to understand those changes brought about in contact and post contact histories, we need to understand time not only from the archaeological perspective, itself a Western discourse with colonialist origins (1999: 16), but we need to disentangle the colonial time-knot to understand indigenous historical processes. In this respect, by tacking back and forth between archaeology and ethnography, anthropological archaeologists – and archaeological anthropologists – can move beyond the boundary between prehistory and history to enhance their understandings of the indigenous past without the need for a false field disciplinary divide.

## *Acknowledgements*

I would like to thank Manuel Arroyo-Kalin, Nadine Boksmati, Richard Bradley, Rick Bury, Carole Bury, Christopher Chippindale, D.C. Clendenen, Sheryl Clendenen, Anwen Cooper, Vicki Cummings, Mark Gillings, Michael Glassow, Dan Hicks, John Johnson, Unika-Delpino Mark, Breck McAlexander, Antoinette Padgett, Jennifer Perry, Rick Peterson, Dan Reeves, Rick Peterson, Gale Grasse-Sprague, Jack Sprague, plus Dan York, the Wildlands Conservancy, and the staff of the Wind Wolves Preserve for their permission and kind support for field research. Thanks also to Duncan Garrow and Tom Yarrow for their editorial eyes, and to two anonymous reviewers for their useful comments. I am indebted to St John's College, Cambridge, and the institutions that provided funding and support: the Ridgeway-Venn Trust, Dorothy Garrod Trust, Bonney and Dr. Philip Frank Hutchins Funds Scholarship, Robert Slowly Award, Cambridge Overseas Trust, and Overseas Research Scholarship.

*Notes*

1. The term 'pictograph' refers to rock-art images that are additive in the sense they are made up of some form of pigment and painted onto a rock surface. The term 'petroglyph' refers to rock-art that is reductive in the sense that they are made by carving, pecking, or using other means of engraving into a rock surface. The rock-art images discussed here are almost exclusively pictographs.
2. Research included a 6 month walk-over (pedestrian) survey of the Emigdiano territory, including sample survey of valley floors, canyon apertures, creek terraces, grasslands, woodlands, and upper elevation ridge-lines and difficult access rock formations (see Robinson 2006; 2007).
3. A Geographic Information Systems (GIS) cost-surface analysis uses topographic data to compute slope values in a given journey, thus defining the easiest route through a landscape in terms of effort (see Robinson 2006 for all cost surface analyses performed in the Emigdiano case study).
4. The Tubatulabal went to war when visiting Yokuts from Porterville improperly took seeds from a woman who was busy pounding (Voegelin 1938: 50).
5. Spirit sticks (or witch sticks) are forked sticks typically set in an up-right position in cache caves. Some 'ethnographic sources suggest the sticks protected cached artefacts, or delineated ownership of the cave, or both' (Goller 1996: 50).

## *References*

Basgall 1987. Resource intensification among hunter-gatherers: acorn economics in prehistoric California. *Research in Economic Anthropology* 9: 21–52.

Beals, R.L. and J.A. Hester 1974. *American Indian Ethnohistory: California and Great Basin Plateau Indians – California Indians I: Indian Land Use and Occupancy in California. Vol. 2.* New York: Garland Publishing.

Blackburn, T.C. 1975. *December's Child: A Book of Chumash Oral Narratives*. Berkeley, Los Angeles and London: University of California Press.

Blackburn, T.C. 1976. Ceremonial integration and social interaction in aboriginal California. In L. Bean and T. Blackburn (eds) *Native Californians: a theoretical perspective*, 225–243. Romona, California: Ballena Press.

Chakrabarty, D. 2000. *Provincializing Europe: Postcolonial Thought and Historical Difference*. Princeton: Princeton University Press.

Cummins, M.W. 1992. *How Coyote Stole the Sun: The Myth, the Music, and Other Features of the Yokuts Culture*. Fresno: Braun-Brumfield.

Fagan, B. 2003. *Before California: an archaeologist looks at our earliest inhabitants*. Lanham, Maryland: Rowman and Littlefield.

Gayton, A.H. 1930. Yokuts-Mono Chiefs and Shamans. *University of California Publications in American Archaeology and Ethnography* 24(8): 361–420.

Gayton, A.H 1935. Areal Affiliations of California Folk Tales. *American Anthropologist* 37(1): 582–599.

Gayton, A.H 1945. Yokuts and Western Mono Social Organization. *American Anthropologist* 47(1): 409–426.

Gayton, A.H 1948a. Yokuts and Western Mono Ethnography: I: Tulare Lake, Southern Valley, and Central Foothill Yokuts. *Anthropological Records*, 10(1). Berkeley: University of California Press.

Gayton, A.H 1948b. Yokuts and Western Mono Ethnography: II: Northern Foothill Yokuts and Western Mono. *Anthropological Records*, 10(2). University of California Press: Berkeley.

Gayton, A.H. 1976. Culture-environment integration: external references in Yokuts life, 79–97. In L. Bean and T. Blackburn (eds) *Native Californians: a theoretical perspective*. Romona, California: Ballena Press.

Gayton, A.H. and S.S. Newman. 1940. Yokuts and Western Mono Myths. *University of California Anthropological Records* 5(1). Berkeley and London.

Gifford, E.W. 1923. Western Mono Myths. *Journal of American Folklore* 36(142): 301–367.

Gollar, B. 1996. *Chumash Indian Cache Caves of the Santa Barbara Backcountry: Evidence for Inland Subsistence and Ceremonial Activities*. Unpublished BA Thesis, University of California, Santa Barbara.

Gosden, C. 1999. *Anthropology and Archaeology: a changing relationship*. London: Routledge.

Gosden, C. 2004. *Archaeology and Colonialism: culture contact from 5000 BC to the present*. Cambridge: Cambridge University Press.

Grant, C. 1965. *The Rock Paintings of the Chumash*. Berkeley: University of California Press.

Guthrie, G. 1950. KER-93. *Archaeological Site Survey Record*. Filed at the California State University, Bakersfield Archaeological Information Center.

Harrington, J.P. 1927. Archeological and Ethnological Researches in California. In S.I. Smith (ed.) *Smithsonian Miscellaneous Collections* 78(7): 232–237.

Heizer, R.L. 1978a. History of Research, pp. In R.F. Heizer (ed) *California Handbook of North American Indians, Vol. 8*, 6–15. Washington, D.C.: Smithsonian Institution.

Heizer, R.L. 1978b. Mythology: Regional Patterns and History of Research. In R. Heizer (ed.) *California Handbook of North American Indians, Vol. 8.*, 654–657. Washington, D.C.: Smithsonian Institution.

Horne, S.P. 1976. Analysis of Chumash Rock Art from Sierra Madre Ridge, California. *American Indian Rock Art* 2:114–125.

Horne, S.P. and M. Glassow 1974. *Archeological investigations, Sierra Madre Ridge, Los Padres National Forest.* Manuscript on file, Los Padres National Forest.

Hudson, T. and T. Blackburn 1983. The Material Culture of the Chumash Interaction Sphere, Vol. II: Food Preparation and Shelter. *Ballena Press Anthropological Papers No. 27.*

Hudson, T. and G. Lee. 1981. Function and Purpose of Chumash Rock Art. *Masterkey* 55(3): 92–100.

Hudson, T. and G. Lee. 1984. Function and Symbolism in Chumash Rock Art. *Journal of New World Archaeology* 6(3): 26–47.

Hyder, W.D. 1989. *Rock Art and Archaeology in Santa Barbara County, California.* San Luis Obispo County Archaeological Society Occasional Paper No. 13.

Jackson, T.L. 1984. Predictive Model of Prehistoric Settlement Patterning in the Southern Sierra Neveda. In Theodoratus Cultural Research, Inc. and Archaeological Consutling and Research Services, Inc. *Cultural Resources Overview of the Southern Sierra Nevada*, 174–303. Fresno, CA: USDA, Sierra National Forest.

Jackson, T.L. 1991. Pounding Acorn: Women's Production as Social and Economic Focus. In J.M. Gero and M.W. Conkey (eds) *Engendering Archaeology, Women and Prehistory*, 301–325. Oxford: Blackwell.

Johnson, J. 1988. *Chumash Social Organization: An Ethnohistorical Perspective.* Ph.D dissertation, Department of Anthropology, University of California, Santa Barbara.

Kroeber, A.L. 1907. Indian Myths of South Central California. *University of California Publications: American Archaeology and Ethnology* 4(4). Berkeley: The University Press:

Kroeber, A.L 1925. Handbook of the Indians of California. *Bureau of American Ethnology Bulletin* 78. Washington, D.C.

Kroeber, T. 1970. *Alfred Kroeber: a personal configuration.* Berkeley: University of California Press.

Latta, F. 1936. *California Indian Folklore.* Santa Cruz: Bear State Books.

Lee, G. and S.P. Horne 1978. The Painted Rock Site (SBa-502 and SBa-526): Sapaksi, the House of the Sun. *Journal of California Anthropology* 5(2): 216–224.

Lightfoot, K. 1995. Culture Contact Studies: Redefining the Relationship between Prehistoric and Historical Archaeology. *American Antiquity* 60(2): 199–217.

Lightfoot, K. 2005. *Indians, Missionaries, and Merchants: the Legacy of Colonial Encounters on the California Frontiers.* Berkeley: University of California Press.

Lightfoot, K and O. Parrish. 2009. *California Indians and their Environment.* Berkeley: University of California Press.

Lucas, G. 2004. Modern Disturbances: On the Ambiguities of Archaeology. *Modernism/modernity* (11) 1: 109–120.

Mayfield, Thomas J. 1993. *Indian Summer: Traditional Life among the Choinumne Indians of California's San Joaquin Valley.* Berkeley: Heyday Books and California Historical Society.

Robinson, D.W. 2004. The Mirror of the Sun: Surface, Mineral Applications, and Interface in California Rock Art. In N. Boivin and M. Owoc (eds) *Soils, Stones and Symbols: archaeological and anthropological perspectives on the mineral world*, 91–106. University College London Press: London.

Robinson, D.W 2006. *Landscape, taskscape, and indigenous perception: the rock-art of South-Central California.* Unpublished PhD dissertation: University of Cambridge.

Robinson, D.W 2007. Taking the Bight Out of Complexity: Elaborating South-Central California

Interior Landscapes, 183–204. In S. Kohring and S. Wynne-Jones (eds) *Socialising Complexity: Structure, Integration, and Power*. Oxford: Oxbow.

Taçon, P. and C. Chippindale. 1998. An archaeology of rock-art through informed methods and formal methods. In C. Chippindale and P. Taçon (eds) *The Archaeology of Rock-Art*, 1–10. Cambridge: Cambridge University Press:

Trigger, B.G. 1981. Archaeology and the Ethnographic Present. *Anthropologica* 23: 3–17.

Voegelin, E.W. 1938. Tübatulabal Ethnography. *Anthropological Records*, 2(1). Berkeley: University of California Press.

Walker, P.L., and T. Hudson 1993. *Chumash Healing: Changing Health and Medical Practices in an American Indian Society*. Banning, California: Malki Museum Press.

Weinberger, G. 1983. Four Forms of Yokuts Rock Art from Tulare County, California. In F. Bock (ed.) *American Indian Rock Art* 9: 72–76.

Whitley, D.S. 1987. Socioreligious Context and the Rock Art in East-Central California. *Journal of Anthropological Archaeology* 6: 159–188.

Whitley, D.S. 1996. *A Guide to Rock Art Sites: Southern California and Northern Nevada*. Mountain Press Publishing.

Whitley, D.S 2000. *The Art of the Shaman: Rock Art of California*. Salt Lake City: University of Utah Press.

Whitley, D.S. and J. Clottes. 2005. In Steward's Shadow: History of rock art research in western North America and France. In L. Loendorf, C Chippindale and D. Whitley (eds) *Discovering North American Rock Art*, 161–180. Tucson: University of Arizona Press.

Willey, G.R. and J.A. Sabloff. 1980. *A History of American Archaeology*. San Francisco: Freeman.

Wobst, H. W. 1978. The Archaeo-Ethnology of Hunter-Gatherers or the Tyranny of the Ethnographic Record in Archaeology. *American Antiquity* 43(2): 303–309.

Wylie, A. 1989. Archaeological Cables and Tacking: The Implications of Practice for Bernstein's 'Options Beyond Objectivism and Relativism'. *Philosophy of the Social Sciences* 19: 1–18.

Zigmond, M.L. 1977. The Supernatural World of the Kawaiisu. In T. Blackburn (ed.) *Flower of the Wind: Papers on Ritual, Myth, and Symbolism in California and the Southwest*, 59–96. Ballena Press: Socorro, New Mexico.

# 8

# Words and things: thick description in archaeology and anthropology

*Chris Gosden*

## *Introduction*

Academic studies of material culture face a paradox. Things are important because of their immediacy to the body, the impact they have on the senses and the activating force to human muscles when held or used. Many of these bodily engagements with objects are hard to put into words. We can instantly recognise the subtle interplay between heat, weight, and smoothness to the touch of picking up a full coffee mug but to describe in words this complex set of sensations and muscular changes is to lag well behind our body's appreciation. Archaeology and anthropology are together trying to understand human engagements with material things, being joined in this attempt by a variety of other disciplines such as art history, cultural studies, geography, music and philosophy. Of all these disciplines, archaeology is the one that has put most effort into dealing with mundane objects, through describing them in words, classifying or codifying them, weighing or measuring them, or analysing their material components. None of this really overcomes the gap between bodily experiences of objects and words but does provide some insights into our ineffable connections with things.

Archaeologists have sometimes been envious of anthropologists. This emotion has a number of sources, one of which is the social anthropologist's ability to engage in 'thick description' (Geertz 1975), rendering the texture and detail of other people's lives, thereby both feeling and conveying the emotional impact of difference. Archaeologists occasionally manage such detailed engagements, sometimes aided by text or oral history, but generally produce what might seem a thinner account of the past. But much less acknowledged, within the discipline and beyond, is archaeology's own form of thick description, which concerns artefacts, sites and landscapes. Stemming initially from nineteenth-century needs to build chronologies based on typological differences, archaeologists have taken very seriously the minor variations in stone, pottery and metalwork. Words have been used to define the difference between a flange-hilted and solid-hilted sword in Bronze Age Europe, for instance, with verbal definitions linked to illustrations, maps and chronological charts. The full panoply of archaeological techniques was put together in the middle twentieth century when statistical techniques were modified for archaeological purposes, based on variations in attributes, artefacts and assemblages. Such analyses can tell us about change through time, help define functional groups, hint at status differences through grave goods and so on. Numbers, showing differences, trends or random variations, carry their own powers of conviction for those inclined to believe. But in archaeology they are predicated on verbal definitions of attributes, types and assemblages so that words are primary. I won't dwell on numbers, but will return to them at the end to make a point about archaeologists' abilities to track long-term movements in material forms.

Rather than celebrating our ability as archaeologists to provide a thick description of the material world, archaeologists of a theoretical inclination have become embarrassed by an obsessive concentration on material details and differences (Hodder 1991). But it is not so much the thickness of the descriptions that have been decried; rather the suggestion is that the mere cataloguing of difference does not enhance understanding of human action.

Conversely, attempts to understand materials by other social sciences, including anthropology, have seemed rather immaterial, lacking convincing descriptions of material differences. It is one thing to acknowledge that mobile phones, soft furnishings or clothing are important to human relations (Horst and Miller 2006, Miller 2001), but unless one can engage with forms, functions and differences at a detailed level, it is hard to say how they are important. Anthropology now regularly incorporates material things into its analyses, but these are still subordinate to the primacy of social relations or act as an insufficiently differentiated raw material mobilized to create these relations. The same is often true of science and technology studies. The mantra of symmetry between all actants doesn't of itself allow the non-human components of networks to be fully acknowledged if there are few disciplinary devices to allow this to happen. I take this to be the point that Ingold (2007) is moving towards when asserting the concrete importance of the properties of materials against a more abstracted notion of materiality. The areas of anthropology most engaged with the material are the anthropology of art (see the rather different but equally serious treatment given to form, material and decoration by Layton 1991, Morphy 1992 and Gell 1998) and museum ethnography (Gosden and Larson 2007).

In this brief contribution I shall stick with this one point – archaeologists are practiced and sometimes very good at rendering material things into words. This is not so true of many other disciplines, including anthropology, now interested in material things. Archaeology has tended to become trapped in a spiral of description, with limited aims of creating chronology or defining regional differences. We are now becoming interested in the impacts that things can have on the senses and the emotions, the nature of their affects and their mood-creating abilities, which are consequential to how people relate one to another. But we have yet to fully realize that the old techniques of the discipline are unusual and useful to many others trying to come to terms with the entanglement of people and things. There are lots of other topics that might be raised in relation to words and things, such as whether material culture can be understood to act as language does (Gell 1998), or how metaphor might work in words and objects (Tilley 1999). In this chapter I focus solely on the important but often overlooked role of description in the archaeological process and consider the contribution this might make to the on-going collaboration between archaeology and anthropology.

## *Describing words*

> The masklike but sharp expressive face with popping eyes ... is created by the simplest of means: a long curved triangle, a schema giving a formalized flat-surfaced nasal, divides symmetrically from its top point to sweep round into flat-terraced volutes ending in the plain eye-bosses, the expression intensified by shaping these terraced volutes in order to set the eye-bosses towards each other ... glowering from either side of the narrow deep-furrowed nose bridge (Jope 2000: 63).

This is a small but representative extract from a very long and complex set of descriptions – which altogether take up four A4 pages – of an item of so-called 'Celtic art', the piece known as the Wandsworth Mask Shield, by Martyn Jope. Jope's work is a mammoth two-volume tome. The first is dedicated to descriptions of objects either as groups (shields, mirrors, etc.) or individually, with attempts made to understand the chronological changes 'Celtic art' underwent from the earlier Iron Age in the fourth century BC to the early Roman period in the first century AD. The volume also looks at the nature of ornament, spanning human or animal figures and more abstract forms, including how items were made. The impact 'Celtic art' objects might have had on those using them is less discussed.

Jope was very much concerned with language, realising that the 'Celtic art' of Britain required an extension of existing vocabularies. His work was motivated by the idea that 'For the details of Celtic formal ornament ... there is no accepted language adequate to carry us much beyond the shapes, conventions and compositions familiar to the ancient civilized world of the east, of the south, of Greece, and Italy' (Jope 2000: 3). He wanted to draw on vocabularies derived from art history, but to then add to these. Outlining his approach to description he explains:

> We have taken some advantage of the more richly developed terminology in some other arts and sciences, notably the biological and molecular sciences, and of musical composition, where closely argued interrelations are of primary importance (Jope 2000: 3–4).

At the end of Volume I he provides a glossary of descriptive terms, complemented by little drawings. The entry for Volute, used in the quote at the beginning of this section, reads as follows – 'VOLUTE. A spiral conformation, usually the terminal part of palmette –, S –, or other figuration' (Jope 2000: 385). The complexity of Jope's descriptions can be frustratingly difficult to follow, but they are both reasonably internally consistent and often evocative of the object. Indeed there is an excitement in some of his object descriptions which is almost erotic in its sensibility – 'This flashy ornament is all done in triple outline ... This swelling opulent flow, with its almost yinyang evolutions in the clasping scroll ends' (Jope 2000: 22) is part of his description of the so-called Wisbech sheath from an early Iron Age dagger. Jope's real sensory and sensual engagement with objects led to a desire to understand, explore, compare and evoke complex items of metalwork in a direct and detailed manner. And while I wouldn't want to push notions of re-enactment and reliving at all far (Collingwood 1946), it may be that, as a result, some of the original Iron Age charge of those objects comes through in Jope's work in the later twentieth century.

Jope's work is unusual in the scale and scope of his attempts to come to terms with objects, deriving partly from archaeological tropes and techniques, partly art historical modes of description (his mentor was Paul Jacobsthal, an art historian, who wrote a work on continental European material (Jacobsthal 1944) to which Jope's own work was a successor). The descriptions in Jope are partly typological – daggers, swords, shields, brooches and so on are first treated as separate categories, within a temporal span – but he also looks at modes of ornament, either figurative which includes people, animals and plants, or formal, taking us through a series of spirals, palmettes, peltae, keeling, lobes and finials. These are complemented by a chapter on craft and an attempt at summation. Major pieces are discussed several times, either individually as an example of a shield or a torc, or then as bearing ornament of different kinds and finally as exemplifying techniques. 'Celtic art' is famous for its convolutions and complexities. Jope's book echoes its subject matter, not having a linear form, but doubling back on itself innumerable times to approach the same pieces from varying directions. It is not a book to be read in a linear sense. Rather it must be navigated with a constant danger of getting lost.

Archaeology is a discipline that puts an enormous amount of effort into material descriptions, which start on the excavation and never stop. 'Light brown loam with fragments of chalk ranging in size between fragments and lumps 2cm in diameter which are spread evenly through the soil matrix' is an invented description of an archaeological context which might actually exist on a context sheet somewhere. Out of this invented context might come a fictitious fibula [a safety-pin type brooch], the potential subject for thick description being part of a predefined class which has a 'construction, with the foot-return cast in one with the bow, their chubby shape, and the bird allusions of one ... recall the Early La Tène brooches which include the *Vogelkopffibeln*, many with similar foot construction' (Jope 2000: 44). In this description of non-fictitious pieces we can see the individuality of objects placed against a series of defined classes, such as the bird's head fibulae (*Vogelkopffibeln*). The effort to create those classes goes back to the earlier nineteenth century when people were attempting to order objects for museum displays. The ultimate outcome of this effort is the Three Age system of Old and New Stone Ages, Bronze and Iron Ages which is still in common use despite many worries that it is constraining our thought rather than enabling it.

Archaeology has a deep stratigraphy of descriptions from the overarching schemes such as the Three Age system down to a lone individual with a single object or layer in an archaeological site. Two opposing impulses are in tension here. At the individual level it is necessary for the investigator to respond to the object or soil matrix in an intelligent and flexible manner appreciating the unusual features of what they are dealing with, or how far an item might be placed in a larger class. The sensorium and creative powers of evocation need to be engaged here. On the other hand, is the need to make any one description accessible and appreciated by others. Here standard vocabularies, modes of writing or drawing and sets of types defined by others come into play to cast our observations in a form which other people can assess, critique or accept. As we shuttle backwards and forwards between the poles of the idiosyncratic and the routinised we hope novel, insightful observations might be achieved but then conveyed in a manner which others, who have not made the direct observations themselves, can grasp.

There has been considerable discussion in recent years of the descriptive process, especially during excavation (Hodder 1999, Chadwick 1998) with the key questions being how to save observations from becoming too routinised so as to open up multiple and changing forms of interpretation. This discussion missed a broader point, which is that compared to many neighbouring disciplines archaeology is deeply descriptive. Very few other disciplines have developed the vocabularies, the modes of visual representation, the statistical analyses and the physical analytical techniques that archaeology has. Jope pointed out the eclectic nature of his vocabulary, drawn from both humanities and science subjects. Archaeology as a whole has benefitted from this mix of approaches. However this benefit has been vitiated somewhat through the recent embrace of perspectives that in highlighting the subjective, culturally influenced viewpoints from which interpretations are arrived at, shift focus away from objective description. Now that the general science and technology studies push to make use of the richness of the melding of the objective and subjective stances has come to the fore (Latour 2005), archaeology should be able to make use of its own traditional forms of description in a more theoretically informed way.

## *The point of description*

Description for its own sake is pointless. An emphasis on materials without the ability to develop thick descriptions is empty. Once one can combine a theoretically informed interest in things with an ability to describe (a process which is potentially endless), we can then ask a deeper question about what it is we want to know about people's interaction with things.

In this respect there are two key things we do not know. We are not sure what the human body can do – neuroscience, anatomy and robotics are all throwing light on the connected nature of human sensorimotor systems and how low level skills build up into complex forms of action (Clarke 2008). We have also not explored the full possibility of materials. The 'we' in both cases refers to analysts. Living human beings over the last 2.3 million years and in many different places in the world have carried out fuller applied experimentation than we are yet aware of. In reality, these two questions of what bodies and what materials can do are really one question – what can bodies and things do in combination?

## *Description in archaeology, anthropology and beyond*

Within the complex ecology of the social sciences, archaeology has a new and particular role to play as a provider of descriptions, which can lead to an appreciation of really salient material differences. Jope's work is useful here as it derives from an odd combination of influences, starting from the typological tradition, dividing shields from swords, fibulae from neckrings, and delineating the details of decoration. This potentially dull description is then infused with Jope's own sensual enthusiasm for the artefacts, which might be seen partly as an attempt by him to evoke the sensory and emotional impact of marvellous objects in the Iron Age. At the start of Jope's book is a chronological chart running from 600 BC to AD 100, outlining trends in the developments of the major artefact types as Jope understood them (Jope 2000: frontispiece). The chart exemplifies common archaeological attempts to understand changes in artefacts over the longer term. These changes are so long term that they occur out of the straightforward control of people (a point I have developed a little more elsewhere – Gosden 2005). In this sense things can be seen to make people as well as the other way round. Other disciplines make such statements, but lack the ability to chart and consider the nature of long-term change (see Feuchtwang and Rowlands, this volume).

These two levels of relationship between people and things – the trans-generational and the more immediate – interact, because the momentary sensory engagement with a thing will depend upon the broader educations of the human sensorimotor system by artefacts. The long and the short combine in a series of complex mutual effects between the human organism and the materials with which it is involved.

There is a lot of describing that could be done, so that we have to make sure the effort is worth it before we begin on tasks which could be endless. The larger end, for me at least, is the mutual production of human beings and material worlds, where both are active, influential and determining. Archaeology has developed very impressive powers of description which it has not always used wisely. But in the on-going collaboration between archaeology and anthropology (and indeed many other subjects in the social sciences) these are one form of practice from which anthropologists might learn. With suitable modification, such forms of description might help contribute to a richer understanding of the material embeddedness of human life in more contemporary forms of sociality.

## Acknowledgements

I would like to thank Duncan Garrow for his invitation to the conference that this volume derives from. He and I have wrestled with Jope together on a joint project on Celtic Art, funded by the AHRC. Tom Yarrow has provided very useful feedback, as have two anonymous referees.

## References

Chadwick, A. 1998. Archaeology at the edge of chaos: further towards reflexive excavation methodologies. *Assemblage* 3. Available at: http://www.assemblage.group.shef.ac.uk/3/3chad.htm.
Clark, A. 2008. *Supersizing the Mind.* Oxford: Oxford University Press.
Collingwood, R. G. 1946. *The Idea of History.* Oxford: Clarendon Press.
Geertz, C. 1975. *The Interpretation of Culture.* New York: Basic Books.
Gell, A. 1998. *Art and Agency.* Oxford: Clarendon Press.
Gosden, C. and F. Larson (with A. Petch). 2007. *Knowing Things: exploring the collections of the Pitt Rivers Museum 1884–1945.* Oxford: Oxford University Press.
Hodder, I. 1991. *Reading the Past.* Cambridge: Cambridge University Press.
Hodder, I. 1999. *The Archaeological Process.* Oxford: Blackwell.
Horst, H. and D. Miller 2006.*The Cell Phone: an anthropology of communication.* Oxford: Berg.
Jacobsthal, P. 1944. *Early Celtic Art.* Oxford: Oxford University Press.
Jope, M. 2000. *Early Celtic Art in the British Isles.* Oxford: Oxford University Press.
Ingold, T. 2007. Materials against Materiality. *Archaeological Dialogues* 14, 1 – 16.
Latour, B. 2005. *Reassembling the Social. An Introduction to Actor-Network Theory.* Oxford: Oxford University Press.
Layton, R. 1991. *The Anthropology of Art.* Cambridge: Cambridge University Press.
Miller, D. 2001. *Home Possessions: material culture behind closed doors.* Oxford: Berg.
Morphy, H. 1992. *Ancestral Connections.* Chicago: Chicago University Press.
Tilley, C. 1999. *Metaphor and Material Culture.* Oxford: Blackwell.

# 9

# Re-evaluating the long term: civilisation and temporalities

*Stephen Feuchtwang and Michael Rowlands*

## *Introduction*

In 1923 in what was seen at the time as a path-breaking essay, Radcliffe-Brown (one of the key founders of British Social Anthropology) set out the distinctions between Ethnology and Social Anthropology as more or less the difference between history and science. The essay was path-breaking since it firmly established the break between a new inductive methodology for anthropology as a social science and its previous identity as a form of conjectural history (Radcliffe-Brown 1923). Anthropology was not alone in 'freeing itself' from the stranglehold of historical consciousness. The 'dangerous surfeit of history' which had been bemoaned fifty years before by Friedrich Nietzsche, was warned against in the same year as Radcliffe Brown's lecture was delivered in South Africa, by Ernst Troeltsch, the German Protestant theologian, who spoke out against the dangers of the 'historicisation of all our knowledge and perceptions'. Europeanised secular historical consciousness had freed itself from long standing theological conceptions of history at the end of the eighteenth and beginning of the nineteenth centuries. Now at the beginning of the 20th century, the crisis of 'historicism', the turning against that knowledge as an epistemological question, would be the recasting of historical knowledge by Heidegger into an ontological question about the meaning of historical existence.

Theologians, both Jewish and Protestant, were the principal anti-historicist critics in post World War 1 Europe. This may seem strangely paradoxical since historical scholarship at the beginning of the 19th century had been the 'handmaiden of theology', designed to demonstrate the truthfulness of the bible. The importation of Rankean modes of historical scholarship into 19th century biblical inquiry was encouraged by many theologians as the means of demonstrating that the veracity of scriptures could be attested by independent rational judgment. But the challenge to faith this represented had converted the debate from a matter of veracity into a broader appeal to faith versus knowledge. European cultural life has indeed experienced various processes of secularization and historicisation whereby religious symbols and ecclesiastical authority have undergone disenchantment only for the theological to creep back in. If transcending the hermeneutic spiral from biblical scholarship to ontology was to lead to Heidegger, then Radcliffe-Brown represented the alternative trend: to save rational judgment by dumping historicism and history altogether in order to create an inductive science of society.

At the beginning of the 21st century, perhaps we have a crisis of another kind. The Eurocentricity of the transformation to modernity is challenged by alternative historical trajectories that simply do not follow the same path. One of the key features of this historicism was its identification with relativism. This entailed recognizing the particularity of Western values and beliefs as only one form of historical development and a deep antipathy to a universal historicism, for instance to *a priori* Hegelian assumptions that all other histories would eventually satisfy the same *telos*. A revival of certain aspects of historicism appears now to be quite compatible with a modified world system approach (Wallerstein 2004) in which European expansion is no longer seen to be a key determining historical event and through which alternative histories and their own historicisms might be written. Subaltern historians in India have already done this, and similar movements now constitute profound alternatives to Eurocentric historicism. Yet, we argue that there is more involved than simply detecting multiple and rival historicities. The historicism or teleology of modernizing projects, the projections of revolutionary or reforming movements and governments, could be considered as a particular temporality that has become a feature of most governments and their economic management in the world system. It is a temporality of breaking from a past to manage movement toward a future, a presentism designed for progress, measured as growth, welfare, emancipation or liberation. But it is grafted on to other temporalities that beg the question of the break with the past, hence the notion of multiple modernities or antipathy to the concept of modernity altogether where its use of 'tradition' entails rupture. These questions of temporality are the starting point of our re-evaluation of the long term.

Others have also been re-evaluating the long term. Goody has crowned a series of books on cuisines, on flowers, on writing, on capitalism, and on modernity, with an attack on great historians and sociologists who read back from the finance and industrial capitalism of Europe and its global spread, to find this end result in every earlier period of European civilisation. This makes that end result a destiny, from the very beginning. To rectify Eurocentrism, Goody turns to the kind of long-term history that archaeologists write, covering very long time-spans. In particular he builds on the history of human civilisation put forward by Childe in his 1951 book, *Social Evolution*. To this he adds the findings of anti-Eurocentric economic historians, such as Pomeranz (2000) and Fernandez-Arnesto (1995). There may be better archaeological materials available for such a task but the point is that we see a convergence of our project with Goody's, in a notion of history that seems genuinely attentive to the significance of long term pasts and their singularity.

Our focus is on what might constitute a more satisfactory conceptual framework for studying long term temporalities in which due weight is given to alternative geocultural centres which, through interaction with each other, have constituted cosmologies that both differ and share elements. In addition, we must meet the challenge of deciding whether there are widespread irreversible changes that have affected social evolution everywhere. The challenge is to acknowledge and describe this without teleology, without reading end-results to human origins, and without ethnocentricity, which is to say without reading all results as if they end up where we, as a defined identity, are now, making us stand out as being exceptional. To do this we have to be conscious of how much these historicising debates within a Eurocentric framework have been shaped by the relationship between history and religion and in particular by histories written from competing theological perspectives. The secularising thesis on which Western modernity prides itself is faithful to a struggle to separate politics and religion but is a conceptual failure in terms of understanding how long term histories have been written from alternative perspectives. Historicist relativism distinguishes as western a logocentrism and its critiques that have defined the limits of rationalism, as well as its corollary of re-enchanted worlds as a particular historical ontology. It should no longer be surprising to see that these debates are not of universal significance but peculiar to a certain philosophically defined notion of difference. Reconciling historicism and historical ontologies and re-asserting the value of long term temporalities are combined in our approach. Whilst we recognise that various forms of understanding long term change relate to different perceptions of temporality (neo-evolutionary, evolutionary biology, phenomenology, etc.), it is the co-occurrence of different temporalities and how they interact with each other that suggest to us greater insights.

The closest analogue to our approach is not surprisingly Braudel's form of 'structural history' (Braudel 1972) for whom the past is conceived as an interacting set of temporal processes combining the short term (events), the medium term (economic cycles and demographic cycles) and the long term (ecological adaptation and continuities). Our starting point, by reintroducing the concept of civilisation, is perhaps an inversion of the adaptationist logic in Braudel and other cultural evolutionary theories (e.g. Carneiro 2003). We would agree with Braudel's focus on 'civilisation' as a spatial and temporal mapping of combinations of material practices, often quite mundane and everyday, that articulate ways of making and doing things that link culture and production in ways that are reproducible over long periods of time. Our intellectual association with the '*techniques et cultures*' tradition in French anthropology is equally not surprising, given its focus on how local taxonomies concerning materials are conceptualised and organised (Lemonnier 1993). What emerges are striking continuities in the distinct forms of civilisations, often persisting over thousands of years and across the transition from prehistoric communities to dynastic states. On the other hand, we acknowledge that events of great turbulence or of extended duration can occur at any of the levels Braudel wrongly distinguished into short, medium and long. Events at any of these levels can create irreversible change not only at their level but affecting the other levels, a criticism already made by Corfield (2007: 208–210).

## *Civilisation: an anthropological reintroduction*

As an idea, civilisation has always been linked to Enlightenment ideals of progress and the achievement of a universal history whose destiny was not in doubt. Projected backwards in time to beginnings associated with technological progress, writing and urbanism, and forwards with ideals of maintaining a synthesis of scientific reason with moral progress to maintain a single idea of humanity, civilisation has, since the 1960s, been a rejected concept in anthropology and sociology, because of its past evolutionary and Eurocentric misuses. More recently the concept has been revived by Samuel Huntington, late Professor of the Science of Government at Harvard University. In 1993 he published an article entitled 'The Clash of Civilisations' and defined civilisation as the highest level of cultural grouping, defining 'culture' in the holistic terms of 1960s cultural anthropology. He argued that there had been an historical evolution of war from the wars of kings, to the wars of peoples, to the wars of ideologies, and now the wars of civilisations and identification with them.

Singular and unified, merely differing in matters of scale from the classic idea of culture, Huntington used this definition to criticize the west for maintaining a monolithic idea of universal history of civilisation in the face of what he described as the emergence of a number of 'civilisations' (e.g. Muslim and Sinic) as the veil of the 'Cold War' was stripped away revealing the reality of these differences. Huntington's prediction of a future of endless conflict and difference has not gone uncriticised. Said (2001), for example, condemned the espousal of the idea of plural monolithic civilisations and stressed instead a reality of distinction but also one of exchange, cross-fertilization and sharing.

But the question of scale remains significant and, more recently, other more historically informed approaches have resuscitated the concept on more sustainable grounds (cf. Arnason 2006). To renew a discussion of its usefulness as a concept, we will start with the most promising, least Eurocentric, conception of civilisation in classical sociology and anthropology, the one forged by Durkheim and Mauss. Durkheim did have a theory of social evolution, which was singular (from mechanical to organic solidarity) and you might therefore expect that he would have a singular theory of the evolution of civilisation. But his collaborator and nephew, Mauss, stressed the histories of civilisations in the plural and rejected the notion of connecting them to some hypothetical general evolution of humankind (2006: 58). Adopting the methodology of Adolf Bastian, Mauss sought not only to trace spread from an origin. He added pluralism to the evolution of any one civilisation over time and in any one location or to people who distinguish themselves and are politically, customarily, linguistically, or religiously distinct (2006: 59). He wanted to preserve the holism central to his and Durkheim's concept of a social organism, but at the same time he acknowledged that a civilisation's boundaries are difficult to determine (2006: 60).

As Mauss defines it, a civilisation consists of 'those social phenomena which are common to several societies'. Notice, however, how he then insists that they are socially linked by adding that they must be 'more or less related to each other' by lasting contact 'through some permanent intermediaries, or through relationships from common descent' (2006: 61), such that on the next page he further refines the concept and calls a civilisation a family of societies (2006: 62). We can imagine what these permanent intermediaries are when we think of tributary or diplomatic or trading or marital relations. In the technical terms of his and Durkheim's sociology, a civilisation is the spread of collective representations and practices, which are the social aspect of the materials of civilisation. He says they are 'arbitrary', by which he means they are not universal but preferred modes of making and doing things. In the actual order of analysis, to say these things belong together as a civilisation is to infer from archaeological and historical evidence a common set of practices and meanings, not one dominant characteristic, design or thing, but the way they all hang together and their evolution over time and their variation in space.

Note that these mark the boundaries of civilisational spread. Beyond them are the spread of bartered or marketed goods that are accepted for their strangeness, or exoticism, rather than their symbolic meaning or the practice and conduct that goes with them within the civilisation from which and within which they are produced. Within a civilisational spread there are other boundaries of more coherent social structures and their centres. In the present day, as Mauss already noted in 1920, the language and spread of scientific knowledge, means of communication of information and of the arts, and forms of state have become universal. He saw them amounting to a single civilisation entering all other civilisations and spreading them or knowledge of them:

> The history of civilisation, from the point of view that concerns us, is the history of the circulation between societies of the various goods and achievements of each. … Societies live by borrowing from each other, but they define themselves rather by the refusal of borrowing than by its acceptance (Mauss 1920: 242–251).

Mauss' writings on civilisation are important because they represent his most non-sociological approach. His inspiration in thinking about civilisation is clearly Ethnological (i.e. he resists creating the division between Ethnology versus Sociology that was necessary for the paradigm break leading to the foundation of sociology/social anthropology in the 1920s). Instead he constantly emphasizes that there exist phenomena that are not limited to a specific society. Instead they are phenomena common to a larger or smaller group of societies. These are phenomena – particularly material practices – that are what he calls 'fit to travel', i.e. they overflow boundaries or do not have fixed boundaries.

Accordingly, large scale unitary spreads prior to formations of 'society' are included in his non-sociological definition of civilisation. For example when he says phenomena of civilisation are international or extranational, he also says it is on the basis of civilisations that societies develop their distinctive features, their idiosyncrasies and their individual characters. That is, he implies that societies, hierarchies, etc. emerge out of larger – already existing – shared sets of material practices and characteristics. It is not the Durkheimian principle of order that fascinates so much here; rather it is the chaos/order and inside/outside binaries that are deemed necessary for the emergence of society. Mauss is making the startling point that far from civilisations being forms of society, civilisations are prior expositions of the binaries that are necessary forerunners of the societies that form within civilisational spreads, historically.

> The form of a civilisation is the sum of the specific aspects taken by the ideas, practices and products which are more or less common to a number of given societies. We could say that the form of a civilisation is everything which gives a special aspect, unlike any other, to the societies which compose this civilisation (Mauss 1929/30 reprinted Mauss 2006: 63).

Possibly the most interesting characteristic of the concept is one that Mauss would consider to be a weakness. It is the *loose* integration of its elements, not a holistic integration. Even though it can be said of a civilisation that it is reproduced, just as social relations, or systems of meaning and material practices are reproduced, we need not feel compelled to put all these together into a single totality and its reproduction. Civilisation is like 'culture', but it emphasises the *spread* of culture. It is like 'society', but it is partial, forcing us to think and to infer how elements of a culture carry with them habits of relating to others. Contra Huntingdon (1993) these are practices and ways of making things, but transformed with different additions from elsewhere, from other cultures in a civilisational spread and further transformations and creations of new civilisational centres out of the results of civilisations spreading into each other. 'Civilisation' is a grand, but not a totalising concept of social, cultural and material life. It forces us to analyse *mixtures*, the spreads of culture into each other and in combination with each other. To identify such a spread it is usual to identify a centre of material production and its spread of influence. But it is necessary to add that over time there can be several centres that have achieved influence on what is spread and they are related to each other as a civilisation. We also wish to highlight the fact that claims to the same civilisation are made from several centres, critical of the established centres. Civilisation is not only a spread of styles, norms of conduct, distinction and knowledges. It is also an arena of contention to the same spread, from several centres of the same civilisation, in the same way that the charismatic promise of a religious tradition is taken up outside its established centres.

So what might be shared in a civilisational spread? One, possibly the most important thing, is what we currently use the term 'cosmology' to describe: ways of knowing and transmissions of knowledge about the origins of the universe, which is existence as a shared set of dispositions. Since these usually relate to creation myths (myths of origin etc., particularly pertaining to chaos, misfortune and disorder as well as to the emergence of order) it is not surprising that in the tradition of Durkheimian sociology and anthropology the term cosmology has been collapsed to the study of society and reserved for the attachment of moral principles to knowledge as order. The concern of this tradition has been to show the ways people make societies or create social groups by making categories, closing off the inside from the outside as part of a sense of cosmological ordering. For writers in this tradition, allowing closure also meant that civilisations were the cosmological materials that encouraged certain kinds of hierarchy for the promotion of closure and order. Hierarchies allowed certain kinds of cosmological centre and encompassment to emerge, promoting the well worn theme that power – conceived in a certain sociological way (coercion, etc.) – will strive to internalise the closure of cosmological being to the operations of a single centre, which may or may not also be a political centre. We on the contrary set our sights on the chaos/order binary of cosmologies and on the always partial nature of a culture and a society in a spread of civilisation, in which one is a version of the next and refers to, even as it distinguishes itself from, the other (neighbour, outside, chaotic), using this and other binaries. In re-setting our focus in this way we believe we remain more true to Mauss' concept, even when it disconcerted his own stress on order.

The problem of recognising uniformities over large areas but also taking into account localised differences has been considered creatively within the framework of social knowledge. Barth (1987), for example, accounts for cultural variation by showing how many different groups draw from a similar vocabulary, material cultures and social practices. For him scale is an issue in defining a tradition as an overall pattern in the distribution of knowledge and ideas (Barth 1987: 78). He recognises that differences occur in the modes of transaction and handling of knowledge over time so that detecting commonalities between Bali and Melanesia shows how different modes of transmission have channelled their development in very different trajectories. In Bali, *gurus* increase cultural capital by disseminating knowledge widely and by objectifying it in complex temple and court systems to which there is relatively open access. In Melanesia, elders who have been initiated into secret knowledge hoard and control access to it as a means of retaining status.

A similar attempt to grasp a sense of higher unity shared by particular local traditions can be seen in Tambiah (1990) who writes on Therevada Buddhism in Thailand, Burma and Sri Lanka as a collective tradition that takes different forms or divergent trajectories in these three settings. In other words, Barth and Tambiah both argue that cultural difference occurs as a result of the transmission of knowledge and of distinctive modes of transmission of knowledge although this is only possible because they share cultural commonalities. The particular attraction of Barth's approach lies in the recognition of how deep analogues in substantive ideas – in his case between Bali and Inner New Guinea – can be combined and shown by comparing the modes by which knowledge is transmitted, adopted and transformed over time (Barth 1990: 640). He suggests that the processes that result from these interactions 'generate regional trends over time, but also discontinuous variation and incompatible syntheses in different parts of the same region' (Barth 1987: 80) and 'culture areas are then not only the product of past history; in a very real sense they are being made now, by the efforts of different intellectuals elaborating different kinds of knowledge' (Barth 1990: 650).

We now turn to two, more extended illustrations to show how our re-evaluated version of Mauss' 'civilisation' might be useful. We dwell in particular on the making of material objects and the performance of ritual as ways within each civilisation of making visible the invisible, the world of the dead and of invasive powers. In this way we are both anthropologists and archaeologists, as well as historians, using archival documents and the materials of written chronologies and histories, ethnographies of ritual and political authority, and material objects, the material culture that is the substance for archaeological enquiry.

## *Civilisation and temporalities: Africa*

In Africa, 'civilisation' connotes recognition of the argument made by such African leaders as the Senegalese historian Cheik Anta Diop and more recently by Thabo Mbeki, former president of South Africa, that 'Ancient Africa' was originally a unity with its own civilisation recognised from Ancient Egypt to the ruins of Great Zimbabwe, having its own internal dynamics and relations of exchange with the outside – in particular the Indian Ocean (see Chami 2004). For many Africans, the 'long term' is desired as a sense of past that denies the 'barbarism' corollary of 'civilisation' and the epithet of 'late comer' to technological and social developments (agriculture, metallurgy, urbanism, etc.) and countering African irrelevance for understanding 'world prehistory' (see Stahl 2005: 9). It connotes equally an irritation that even sympathetic histories of Africa are written from the perspective of the impact of Europeans on the continent, usually the slave trade, colonialism and postcolonial misgovernance rather than from an 'internalist' perspective of 'civilisational' achievement. What Stahl calls the long term exclusion of Africa from the 'circle of we' combined with general pessimism became the rallying cry for historians and archaeologists to prove that Africa has a progressive history. There is much that is new in African archaeology because of this. There is also the need to emphasise the originality of concepts developed in Africa. The association of civilisation with evolution has, however, for a long time shrouded such discussion in the African context in either pejorative terms or been seen as a wish to prescribe dignity and respect for a difficult past. The perspective adopted by us is that there is no single temporality but multiple temporalities, each with ruptures, and that internalities and externalities are matters of reflection and contention, forming the realities in which knowledge of pasts are created. Here, we want to stress that making history through stressing alternative temporalities has been and remains a localised phenomenon in Africa, as in any other geography of civilisational spread.

Since Frobenius (1898; 1913), there have been numerous attempts to describe a symbolic repertoire of common elements for Africa as 'ways of knowing' that can pass back and forth across different regional and social boundaries (e.g. Herskovits' 1926 study of the East African 'cattle complex'). In his study of Mueda sorcery in Mozambique, Harry West discovered that the life-world Muedans make through sorcery discourse comprises two domains, one visible and one invisible (West 2005: 47). A specifiable mode of distinguishing and joining two domains, one visible the other invisible, is a way of knowing repeated across several African cultures and societies. Muedan sorcerers use a medicinal substance *shikupi* to make themselves invisible and get outside the visible world normally experienced. Sorcerers can act upon the visible world of their victims without being seen and, at night, carry out their depredations of the living. But those who can detect and defend people against sorcery can also enter the invisible world and reverse or overturn the actions of sorcerers and expose their activities in the visible world of the living. The ambivalence of sorcery power comes from the belief that sorcerers and anti-sorcerers must share the same power through their ingestion of medicinal substances but it is their intentions that separate them. Stoller (1984) describes the 'fusion of worlds' in possession cults among the Songhay in Burkina Faso as also dependent on the means of spirit mediums to move between separate visible and invisible worlds. The point is that those with the authority to mediate should show that they have the power to do so. More than that, the power they have should be displayed through the benefits that accrue from having these powers.

The invisible/visible dichotomy and their mediation/interpenetration is core to many versions of African civilisation. It is the basis of statements (e.g. MacGaffey 2000) on the fundamental powers of life and death that are thought to be general among Western Bantu speakers from Cameroon to Angola. In one part of this vast area, in the forest region of the Cross River (Nigeria border) and in the Cameroon Grassfields, the interface between visible and invisible worlds takes the form of ritual cults and associations. This is a polycentric landscape in which demographically smaller or larger local communities each have their own cult and warrior associations with different names and minor local variations but with similar concerns. Exchange and trade in cults – drawing from the same 'symbolic reservoir' – circulate the objects and paraphernalia even more widely as esoteric objects than the circulation of knowledge needed to produce them. The visible, taking the form of masquerades and cult associations, is the materialisation of the invisible – a means of locating it and grounding it both as a means of controlling and of managing it.

Associations and cult agencies materialise the invisible in several ways. By 'cult agencies' we mean both objects and the powers they have been endowed with by secret rituals, and the rituals themselves, their leading authorities and performers. Through objectification of the spirits of the invisible world, in masks, statues, and other objects, they make the invisible concrete. The associations and leaders of the cults penetrate invisible worlds of sorcery/witchcraft/forest spirits and ancestors and return with them to the visible world. By these means the invisible can, potentially, by those with requisite authority and skill, be managed and controlled and their powers disseminated.

The invisible materialised as cult agencies and associations shares considerable continuities in form over the whole area of the Cross River and Grassfields regions.

Cults and associations can be separated in a division of function and power. But all, in different ways and for different purposes, objectify the invisible by seeing or hearing or rousing invisible agencies whether by day or night or by timing in a ritual cycle and so controlling them when they can be encountered. Mediations of the invisible and their dangers and benefits are constituted as knowledge, and that knowledge is disseminated through means that, by their dissemination, describe a moral community.

There are several local ways of classifying cults and associations. For example keeping them and those who have expertise in them separate; that is separating the ambivalence of witch finding functions from those of divination, healing and cure and who controls these functions, serves to maintain more egalitarian forms of association since it also separates control over the exercise of these functions. Fusing them together – as happens with the Grassfield palaces – instead creates hierarchy. Wide spatial and temporal continuities in the mediation of invisible and visible worlds, objectified as material forms of cults and associations dealing with the basic ontologies of life, death and misfortune can be contrasted with strong differences in social forms. Hierarchies and palace organisations in the Grassfields contrast with acephalous, more egalitarian social forms in the forest zone. In the forest zone agencies possessing medicines that protect against witchcraft are kept separate from associations that heal and cure; in the Grassfields the two are fused in the same complex of cults. Their separation in the Cross River forest zone produces egalitarian village structures, in the Grassfields their fusion resulted historically in palace hierarchies.

We have emphasised the role of ritual in maintaining the separation and mediation between realms that also allows us to see both continuities and variations in the materialisation of the invisible as forms of visible cult agencies and associations. Such a conception of 'civilisation' displays long term similarities over large areas, yet accommodates their concrete and particular historical circumstances. For example, the European inspired slave trade created new associations and cults based on a pre-existing repertoire of elements that now combined in new and quite distinctive forms. Some time during the early 19th century, the Ekpe cult association (which first materialised in the south west of the Cross River region near Calabar and subsequently spread to the edges of the Grassfields) borrowed elements of dress, music and ritual objects from Europeans, creating a powerful cult agency that was sought by and subsumed or syncretised with existing cults over a much larger area than had ever existed before. This new kind of association involved prestige for its members, high payments to belong to it and the transformation of a man into chiefly status over his lifetime – in other words an opening up of hierarchies to membership based more on trade wealth and external contacts than had previously been the case. Integrated through the development of

European trade within its hinterland of this part of West Central Africa, associations were the principal vehicle for the development of trade partnerships and the necessary conditions of trust and security that first the trade in slaves and then subsequently the late 19th century trade in palm oil products could be secured.

The imposition of colonial rule changed all this, first in Cameroon by Germany until the end of the First World War and then subsequently Britain and France when the Cameroons were administered as mandated territories (part of Nigeria and French Cameroon). Whilst cult associations and agencies continued in less overt and secret forms, often suppressed by missionary activity and later supplanted by the new churches, a new historicising process developed to encourage more varied forms of cult association. One of these was the appropriation of the European idea of the museum.

In 1923, the same year that Radcliffe Brown and Troeltsch were overseeing the demise of historicism in Europe, Mose Yeyab, a Christian interpreter and secretary to the new French colonial administration in Cameroon, established in Foumban a Museum for the Arts and Traditions of Bamum. Already in 1920 he had built a 'personal museum' to house the ritual objects he had collected from various palace cult associations, which, due to the intensification of the conversion of the court of Sultan Njoya to Islam, were flooding on to the market and serving an active tourist trade among French colonial officers and administrators. Since the 1890s the Bamum court had been an active supplier of 'African art' to the European markets with court artisans making sculptures specifically to meet European museum and private collector demand (Schildkrout and Keim 1998). Besides the commercial benefits involved in turning ritual objects into African art, as a Christian convert Yeyab's purpose in building a museum was political. Working with the new French administration in order to undermine the court ritual and power of Sultan Njoya, he had established for himself a key role in creating 'administrative chiefs' in Bamum based on appointment rather than hereditary position. Njoya, once the favoured 'African King' of the German administration, was then condemned by the French as an 'African despot' and the chief practitioner of the 'animistic practices' used by his court to rule the Bamum people. Njoya was finally to be exiled to Yaounde by the French in 1931 and to die there in 1933, but not before he had established a palace museum, to counter Mose Yeyab's museum of African art (Geary 1984).

Paul Gebauer, a North American head of mission visiting Foumban in 1931, recognised the role of the museum in this political struggle when he remarked:

> This enlightened sovereign (Njoya) possesses a private museum in his palace in Foumban, a town in which we also find another museum at the top of the avenue where the art shops of the capital can be found. The best of Bamum art and artisan work are displayed here for the immense pleasure of amateurs and visitors. In 1931, the palace museum contained a valuable collection of objects both from the Sultanate and other parts of Cameroon. The passion of Sultan Njoya for these fine things is shared by his 60,000 subjects (quoted in Geary 1984 :18).

In 1931, therefore, there existed two museums in this Cameroonian town, one a royal palace affair safeguarding the traditions of the Bamum people and the other a public, artisanal museum involved in the buying and selling of art objects. Both of these museums still function today in Foumban, the palace museum built by Sultan Njoya housing palace ritual objects and documents that would recount the history of the Bamum kingdom, and the museum of Mose Yeyab, which is now the focus for one of the largest centres of artisan production of African art in contemporary West Africa. It is unclear exactly when Njoya created a palace museum but probably sometime between 1917 and 1922 when he had also written a book on the history and customs of the Bamum people and encouraged the development of a separate and unique Bamum writing script. Njoya's historicism was therefore not only consistent with the experience he had acquired of the European idea of 'writing a past' from previous, German visitors, but also, for him, the interregnum between the end of German rule and the full imposition of French administration was an opportunity for his historicised perception of the power of Bamum tradition to be materialised in a museum and in the development of a writing system. Njoya's concern in writing the history of the Bamum peoples was in part 'self justification'; he firmly believed that he had saved his people from conflict and destruction during the German period. But more significantly, his concern was to write the dynastic history of his predecessors as 'Kings' of Bamum. For Njoya, chronological sequence and dates mattered; so did collecting the royal objects of his predecessors and ensuring that cult objects were preserved in the 'palace museum' and their secrecy maintained. In other words, the cult objects maintained their function of making the invisible visible and as a way of knowing life, death and misfortune, but were now associated with a new temporality of chronological sequence and a new kind of authority. Making a collection for the palace museum in the 1920s did not therefore have at stake the desirability of display to all visitors, including tourists; nor was it to do with recognition of the role of the public space as a legitimation of a dynastic tradition. It was about the preservation of the objects and texts that could be associated with the reigns of his predecessors and their achievements; and it was about the significance that ancestral power and its temporality had for the living. There is a wider perception implicit in many other studies of ancestral temporalities, namely that these are active objects and texts potentially possessed by spirits of dead ancestors and dangerous if ignored or allowed to rot and decay. Njoya's historicism and the compulsion to record a past followed the tradition of preserving the things of the past as a form of ancestral stereotypical reproduction (cf. Peel 1984). Equally, no doubt, it was also based on a brilliant perception of what lay behind the power of German rule and, as Gebauer's quote suggests, this was not a minority view of the power of the past in the kingdom. We are not too far away therefore from the role of 'traditional' cult associations, but now transformed into modern institutions that act correctly as store houses and a means of materialising and displaying the invisible power of colonised ancestral power.

The legacy of Njoya's historicism is therefore quite different from reviving an orthodox sense of historiography. As part of their crushing of Njoya's historicism, the French banned the performance of ancestral rituals in the palace in 1922. But in 2003 the *nguon* festival was revived, using the descriptions of the ritual recorded by Njoya and bringing objects from the palace museum on to the ceremonial ground for the current Sultan Seidou to use. The alacrity with which an eighty year gap was bridged and rituals in quite complex detail 'remembered' suggests something other than social memory. It suggests instead the presence of an indigenous historicism based on objects rather than texts and implicit forms of heritage memory embedded in these technologies. The presence of politicised memories and the temporalities they generate form the basis for a reappropriation of civilised pasts in Africa.

## *Civilisation and temporalities: China*

The African example of long term historicity takes one vital step in the direction of suggesting multiple historicities. There are further steps to be taken in any project of writing a history that considers several historicities, and such steps include consideration of what temporalities are involved in each. In the following sketch, using an example of claiming a Chinese historicity similar to the Cameroonian claim to a continual sequence of kings, we want to consider what such further steps entail.

First, we have to consider the temporality of the history of historicities that we are writing. The temporality of such a history envisages transformation that is irreversible, in which certain temporalities, which can be inferred and reconstructed, are no longer lived or used. We should envisage irreversible change despite the fact that the civilisation we seek to know may not entertain the idea of irreversible change and social transformation. Such reconstructed and redundant temporalities must have existed in the topical civilisation. It is also important to note that one element, such as a temporality of death, may cease without the other elements of a civilisation ending. We cannot assume totalities in 'civilisation', and so we do not entertain totalities of transformation.

Let us first consider the temporality of a break from a past itself. It is the common-all-garden break that makes a past into a tradition coupled with modernity. Mauss' concept of civilisation encompasses what he considers, as very many writers (such as Wallerstein) still do, a 'modern', 'world' or 'global' civilisation (Wallerstein 2004 calls it a 'geoculture'). As we have already pointed out, its characteristic temporality is a narrative of a break from a past and into a progressive time. This is the temporality of modernity as a project, variously performed and heralded as that of national liberation, revolutionary emancipation, or development. It is a teleology of perpetual change breaking through and released after a break from or superimposition upon other civilisational temporalities. We have already pointed out that the posited break begs

the question of continuity through it. And we have also, through our preference for the concept of civilisation, discarded the tyranny of social or any other totality and therefore of total transformation. We have further acknowledged that the historicity and politics of repossessing a civilisation opens a field of contention between pasts and futures. But it remains true to say that in each instance of repossession of long term historicity, such as the African example already described, the appropriation is an inflection and a renewal of the characteristic temporality of a global civilisation of perpetual change, introduced in different ways and at separate times in each of its eventual contexts. Relativised historicity is nearly always a teleology of the present and future of a region or a people.

The modernising project is a temporality of secular calculation for betterment, usually in a present of disappointment and the necessity to confront denial of the transformative promise. In each instance, a politically high moment of such confrontation, such as the twenty five years of a fully-formed Maoist state in China (1953–1978), has been followed by a longer look backwards and forwards in the same temporality – backwards to what remains and might be continuous with the country's civilisation(s), forward to a more gradual transformation, including the turning of the past into a present pride (museums) and an industry (tourism). The political high – the establishing of an independent nation and a secular state of a people, be it revolutionary or not, be it a dictatorship in practice or not – is then an episode in the 'modern' transformation. It is measured and lived in the modernising project, a temporality in various modes, historiographical, political-rhetorical, commemorative, and spectacular (in shows and displays, in exhibitions and festivals).

Beside this break, or rather temporality of a break, transforming previous temporalities, there is no good reason to assume that there have not been such irreversible changes before, in which an older temporality was irreversibly abandoned or else contextualized by another, newer temporality. The work of anthropological and archaeological historians should include, infer and reconstruct such distant past temporalities as well as the more recent past, starting as we inevitably must, in a present in which we are formed by whatever immediate pasts we take on, calling them 'tradition'. Taking on tradition is all the more self-questioning by dint of such reconstructions of irretrievable pasts, of knowledge or of eschatology (knowledge and doctrine of life and death), and indeed of histories and historicisms. History, archaeology, and museums are our ways of making the invisible visible, the dead including the very long dead evident, according to the empiricism of the visible in fields of visibility as evidence. Latour (1993: 68–76) would have them be objects as witnesses of multiple times. But for what he calls 'moderns', who include us all, they are displayed in a visibility of both record and evidence, be they experimental or of authenticatable historical/archaeological finds.

A good example of both, the transformation into modern spectacular temporality and the reconstruction of a long-gone temporality, was evident in the recent British Museum exhibition of the First Emperor, in fact an exhibition of some of the figures

from excavations at sites surrounding his tomb. It was a show, constructed jointly by Chinese and British curators, although its dramatic design had been contracted out to a firm called Metaphor. Metaphor made an impressive drama of the display. The visitor had first to walk through a narrow and dark passage, then climb some stairs into an ante-chamber-like space beneath the dome of the Reading Room. The ante-chamber provided well-captioned small exhibits of the period preceding and contemporary with the burial, including a decorated tile from a kiln and a full model of a palace for which it might have been intended, before entering the main chamber. The main chamber was entitled 'the mystery of the tomb'. It was directly under the dome, and its central spaces contained spot-lit standing figures of warriors and the remains of a chariot, as well as a full-scale model of what it must have been when first buried. You stood before any one of these figures, looking into their faces, slightly above your own, experiencing a frisson of meeting an unseeing stranger from more than two thousand years ago.

Of course, this mystery chamber was not the emperor's tomb, even though it was under a dome and his tomb is domed under a tumulus the size of a substantial hill. All the objects on display came from chambers on the fringes of the area that has the tumulus at its centre. And the spotlights individuated as well as lit figures that had been serried in ranks underground and were never meant to be seen. This is the modern temporality of spectacle and personality at play, principally in the naming and making of the First Emperor into a so-called 'genius', claimed as a fore-runner of the present genius of resplendent China. It made spectacularly visible what was intended to remain invisible. Meanwhile, the Emperor whose historical power is made visible for and by the government of China, is kept invisible. The viewer was drawn into an implication and speculation on the huge potential of what could be displayed in the same way. But the domed chamber where the emperor is supposed still to remain has not been excavated. As Dr Wu the director of the Terracotta Warrior museum in Xi'an, China, wrote for the British Museum exhibition catalogue: 'we should respect our ancestors and our cultural heritage... and so we should proceed in our scientific enquiries and conservation without disturbing the sleeping emperor' (Wu Yongqi 2007: 157).

Here is the curator as preserver of a current historicity, in the same mode as Sultan Njoya placing behind him a line of predecessors by curating his palace museum.

The sleeping emperor whose own title The First Emperor (Shi Huangdi) named the show in London is important to the current government of the People's Republic of China as one of a number of origin figures for its own version of Chinese civilisation. The importance of the tomb to the current state requires a continuity that provides a pedigree.

The importance of rulers' tombs as authentifications of civilisational and political pedigree seems to have been maintained from the past. But authenticity is now claimed through 'scientific enquiries' and exhibition, in a temporality entirely different from that of the tombs of the monarchs of the Warring States (475–223 BCE), out of which the monarch of the state of Qin emerged as the victorious conquering unifier and self-

designated First August Emperor, which was one of awe through *in*visibility and the achievement of immortality by ritual techniques. Nor is this temporality the same as that of subsequent dynasties. It was transformed when the afterlife of emperors and the common people alike became treatable by Daoist and Buddhist ritual experts who by the fifth century had succeeded the older ritual experts (*fangshi*) who had advised the First Emperor at court.

The First Emperor's tomb, like those of the other monarchs of the warring states, and of the Zhou state in particular, replicated the state over which he ruled, except that in this case it was one that included all the other states, the court from which he ruled, and the mountains and rivers through which he communicated with the eternal and highest principle of the universe, Tian [Heaven] (Rawson 2007). Most significantly, it included the materials – such as mercury – and the bodies of other people – such as concubines who had not yet given birth to his descendants – by which, through alchemical and sexual techniques he sought to attain everlasting life (Lewis 2007: 90, Strickman 1979). Even though the fact of the death of the living body and its succession by a son was of great ritual importance, the tomb put into effect the same ritual techniques that the emperor had been advised to practice when alive to achieve everlasting life.

His tomb and its buried world were as invisible as his ritual and governmental advisers said he should be when he lived, such that the emperor had high towers raised and covered walkways built on the advice of his *fangshi* so that he could see but remain unseen except for carefully controlled appearances for selected audiences. This and other pieces of advice were made with the aim of raising the emperor and his lineage above the lineages of the landed grandees, who lorded it above the rest of his subjects, along with the monarchs of former states and of the principalities that made up the empire.

The temporality of immortal imperial afterlife, wrecked if (usually when) tombs were raided and their contents made visible and sold or hoarded, was finally ended by the republican overthrow of dynastic rule in 1912. The republican governments that followed eventually made the tombs their heritage. But the temporality of the original burial had already been so modified that we can consider it to have long been transformed into another, while keeping some elements that continued into even the present day. The material culture of the imperial court included shrines at which emperors of this and of previous dynasties were venerated with elaborate offerings. But in the tombs of the last twelve emperors of the Ming dynasty (1406–1644) imperial self-cultivation to reach immortality had become similar in form but now modulated into a respect for ancestors to be treated in death as in life through offerings at their graves as well as in their ancestral halls. This veneration of ancestors at gravesites as well as domestic and hall shrines had already by then become, from the Southern Song dynasty onwards (1127–1279), as true for commoners as it was for emperors, so that emperors had to guard against the tombs of commoners being more auspicious than

their own in case they promised the ultimate, a future imperial dynasty. We can infer from this a transformation of a conception of afterlife and eschatology, ending the imperial tomb temporality of the first emperors.

The new temporality involved the treatment of the bodies of the dead as the earth-bound remains of ancestors affecting their descendants according to the siting of the tomb by calculation of its *fengshui* and lasting just so long as the descendants cared for the tomb with offerings on site. This was, as before, distinguished from the same person's immaterial soul (*hun*) as ancestor in a tablet for veneration at home or an ancestral hall. But by the Ming this had become the privilege and duty of the common people in the same civilisation as the emperor. There was an equally, or more important addition, modifying if not replacing the cultivation of immortality and so changing it into another temporality. This was a performed conception of the same soul being brought, by Buddhist and Daoist rituals, across (*du*) from purgatorial judgment into rebirth or the various versions of the realm of release from the karmic cycle, the Pure Land or Western Paradise. Ritual and its objects, shrines, ancestral tablets, offerings and their vessels, maintaining many of the designs and features of the bronze vessels of the time before the First Emperor, the statues of gods, the pictures of purgatory, incense and fire were and remain ways of making the invisible visible, in which the invisible are the powers of Heaven and Earth, and the spirits of predecessors, not just emperors, but heroes of skill – of medical treatment, or of building, or of making paper and writing – and salvation. Material forms continue, such as the bronzes for the heating and presentation of offerings. But they have over time conveyed new ritual techniques and new temporalities.

This brief sketch is meant to serve the purpose of suggesting how a conception of civilisation as a set of temporalities, into which other temporalities enter, as through Buddhism in this instance, might be worked out. Other details could be provided to indicate the historicism of the civilisation that was transmitted by the Chinese empire, on the twin premises established by the time of the First Emperor and that continue, though transformed, to this day. The first premise is that of sage rule and its task of adaptation in a cosmology of constant principles of constant change, failure of which brought about chaos and confusion, a temporality of fluctuation from clear and sage to confused and chaotic and the restoration of sage rule (see Wang Mingming forthcoming). The second premise is that of self-cultivation, bodily and spiritual ritual techniques and exercises for long life that can extend to perfection and that include the arts of writing (calligraphy and composition). The point of mentioning them here is that they exemplify the problem of continuity in such long term civilisational histories as we are trying to suggest.

Some of the characteristics of the expectation of rule to be sage have informed the socialism that Mao established in China (see Lin Chun 2006: 140–142). While very many of the exercises of self-cultivation have been continued in popular culture (see Yen Yueh-ping 2005, Farquhar and Zhang 2005). So too have the rituals of ancestral veneration and of passage from purgatory to the Western Paradise. What do we make of these continuities? It is probably necessary to say two quite different things about them as conveyors of temporality. One is that they convey the temporalities of self-cultivation toward perfection, of ancestral reproduction, and of karmic retribution or release as before. The other is that they are now in conjunction with the transformed, secular historical temporality of popular rule and self-strengthening in a patriotic project or a personal project of betterment and a way of knowing that is evidential and spectacular.

## *Conclusion*

We hope by these examples to have shown how a concept of civilisation opens out a field of joint anthropological, archaeological and historical enquiry. The concept of a history of temporalities is inevitably formed in a current temporality. However, this can open that temporality out into a view of several historicities, of which Eurocentricity is just one, and lead to a reconstruction of past temporalities.

Our re-introduction of civilisation and opening out of the topic of temporalities has led to the definition of two problems. One is the problem of continuities. Have they been incorporated into the new temporality as its sequence of origins, or do they continue, modified or not, separately alongside? In any case, what our proposed view opens up is one of different temporalities coexisting in the same people and in the same context, a space of different but interacting temporalities. The other is the problem of the reconstruction of temporalities that were abandoned and superseded long before. We do not propose a necessarily sudden break. Indeed what we propose are longer processes casting older temporalities into an irretrievable past of a past, an irreversible change. Comparisons of civilisations and their temporalities might reveal similar processes and similar past temporalities. But that is to be shown, not assumed from any theory of social and cultural evolution.

Neither of these are new problems. They have been broached in histories of knowledge, the reconstruction of the generalities of sciences or of cosmologies. Such histories ask how knowledge and truth were constituted as such, rather than as fore-runners of what we now call science and religion. But we have drawn particular attention to the designation of temporalities, the coexistence of more than one such sense and performance of long term repetition and change, and their place in the knowledge denoted by the term 'historicities'. Through a Maussian concept of civilisations as spreads of material culture and what they convey, cosmologies and temporalities, ways of creating socialities, the formation of centres of different kinds of hierarchy, their transformation over time and their variation in relation to each other in space, we hope we have suggested an agenda of the long-term for archaeology, history and anthropology combined.

## *References*

Arnason, J. 2003. *Civilisation in Dispute.* Leiden: Brill.

Barth, F. 1987. *Cosmologies in the Making: a generative approach to cultural variation in Inner New Guinea.* Cambridge: Cambridge University Press.

Barth, F. 1990. The Guru and the Conjurer: transactions in knowledge and the shaping of culture in Southeast Asia and Melanesia. *Man* 25: 640–653.

Braudel, F. 1972. *The Mediterranean and the Mediterraean World in the Age of Philip II 2 vols.* London: Fontana.

Carneiro, R 2003. *Evolutionism in Cultural Anthropology*. Boulder: Westview Press.

Chami, F. 2004. *The Unity of African Ancient History*. Dar-es-Salaam: E and D Ltd.

Corfield, P. 2007. *Time and the Shape of History*. New Haven and London: Yale University Press.

Farquhar, J and Zhang Q. 2005. Biopolitical Beijing: Pleasure, Sovereignty, and self-cultivation in China's capital. *Cultural Anthropology* 20, 303–32.

Fernandez-Arnesto, F. 1995. *Millenium: a history of our last thousand years*. London: Black Swan.

Frobenius, L. 1898. *Der Ursprung der Afrikanischen Kultur.* Berlin: Reimer.

Frobenius, L. 1913. *The Voice of Africa Vol 1.* London: Hutchinson.

Geary, C. 1984. *Things of the Palace.* Wiesbaden: Franz Steiner Verlag.

Goody, J. 2006. *The Theft of History*. Cambridge: Cambridge University Press.

Harris, M. 1969. *The Rise of Anthropological Theory: a History of Theories of Culture.* New York: Harper Collins.

Herskovits, M. 1926. The cattle complex in East Africa. *American Anthropologist* 28, 230-272.

Huntingdon, S. 1993. The clash of civilisations. *Foreign Affairs* 72:3, 22–49.

de Heusch, L. 1985. *Sacrifice in Africa: A Structuralist Approach.* Manchester: Manchester University Press

Kuper, A. 1979. Regional Comparison in African Anthropology. *African Affairs* 78, 103–113.

Latour, B. 1993. *We Have Never Been Modern.* Cambridge, Mass.: Harvard University Press.

Lemonnier, P. 1993. *Technological Choices.* London: Routledge.

Levi-Strauss, C. 1970. *The Raw and the Cooked: Introduction to a Science of Mythology.* London: Jonathan Cape.

Lewis, M. 2007. *The Early Chinese Empires; Qin and Han.* Cambridge, Mass.: Belknap, Harvard University Press.

Lin, C. 2006. *The Transformation of Chinese Socialism.* Durham, NC and London: Duke University Press.

Mauss, M. 1920. La nation et l'internationalisme in *The Problem of Nationality: Proceedings of the Aristotelian Society,* 20: 242–251.

Mauss, M. 2006 [1929/30]. Civilisations, their elements and forms. Translated in Mauss, 2006 *Techniques, Technologies and Civilisation* (ed N. Schlanger). Oxford and New York: Berghahn

MacGaffey, W. 2000. *Kongo Political Theory*. Bloomington: Indiana University Press.

Naas, M. 2003. *Taking on the Tradition: Jacques Derrida and the Legacies of Deconstruction.* Stanford: Stanford University Press.

Peel, J. 1984. Making history the past in the Ijesha present. *Man* 19.1: 111–133.

Portal, J. (ed) 2007. *The First Emperor: China's Terracotta Army*. London: The British Museum Press

Pomeranz, K. 2000. *The Great Divergence: China, Europe, and the making of the modern world economy.* Oxford: Princeton University Press.

Radcliffe-Brown, A. 1923 [1958]. The methods of Ethnology and Social Anthropology. In A. Radcliffe-Brown (ed.) *Method in Social Anthropology*. Chicago: Chicago University Press.
Ravenhill, P. 1996. The Passive Object and the Tribal paradigm. In M. Arnoldi, C. Geary and K. Hardin (eds) *African Material Culture*. Bloomington: Indiana University Press.
Rawson, J. 2007. The First Emperor's Tomb: the Afterlife Universe. In Portal (ed), 114–151.
Said, E. 2001. The clash of ignorance. *The Nation*, October 4, 2001.
Schildkrout, E. and Keim, C. 1998. *The Scramble for Art in Central Africa*. Cambridge: Cambridge University Press.
Stahl, A. 2005. *African Archaeology*. Oxford: Blackwell.
Stoller, P. 1984. *The Fusion of Worlds*. Bloomington: Indiana University Press.
Strickman, M. 1979. On the alchemy of T'ao Hung-ching. In A. Seidel and H. Welch (eds) *Facets of Taoism*, 123–192. London: Yale University Press.
Tambiah, S. 1990. *Magic, Science and Religion and the scope of Rationality*. Cambridge: Cambridge University Press.
Wallerstein, I. 2004. *World-systems Analysis: an introduction*. Durham NC and London: Duke University Press.
Wang, M. forthcoming. *Empire, History, and Local Worlds: The Carp, the Imperial Net, and its Loopholes in Quanzhou*, 712–1896. Walnut Creek, CA and London: Left Coast Press and Berghahn Books.
West, H. 2005. *Kupilikula*. Chicago: University of Chicago Press.
Wu, Y. 2007. A Two-thousand-year-old Underground Empire. In Portal (ed), 152–157.
Yueh-ping, Y. 2005. *Calligraphy and Power in Contemporary China*. London and New York: Routledge.

# 10

# Relational personhood as a subject of anthropology and archaeology: comparative and complementary analyses

*Chris Fowler*

## *Introduction*

In this chapter I explore how both anthropology and archaeology approach the study of relational personhood, focusing on the 'translation' of the concept from anthropology into archaeology. In Strathern's terms (this volume) personhood can be seen as a 'boundary object'– a construct that 'holds different meanings in different social worlds, yet is imbued with enough shared meaning to facilitate its translation across those worlds' (McSherry 2001: 69). The concept of 'relational personhood' was developed in anthropology to facilitate comprehension of certain non-western forms of personhood, but has since been applied in anthropology and elsewhere to thinking about personhood in all cultural contexts. A number of archaeologists have recently turned to anthropologists' interpretations of contemporary relational personhood for inspiration in their analyses of how personhood was conceptualised in the distant past (e.g. Brück 2004; Chapman 1996; 2000; Fowler 2001; 2004a; Jones 2002; 2005; Joyce 2001; Meskell and Joyce 2003; Oliver 2009; Thomas 2000; 2002; Whittle 2003). In this 'translation' archaeologists have presented different ways that relational personhood can operate to those identified by anthropologists. I will explore how the methods and interpretations of these archaeologists are different than, yet parallel to, the methods and interpretations of anthropologists. I focus in particular on a point of similarity: how partial information is articulated to produce a synthetic understanding of the communities studied.

The chapter begins by outlining this point of similarity, then discusses the anthropological conception of relational personhood. It then turns to the archaeological adoption of the concept, and focuses in on some of the techniques of analysis by which archaeologists apprehend relational personhood. The discussion moves on to a comparison of how archaeologists and anthropologists compare when they analyse relational personhood in the contexts they examine, before considering the role of core disciplinary differences in how personhood is investigated. I conclude that further comparisons between the forms, media and operation of relationships provides a fertile area for future research in and across both disciplines.

## *Starting points: making connections from an archaeologist's perspective*

When I read ethnographic and anthropological literature, I do so as an archaeologist: at one level I am often attempting to look for specific information in accounts that may document only parts of that information. I am left to piece together understandings of a mortuary practice, for example, based on only a few lines of an ethnographic text, much as I must do from the archaeological remains at a specific site. To me this process feels rather 'archaeological'. But anthropology, in common with archaeology and with all other social sciences, also conducts the study of an incompletely known social world and attempts to construct an understanding of social phenomena from the fragments of daily lives (see Strathern 1991).[1] In their syntheses and in developing site-specific interpretations (of archaeological sites and landscapes or of contemporary communities) both disciplines rely on information from previous studies that is partly incommensurate: some communities build massive monuments while their neighbours do not; some ethnographies, as with some archaeological texts, focus on social organisation while others might examine subsistence, or rituals, or cosmology or exchange. Our knowledge about the British Neolithic, for instance, is based on a composite of sources from the antiquarian to the present day, requiring skilful appraisal of differing sorts of information (e.g. Smith and Brickley 2009). In both disciplines comparing sources requires analysis across different cultural concerns, paradigms, methods and approaches (Strathern 1991: xix, 51–2). Thus, while we could argue that the fragmentary and partial nature of archaeological evidence makes the discipline unique, it also brings to the fore certain similarities with anthropology.

Alongside my interest in the specific social phenomena they discuss, I am equally interested in the theoretical approach to personhood that anthropologists are developing – much as I am interested in the approaches that other archaeologists develop as they research past contexts. Anthropologists share certain interpretative approaches with archaeologists mainly due to the influence of similar theoretical trends (e.g. phenomenological and hermeneutic approaches), but also due to the fact that both archaeologists and anthropologists find personhood to be incompletely 'recorded', and to be 'voiced' as much in the use of material culture as verbally. Practitioners from both disciplines often draw on similar forms of evidence: particularly how practices shape bodies, substances, objects and architecture in the generation of personhood. Both disciplines can focus on the effect of practices on these media, and the effects of media on ongoing practices. Anthropologists can discuss beliefs about these practices with informants, and many have identified how social interactions focused on these media are vital to the understanding as well as the construction of personhood. Archaeologists have made significant contributions to the investigation of relational personhood through these media and these build on, re-assess and afford critical comparison with the work of anthropologists. Archaeological studies necessarily work with the fragmentary remains of the past, and acknowledge that the evidence we have is partial, fragmentary, incomplete. As some of the studies discussed below show, the fragmentary nature of some past evidence may itself be a deliberate product of past social relations, and convey meaningful information about the nature of social relations and personhood. The same may be true among present communities, though far less research has been published on this.

Analyses in either discipline may dwell on the differences between one community or one set of cultural practices (such as *malangan* or building Neolithic chambered long barrows) and another, or on differences between one way of interpreting a phenomena and another, as much as they focus on highlighting similarities between contexts. I use the example of relational personhood as my 'case study' in considering the relationships between the two disciplines. Dealing with what could be seen as broadly a single theoretical paradigm helps throw into relief the disciplinary differences in evidence, methodology and above all the construction of interpretations. The enabling constraints of each discipline are different, and provide different yet complementary points of focus on relational personhood. I will therefore suggest that a fully comparative study of personhood would benefit from the adoption of archaeological comparisons into anthropological discourse – both in terms of the content of archaeological studies and consideration of some of the analytical techniques adopted by those studies.

## *Relational personhood in anthropology*

A detailed review of the history of relational personhood in anthropology is beyond the scope of this paper (see Carsten 2004; Fowler 2004a; in press a; Marcus and Fischer 1999: 45–76), but it is necessary to sketch some key tenets of this area of study in order to understand their translation by archaeologists. A person is generated through fields of social relations in which they actively participate (e.g. Battaglia 1990; Marriott 1976; Munn 1986; Strathern 1988; 1992). There are many different ways that persons may be relational, because many different kinds of relationships are evident across human societies. Persons are composite entities with both seemingly tangible (e.g. body, image) and intangible (e.g. spirit, breath) features, but all of those features are invested in the material world in some way and are manifested not just in the human body but in objects, plants, animals, buildings and so on, in which a person invests labour. A person is a complex composite of these features or aspects as well as of relationships. Scholars and the people they study alike may place emphasis on one relationship temporarily brought to the fore in a certain context in defining a person, or on histories of relationships that have shaped the person in an enduring way.

Persons desire to attain specific states of personhood or to be able to exhibit particular combinations of qualities. Social action may be directed towards attaining these goals, which are socially – and often cosmologically – sanctioned (see Fowler in press a; in press b). The concerns people have in attaining social identities and being effective in relations with others vary culturally. Persons pursue actions which they believe will help them attain or maintain desirable forms of personhood. Personhood is intelligible in relation to other aspects of identity such as gender, ethnicity, religion, age and forms of social differentiation based on kinship like household, caste or clan systems. For instance, drawing on Dumont's (1970) observation that *dharma* (duty) provides the moral, cultural, spiritual and social basis for Hindu existence, Marriott (1976) showed how the ethos and activities of particular castes, age groups and cults form the basis for many such strategies in Hindu communities. Marriott argued that an Indian Hindu person's internal composition depends upon their exterior relations within specific social networks where certain substances are exchanged at specific tempos.

Anthropological analysis stems from the identification of cultural principles structuring the relationships through which personhood is negotiated (e.g. Busby 1997; Marriott 1976; Mosko 1992; Schwartz 1997; Strathern 1988). These principles, metaphors and logics are combined in culturally-specific ways, but, as I will argue, such principles may also recur in unrelated contexts. Some key examples here are the conception of the person as divisible or dividual (Marriott 1976; Strathern 1988; Busby 1997), partible (Strathern 1988; Busby 1976; Mosko 1992), permeable (Busby 1997) and fractal (Wagner 1991). Marriott coined the term 'dividual' to describe how persons are composed through their incorporation of essences, each of which are charged in different ways. Internal personal composition could be altered through interaction with other persons involving the transfer of these essences, so the person was not primarily a fixed and indivisible being but a flexible incorporation of different qualities and relationships. Indeed, Busby (1997) has argued that southern Indian persons conceive of themselves as clearly-bounded but permeable to these flows of essences, and traced how bodies are gendered substantially through their interactions. Strathern (1988) identified Melanesian forms of personhood as constantly modulating between two perspectives: one divided, incomplete and involved in specific dyadic interactions (partible); the other composed, temporarily complete yet potentially partible, and, due to the donation of bodily substance from both parents, androgynous (dividual). The Melanesian dividual person is an image of the relations composing both a single person and a community, but as soon as the person acts within specific select relations with other equivalent persons, partial relations within that scheme are activated. Persons and gift objects (which are extracted from the partible person) are comparable, multiply-constituted entities conveying key qualities of personhood and bringing those to the fore in specific circumstances, such as prestigious gift exchange ceremonies like Highland Papua New Guinea *moka*. Gifts and persons are gendered through such events rather than essentially, and parts are extracted from collectivities, whereas in India flows of charged essences extend across bodily boundaries. In Strathern's (1988) analysis personhood fluctuates as people negotiate a series of dualisms relating to their identity: male and female, single-sex and cross-sex, particular and collective, external and internal, complete and incomplete, partible and dividual. Through such fluctuations the boundaries between each of these dualisms temporarily disappear.

Wagner (1991) presents the fractal person as an alternative image for the dividual person, where the same relations act equally at different scales, so that each person is both presented as a 'whole' and is also a 'part' of a person at a larger scale (e.g. a single person in relation to a clan). The image of the fractal illustrates that there are really no social 'wholes', only unfolding relationships which can be viewed at different scales. Thus, we can observe an individual or a clan or a tribe, but these entities are all incomplete (where does one family end or one clan blend into another?). Each single entity is really a 'set' of relations. The closer we look at them the more we see that the rough fractal edges of each entity are folded into those of other entities. These rough edges (visible, for instance, in exchange practices or the social use of domestic architecture) carry information about the complex relationships composing each entity and its relations with other entities. 'Fractal personhood' provides a term which can encapsulate all of the various forms of relational personhood. It applies equally, though differently, to forms of personhood aspired to in India, and to both 'big man' and 'great man' schemes of relations in Melanesia despite the socio-political differences between these contexts and differences in the forms of persons that emerge (Wagner 1991).[2]

Having briefly sketched some significant features of studies of relational personhood in anthropology, I now turn to equivalent studies in archaeology in order to illustrate the comparability of the subject within the two disciplines and the developments made by taking an archaeological perspective on an anthropological approach.

## *The translation of anthropological perspectives on personhood into archaeology: an example*

Studies of personhood in archaeology originated from several directions and were deployed with different agendas. I would not wish to paint a unified picture of archaeological discourse, nor attempt to delineate specific national or international schools, but, for instance, some prehistoric archaeology in northern Europe underwent a 'phenomenological turn' in the 1990s following a 'linguistic turn' in the 1980s and early 1990s involving a combination of structuralist and post-structuralist perspectives.[3] Discussions of how the subject/object dichotomy (which is fundamental to western thought yet poorly characterises personal experience and is un-representative of indigenous experiences in other parts of the world) could be overcome in our analyses made important reading for many archaeologists, especially (but not exclusively) those working on prehistoric and proto-historic periods. Archaeologists exploring a phenomenological perspective and drawing on theories of practice were able to find inspiration in numerous anthropological texts.

Anthropological studies had established that the principles and relationships through which personhood is generated were manifested throughout the material world, shaping the production of bodies, objects and architecture within the same cultural context. In the late 1990s and early 2000s many archaeologists drew on ethnographic studies of inalienable objects and analyses of gift exchange (e.g. Chapman 1996; Thomas 1996; Tilley 1996) as a way to reconceptualise the relationships between persons, and between persons and things. Influential here were theories of objectification whereby people and things are seen as mutually constituted through social practices (e.g. the production of iron tools makes a smith as well as those tools). Some of these studies discussed the person as a composite entity (e.g. Joyce 2001; Meskell 1999) and some drew on the idea of 'economies of substances' or other perspectives whereby personhood was constituted through the social circulation of objects and materials (e.g. Strassburg 2000; Thomas 1996; 1999). Archaeologists interested in relational identity and personhood have focused on the material media through which personhood is negotiated in specific practices: primarily the construction and use of architecture (e.g. Cummings *et al.* 2002; Fowler 2003; 2004b; 2008a and b); social relations as inferred from settlement plans (e.g. Jones 2005); representations of the body (e.g. Gillsepie 2008; Joyce 2001); the circulation and transformation of objects (e.g. Brück 2001; 2006; Chapman 2000; Thomas 1999), and; transformations of the body, including through mortuary rites (e.g. Fowler 2001; 2004b; Gillespie 2001; Thomas 2000; 2002; Tilley 1996). Despite differences between positions expressed by some authors, each strand has led to the development of culturally comparative analyses of bodies and persons in archaeology.

The kinds of material worlds persons inhabit provide significant information about the way that personhood is achieved and the concepts that shape it because that material world is produced through the same relations that produce persons. By examining the remains of such material worlds, some archaeologists have attempted to distinguish distinct principles in social relations and cultural action which could be said to support specific forms of relational personhood in much the way that anthropologists have (e.g. Chapman 2000; Fowler 2001; 2004a; Harris 2006). Chapman (2000) has translated the concept of fractal and partible personhood into prehistoric European contexts with the aim of tracing the tensions between different ways of relating, and the shift in dominance between competing forms of personhood. In examining the Neolithic and Chalcolithic archaeology of the Balkans, Chapman suggested that a long term tension existed between two ways of relating: one in which persons were enchained by inalienable relations (fostering dividual personhood), and one in which persons accumulated goods for intrinsic value (presenting opportunities for greater individualization). I will analyse how Chapman's translation of these concepts from anthropology has both interpreted the concepts in new ways and provided a view of prehistoric European ways of negotiating personhood that differ from those identified in the present by anthropologists.

Drawing on Wagner's concept of the fractal person and Strathern's concept of partibility, Chapman argues that the curation of fragments of deliberately broken Neolithic objects (sherds of pottery, snapped clay tokens, ceramic figurines and shell rings) indicates a fractal concept of personhood and social relations. He compares these fragmented objects with the fragmentation of the bodies of the dead, and considers the importance of 'parts' and sets (or 'wholes') at various scales – including burials as parts of cemeteries, or whole objects as parts of hoards. While Chapman allows that the articulation of parts and wholes could be mobilised in pursuing a range of forms of relationships and identities, the dominant pattern he outlines is a tension between fractal, dividual and partible relations and those where some special persons attempt to distinguish themselves as owners of collections of intact prestigious objects. For Chapman (subsequently with Gaydarska) communities fragmenting things and bodies are fractal, dividual and egalitarian, while the status of those exchanging and accumulating intact objects (which increases during the Chalcolithic) is identified with more individualizing forms of personhood (e.g. Chapman and Gaydarska 2007: 143, 199–201). Rare anthropomorphic figurines presenting single-sex identities rather than ambiguously-sexed identities are taken to indicate that some people were able to achieve a distinct form of sexual identity predicated on increased personal individuation (2007: 69–70). Chapman and Gaydarska argue that this individualized identity was not presented as inherent from birth but as achieved in adulthood.

Chapman adapts the anthropological understandings of relational personhood to make sense of rather different patterns in the material media of social relations. Intact, often composite goods, are the media of *moka*, *kula* and other Melanesian prestigious gift exchanges – anthropologists do not record people sharing out fragments of broken objects at these events. Furthermore, dividual, fractal or relational personhood does not necessarily involve social equality: in *kula* the circulating gift object 'exchanges' the perspective of the donor for the recipient as it moves and in doing so reverses the polarity of the power relation between them, but inequalities in power relations still exist. Melanesian persons may become 'larger' through their gift-giving as their influence spreads with the mobile exchange object. Fractal personhood can support social differentiation in various ways including hierarchically (Gillespie 2008; Marriott 1976; Mosko 2000; Wagner 1991). Thus, I would suggest that complex forms of fractal personhood, including various kinds of hierarchical relationships may have emerged during each of the periods of European prehistory Chapman studies. Debt could be produced as feast hosts distributed pot sherds among those feasting just as it could be produced in the circulation of intact objects. Armlets and necklaces made from spiney oyster *(spondylus)* have been found across Europe in Neolithic contexts despite the fact that the animal which provides the shell lives only in the Aegean. The increased circulation of intact, brilliant and enduring objects like these shell ornaments and copper axe heads and blades throughout the Neolithic and Chalcolithic could have supported an expansion of forms of relational personhood exhibiting a principle more akin to Melanesian partibility than Chapman allows (cf. Whittle 2003: 63–4), while some of the fragmentation practices of the earlier Neolithic may have no equivalent in the anthropological literature. We could see the changing forms of personhood in Chapman and Gaydarska's study area as all relational, but in differing ways from one another.

While we may not necessarily agree with the precise interpretations of personhood he produced, the translation of fractal and dividual personhood that Chapman has effected brings to the fore how an emphatically archaeological focus on the material media of relations can provide a new appreciation of an anthropological phenomenon. Anthropological studies of personhood have examined the constitution and deconstitution of persons and the movement of intact objects and of flows of substances between persons, but have not often explicitly considered the fragmentation of objects and treatment of fragments.[4] Therefore, archaeological approaches have illustrated a *different* set of socio-cultural practices and ways that personhood might operate to those known by ethnographers while identifying some comparable underlying principles. In the next section I elaborate this idea by comparing how both disciplines locate the interpretation of personhood in the analysis of material things, bodies and substances.

## *The material media of personhood: substance, form and metaphor*

Alongside the consideration of specific techniques by which personhood may be constituted (e.g. giving and keeping fragments of objects, producing hoards of similar objects, exchanging prestige goods, deconstituting bodies and curating bones), studies of personhood in archaeology have also focused on the role of 'material metaphors' which crystallise key principles in social action (e.g. Battaglia 1990: 128–35; Brück 2004; Ray 1987; Hoskins 1998; Tilley 1999). Metaphors are central to the rhythms and forms of social interaction, and the conceptualisation of how persons are shaped by these interactions. In Strathern's (1988) analysis Melanesian relations draw on a horticultural metaphor: we could say that people, like plants, grow and produce buds which can be removed and given to another person who can absorb that bud and grow it – just as a garden can be planted with many taro from other originary gardens so a person can be planted with many parts from other persons. Hindu and southern Indian concepts of the permeable person invoke a 'hydraulic' metaphor (Marriott 1989: 16). Persons direct flows of different essences through bodily vessels in desirable ways: changing the ratio of charged fluids in the vessel changes the internal composition of a person (Busby 1997). In both cases social technologies associated with acts of bodily consumption play a central role, and the production, sharing and consumption of food are key arenas in which social relations operate. Such metaphors can be identified as core to the principles structuring personhood in any context, and there may be many such metaphors in each cultural context with some brought to the fore to different degrees at different times (cf. Fowler 2008a). Material metaphors are the manifestation of key social relations in the design of artefacts, buildings and other media. Anthropological examples include Sabarl axes, lime-sticks and canoes (Battaglia 1990), Malagasy houses (Bloch 1995), Kabyle houses (Bourdieu 1970) and Batammaliba houses (Preston Blier 1987). The same principles and relations as are made manifest in these artefacts and buildings are those made manifest in the body of the person.

Archaeological studies always start with the material (see also Garrow and Yarrow, this volume), and the idea of material metaphor has attracted significant attention (e.g. Brück 2001; 2004; 2005; Ray 1987; Tilley 1999). If we accept that personhood in past contexts was to some degree relational, then studies that reveal the key principles manifested in the parallel treatment of, say bodies and houses, can be developed to inform us about past concepts of personhood. For instance, Bradley (2002) and Williams (2003) have stressed the central role of agricultural cycles in northern European later Bronze Age and Iron Age world-views, including conceptions of life and death. Brück (2001) has demonstrated in detail how middle and late Bronze Age pottery, cereal crops, human bodies, and bronze objects in southern England underwent parallel transformations in their 'life cycle'. She illustrates how at the end of a life cycle each was crushed and burnt. New bodies spring from a share of the remains of the old, as some bronze was resmelted, new pots were tempered with the ground remains of other pots, and some cereal grains were replanted. Brück situates the human life cycle in relation to these practices: after death human bodies were cremated, and some bones were placed in liminal locales around settlements while others were removed from the vicinity or swept into middens – material from which was spread on the fields. Eventually a part of each 'body' would enter the earth, while the ongoing generation of 'bodies' required the fragmentation and redistribution of previous 'bodies'. Furthermore, each type of body shaped, fed and sustained others as the impermanence of the individual life was offset against the permanence of social relationships on and with the land (cf. Brück 1999, 2005). From such studies we can consider the role of objects, houses, and the land in framing relational concepts of the person, and see such material things as constituents of past societies every bit as much as human beings.

Archaeological and anthropological studies like these also involve assessing the cultural appreciation of different substances. Anthropological studies illustrate the cultural specificity of the qualities people associate with specific materials, and, indeed, the range of ways that anthropologists have identified 'substance' (Carsten 2004). For instance, Marriott considered 'substance-codes' to be essences that could take the form of words and knowledge as well as materials like blood. Archaeological definitions of substance are more restrictive: bronze, bone and quartz would all be recognised as substances, but names or knowledge would not (though they might be seen as aspects of the person). While anthropologists can make direct claims about whether substances have a culturally-fixed value or are contextually charged, archaeologists, particularly those working with prehistoric evidence, by and large cannot know definitively whether value or meaning was fixed in substance or relative to action. However, archaeologists can explore patterns in the deployment and juxtaposition of different substances and consider how features of their physical properties were brought to the fore contextually (e.g. Jones 1999; 2002; Keates 2002; Owoc 2002; cf. Clark 1991). This can be developed into a reading of the cultural qualities associated with the properties of certain materials (e.g. colour) which may be shared across several substances such as stone, bone, semen and copper (Keates 2002) or running water, quartz and bone (Fowler 2004b) or red flint, sandstone, blood/flesh and fertile soils (Jones 1999). Archaeological studies can identify how certain transformations of bodies, objects and places draw on such substances in specific ways and can examine how certain substances and forms are presented in specific contexts. For instance, copper daggers in the Chalcolithic Alps may have conveyed an ancestral, luminous quality associated with the male body and the substance it contained (Keates 2002). As daggers appear in male graves and carved on what appear to be commemorative *stelae* decorated with the images of the dead we can see that this quality was one that some members of the community were keen to associate with certain men. We can usefully suggest that male appropriation of luminous substances for objects like axes and daggers suggests that there was an unfolding dialectic between substances and forms in which specific materials became associated with specific genders.[5] As with the archaeological research on fragmentation and personhood, the picture of personhood that emerges from archaeological considerations of substances provides a slightly different yet certainly comparable view on personhood to that from anthropology – one rooted in the physical properties of materials and the cultural transformation of things, materials, bodies and places.

These studies illustrate how the same concepts have been adopted in both disciplines, and provide an excellent point of connection from which to make comparisons about relational personhood across all cultural contexts. Archaeologists focus on: how substances were derived from landscapes and bodies, then transformed into buildings, artefacts and other bodies; how substances moved through those buildings, artefacts and bodies; how those buildings, artefacts and bodies were themselves then transformed back into their materials; and how those materials were then relocated, abandoned or deployed. The patterns that emerge may inform us about the relationships and conditions through which personhood was constituted, negotiated and deconstituted. In the next section I move beyond the parallel nature of analyses of the material media of personhood to consider the ways in which both disciplines carry out cultural comparisons in assessing personhood through these analyses.

## *Comparing comparison*

Much of the analytical framework for the anthropology of personhood has developed comparatively, with each analyst borrowing from concepts formed during analyses of communities elsewhere in the world. Strathern draws on Marriott's analyses in India, and constructs an understanding of Melanesians by comparing many different Melanesian communities. As she acknowledges this provides a series of 'partial connections' between these communities, rather than a complete image of Melanesian beliefs about personhood (Strathern 1991). Strathern (e.g. 1992) also compares English and Melanesian concepts of relationships, persons and communities. Busby (1997) compares Indian personhood with Melanesian and also draws on Marriott's studies of Hindu personhood in framing her understanding of Christian southern Indian personhood as permeable and dividual in contrast to partible and dividual Melanesian personhood. In each case the analyst uses the forms of relations in an external context to frame their understanding of any one context. Unlike Mauss' early comparative analysis of personhood (Mauss 1938), none of the recent anthropological analyses bring historical, ancient or prehistoric communities into their comparisons.

The *way* that this technique is comparative is important because it differs from how archaeologists conventionally deploy analogies in their analysis, but is arguably very similar to how many archaeologists now carry out their comparative analyses of personhood. In archaeology analogies are usually drawn between archaeological contexts and ethnographic ones (though historical or other archaeological contexts may be used) in order to make further inferences about unknown aspects of the archaeological context. Direct analogies compare one present community with one past community on the basis of some observed similarity between them (e.g. village layout and subsistence evidence) in order to make inferences about further features that cannot be directly observed in the remains left by the past community (e.g. social organisation). Although Busby's analysis, to take an example, directly compares two contexts it is not analogical in this sense: Busby is not attempting to interpret something she does not know about the Mariana by illustrating a series of similarities with people from Mount Hagen and then drawing further inferences. However Busby *is* drawing on Melanesian conceptions of personhood as they are understood by Strathern in order to consider a range of comparisons between Indian and Melanesian concepts of the person which illustrate the distinctiveness of each. These two anthropologists identify dividuality as a principle evident in both contexts, but each examines different ways the principle operates in articulation with other principles (partibility, permeability). Archaeological interpretations of personhood *are* comparative in a comparable way to anthropological analyses: they have moved beyond making inferences based on direct analogies and seek to compare trends in relationships which recur across contexts but may be manifested differently, have different effects, and occur in articulation with other differing principles, metaphors and concepts. For this reason I believe there is significant value in drawing further comparisons across contexts which may in many ways be different (e.g. of differing social or economic 'type'). In doing so it becomes possible to illustrate a broader range of differing ways in which personhood may be relational than the sample of human experience represented by analyses based on the contemporary world.

Elsewhere I have argued that we can identify cultural modes of personhood, and suggested that key principles within these may recur in unrelated cultural contexts separated in time and space (Fowler 2004a). For instance, we can postulate that partibility as a principle may crop up in many different cultural contexts combined with supporting metaphors and material media different than those in Melanesia. Equally, the concept that the person is a permeable vessel also recurs in many cultural contexts (e.g. medieval and early modern Europe). Perhaps because I focused on the concepts of dividual, permeable and partible persons developed in Melanesian and south Indian anthropology as examples of key principles in modes of personhood, and even though a wider range of ethnographic instances were considered, the result has been criticised as based on too narrow a range of possibilities for comparison (Jones 2005: 194, 198). It is certainly the case that the examples I used concentrated on exchanges and mortuary practices, dealing only briefly with architecture and landscape (compared to, for instance Fowler 2001; 2003; 2004b; 2008b; Fowler and Cummings 2003). However, this does not weaken the *approach*: my point was that there are many different ways that personhood can be relational, and that we may be able to identify some recurrent trends in the kinds of practices through which personhood is generated. This can also be extended to considering the extent to which persons were individualised by social relations, provided we qualify what may be inferred about personhood from that individualisation (Whittle 2003: 52–4).

Other archaeologists have carried out contextual investigations which compare different cultural contexts from the distant past. These analyses draw out further ways that personhood can be relational, and these again extend our understanding of the relationships that generate different forms of personhood beyond anthropological studies. Jones (2005) illustrates the importance of situating exchange and mortuary practices within a temporal and spatial framework, particularly by considering settlement patterns. He draws his own ethnographic analogies with household communities, again to highlight trends in social relations which recur in many different cultural contexts (cf. Gillespie 2001). Jones' study compares personhood in Neolithic communities in southeast, central and northwest Europe. He emphasises how the distinct practices dominant in each region made different kinds of connections with the past. To outline his analysis of just two of these regions, in southeast Europe c. 6000–5500 BC where people lived in tells which were occupied for hundreds of years and grew through the repeated building, flattening and rebuilding of wattle-and-daub or mud brick houses, the living inhabited the space of their ancestors and traced kin relations locally through household and settlement space. More distant connections were maintained through exchange relations. In central Europe c. 5500–5000 BC settlement patterns were more dispersed, and wooden longhouses (which Jones argues were often oriented towards southeast Europe, the direction of origin for Neolithic products, practices and probably people) were left to stand as decaying monuments while new ones were built nearby. The dead were buried around houses or in cemeteries. Long-distance exchange networks intersected here, and there is evidence for a combination of horticultural and foraging activities and of incoming and indigenous populations. Jones argues that "personhood in this period is grounded less in place than in communities composed of a set of relations, both real – between the living community with differing origins, and ideal – between the living and their ancestors distanced in time and space" (2005: 215). Jones traces changing trends in how personhood was generated, in this case by comparing activities in different regions as well as through time. Unlike Marriott, Strathern and Busby, Jones (2005: 216–7) does not create named categories of relationships or personhood – and, indeed, argues against the temptation to do this.

In a similar comparative vein, Meskell and Joyce explore the specificity and comparability of two disparate contexts. They set Classic Mayan and Ancient Egyptian relational persons (e.g. Joyce 2001; Meskell 1999) in juxtaposition through their examination of 'embodied lives' in these contexts (Meskell and Joyce 2003). Using textual and archaeological evidence Meskell (1999) attempts to grasp how past individuals (a term she qualifies) understood and experienced their lives, and also appreciates that these persons might be understood as dividual persons (Meskell 1999: 33; Meskell and Joyce 2003: 17–18). She outlines the Ancient Egyptian person as consisting of several aspects and illustrates a range of terms that were used to refer to different components of the body and person (e.g. *mtw* as 'conduits' comprising 'blood vessels, ducts, tendons, muscles and perhaps nerves' (Meskell and Joyce 2003: 19). Many of these terms seem to have metaphysical connotations, linking physical and spiritual characteristics, and there are further terms for spiritual aspects of the person which were not tangible, such as *ib* (the metaphysical 'heart' which was the seat of intelligent thought – possibly actually associated with the physical stomach), *ka* (life force or spirit self), *swt* (shadow), *rn* (name), and *ba* (character or individuality). Following death the stomach, lungs, liver and intestines were removed and placed in canopic jars each dedicated to different deities, while the heart remained in the body, which was ritually mummified (2003: 132), presenting an image of completeness from the partial remains of the corpse. Personal deconstitution following death was a matter of significant anxiety and mortuary practices included rituals aimed at reconstituting the aspects of the person in the afterlife. The *ba*, *ka*, *rn*, *swt* and *heka* (magic emergent from a person only following death and which could be invoked by their living kin) extended into the afterlife. Some of these aspects of a person could be attributed to objects (e.g. *ba* – Meskell and Joyce 2003: 69), and bodily substances conveyed specific properties. While Classic Mayan persons are shown to be equally composite and complex, they exhibited different concerns about personal composition, dissolution and commemoration. The body was less permeable to mobile fluids than the ancient Egyptian body yet the person was open to the influence of spiritual forces (2003: 127), and aspects of the Mayan person could be materially and culturally located in the world of the living after death more extensively than in Ancient Egypt (2003: 142–3). Nonetheless in both cases personhood was widely negotiated and commemorated through material culture as well as the body (2003: 161).

These archaeological studies do not draw a firm analytical distinction between the communities they investigate of the sort that Busby draws between India and Melanesia, but rather seek to illustrate the comparable and yet differing nature of personhood in each context. The value of archaeological analyses lies in teasing out trends in practices and relationships: trends in the manipulation of material media, which can be compared with those in other contexts. These archaeological approaches attempt to describe the specific conditions in which persons are embedded – arguably a sort of 'thick description' (Geertz 1973) based on contextual analysis of past practices as understood from patterns in material evidence (and, where relevant, textual information). Archaeological reports describe the bits of evidence we have in immense detail (see Gosden this volume), and these and other archaeological analyses describe how each bit was related to others through past social relations. I would suggest that archaeological approaches to relational personhood are interested in both 'contexts' and 'concepts' (following Viveiros de Castro 2003), including the comparison of and intersections between such concepts as they seem to reoccur throughout time and place. Archaeologists are also interested in how these concepts are bound together with specific practices and material things that can be found in the contexts they study: ways of feasting, transforming the dead, planting and harvesting; the roles of vessels, tombs, fields, etc. Through such studies we can continue to expand on our understanding of the roles that different material media can play in the practices that generate specific kinds of personhood.

As well as comparisons between different non-western contexts, anthropological and archaeological studies carry an implied comparison with the modern western contexts from which the disciplines originate. Relational personhood underlies western experience as well as non-western experience (Fowler 2004a: 33–7; LiPuma 1998; Jones 2005). It seems that in all cultural contexts an *aspect* of the dividual and relational person may convey an individual biographical identity, or be described as individual will, and this may be brought to the fore contextually and temporarily even when the person is not seen as monadic and indivisible. Strathern (1988: 268, 273, 281–2) acknowledges that Melanesian persons do appear as distinct from one another in terms of their biographies, though it is a specific interaction that individualizes each person temporarily. Battaglia argues that '...Sabarl represent and understand themselves as products of social relationship, where individuality serves the very limited and temporary purpose of calling attention to oneself in particular contexts for particular (usually political) purposes...' (Battaglia 1990: 55). LiPuma (1998: 69–74) argues that among the Maring overt individuality was until recently equated with sorcery, suggesting that while some version of such a concept exists, it was hardly celebrated. Munn (1986) discusses how Gawan witchcraft stands for the individualistic will to inequality which the Gawan ethos of equality seeks to suppress. Furthermore, Strathern (1992: chapter 1) illustrates how individuals emerge from relations in British kinship, but in so doing explain individuality as basic and relations as secondary (cf. LiPuma 1998: 67–8). She also demonstrates how degrees of individual autonomy may change in the life course, revolving around shifting relations between parents and children as children grow apart from their parents and leave home (cf. Marriott (1976: 131–2) on how following 'retirement' Hindu persons who enter a stage of 'renunciation' exhibit a higher degree of individuality than at other times of life – in effect, at different stages in life personhood is experienced differently). To summarise, various qualities that fall within our definition of 'individuality' are present in many contexts, but these are not bundled together nor brought to the fore in the same way in differing cultural contexts. It seems to me that the onus is on us to explain what form of personhood we think is being presented in any cultural context and how a certain extent or type of 'individuality' is articulated as an aspect (or aspects) of that personhood via the relationships that support it.

Both disciplines have debated the extent to which specific concepts 'belong to' specific contexts. The scale of comparison adopted by the archaeologists is arguably larger than that tackled by the anthropologists because the timescale archaeology encapsulates is far greater. LiPuma's (1998) concerns about an over-emphasis on the dividual in Melanesian anthropology stem from a volume comparing African and Melanesian concepts of the person, while some other anthropologists I have cited are primarily concerned with single communities or regions (arguably usually comparing these with their own cultural context). Archaeologists debate the extent to which concepts like the dividual person or the individual can be applied to differing past contexts, usually in a modified, qualified and contextualised sense (e.g. see Knapp and Van Dommelen 2008). In the archaeological debate present concepts are tested against a wide range of past contexts. Whenever the scale of analysis expands, the limits (or rather the rough edges) of these stretched concepts become more evident. Such concepts operate best, I would suggest, as heuristic devices we can use pragmatically in order to highlight differences and similarities and appreciate the reoccurrence of certain relationships in many different contexts. Some forms of relationships may be rare, and all variations unique, but all forms of relations can be compared. In the next section I argue that combining archaeological and anthropological accounts of personhood in cross-cultural comparisons provides a more useful – though avowedly incomplete – picture of how personhood can be conceptualised.

## *Discussion: complementarity and the 'collage' of cross-cultural comparison*

Both archaeological and anthropological studies detect generative principles by piecing together repetitions at the small scale of specific practices which instantiate such principles. This piecing together of fragments can contribute to more holistic interpretations of trends in specific kinds or experiences of personhood, and/or an expected life course or a projected cosmology. But both archaeologists and anthropologists have to acknowledge that these interpretations are also partial and draw on disparate forms of evidence. They create a holistic scheme out of fragmentary evidence perceived from a specific point of view. Fragmentary and partial information is arranged to present a complex image from which we can draw new meaning, but which we have to accept is not really the sum of its parts and not a complete whole. Here, an epistemological constraint is shared. But despite parallel interests in how social relations are manifested in and mediated by material culture, in how practices produce people, places and things simultaneously, the methodological differences in how archaeology and anthropology go about their studies are significant. An archaeological study of *kula* exchanges would be concerned with tracing the path and distribution and disposal of the objects as well as the social relations of the people exchanging them. Ethnography may rely on the oral account of the object's origin and be unable to contextualise that alongside a study of the time and place when the object was made. The ethnographer often provides a fixed perspective within a certain community,[6] and, although considering testimonies, ethnographers do not usually follow the paths of key media which may circulate *beyond* that community. By contrast archaeologists frequently shift from one site to another and one scale to another, but can never visit the communities they study or converse with the people in those communities. The archaeologists' informants are the material traces of human action, the material constituents of past communities, not living human beings (see McFadyen, this volume). Archaeologists can only live among the enduring material members of the communities they study – and few of these community members survive in anything but a fragmentary state. Thus, archaeologists cannot ask human beings to explain what they mean in their own words. Archaeological accounts of personhood in the past may therefore be qualified by using terms like 'perhaps' and 'possibly'. They need to be (*pace* Herzfeld 2004: 195–6): archaeologists can discuss the features of past personhood that *seem* to arise from certain relationships evidenced in archaeological patterns, but cannot achieve certainty in this respect. Yet there are also areas that anthropology struggles to reach, but about which archaeology is more informative, such as the long-term effects of particular trends (see Filippucci, this volume). Both disciplines, then, produce partial knowledges.

While each discipline asks different questions about temporal patterns and answers these in differing ways, they can easily complement one another (see Feuchtwang and Rowlands, this volume). A full consideration of long-term trajectories in personhood would be advantaged by a combination of archaeology, history and anthropology: combining different kinds of evidence which reveal different angles on personhood, and combining evidence from different times. For instance, archaeological investigations in the Trobriand region provide evidence that stones used to make axes and adzes and standing stones arranged at the centre of villages were transported between islands. The standing stones were used, though not necessarily exclusively, for burial practices between c. 950 and c. 450 years ago (Bickler 2006). Shell valuables have not been located in archaeological deposits, though this does not necessarily mean that their exchange is a completely recent practice – one shell object now associated with *kula* has been radiocarbon-dated to c. 1200 AD (Bickler 2006). Archaeological research in the region provides the opportunity to consider the changing uses of material culture in maintaining and renegotiating social relations in ways both similar to and different from contemporary *kula* practices, and, ultimately, to reflect on how social relations and concepts of personhood have changed over time.

The distinct enabling constraints of the two disciplines undoubtedly provide productive differences between them, but these differences can also be overstated. More importantly, they can be seen as complementary in a larger project of human cultural comparison (see Ingold, this volume). Relational personhood in all contexts could be better understood by further combination of anthropology and archaeology: for instance, by ethnographically studying the roles played by artefact fragmentation or object disposal and/or recovery in the production of personhood; by incorporating archaeological information into longer-term narratives of local pasts, and by further comparing phenomena from times and places studied through participant observation with those examined through archaeological analysis. Similarities as well as differences in how relational personhood operates between contexts could be better understood by drawing together the knowledge produced by archaeologists and anthropologists (as well as historians, sociologists, etc.).

I would like to summarise the potential of this complementarity by drawing on an image discussed by Strathern in *Partial Connections*: the collage (Strathern 1991). The separate images assembled in any one collage might be very different in nature. Some may be based on participant observation, some on analyses of excavated sites; some may be narratives of long term change, others discussions of life-cycles or annual cycles or single events. Some collages may consist of anthropomorphic pots, others studies of mortuary practices, and so on. But all yield valuable points of comparison that allow us to recontextualise each separate study, each element within our contextual studies, and our understanding of recurrent patterns in social relations. While I am advocating cross-cultural comparison here, I do not suppose that this could ever provide a complete picture of all the different ways that human beings have ever understood personhood. Rather, I expect that assembling any particular collage will present the opportunity to perceive connections between relationships, practices, metaphors and experiences that may not have been made before. These connections are not relations of descent between one community and another. The collage need not arrange relationships by types of society. Instead a collage could focus on a specific type of practice, transformation, form or material. While Mauss' essay on the category of the person (Mauss 1938) was deeply problematic in how it organised communities into evolutionary stages, the comparison of personhood – and the media and practices through which personhood is generated – across time and space is well worth resuming.

## *Conclusion*

The study of personhood in archaeology provides areas of similarity with studies of personhood in anthropology, and the differences between them provide points of strength which can be offered to the other discipline. The two disciplines have been influenced by similar theoretical trends, provide only partial knowledge about the subjects they study, and, in terms of studies of personhood, pay attention to bodies, substances and material culture in their analyses. Human informants provide as partial a basis for analysis as material informants, though each provides a different basis from which to grasp social phenomena. Despite the limitations of drawing inferences from archaeological remains, there is no lack of information regarding the means by which personhood in the past was negotiated. Anthropology provides detailed comparative analysis of communities based to some extent on participant observation within living communities. Archaeology provides analytical approaches to patterns in material culture (in its broadest sense), drawing inferences about past practices and beliefs based on those patterns. Archaeological studies may investigate long term trends and change over time. Some of the patterns archaeologists identify have no present-day equivalents and throw up possibilities for expanding on our knowledge of social relations. Archaeology provides key evidence about periods of time for which no verbal or written records exist, and a comparator for oral histories, therefore offering a key to long term anthropologies.

This chapter has considered a single concept originating in anthropology: relational personhood. The approach embedded in this concept has been examined from an archaeological point of view partly to illustrate what archaeological epistemology has to offer anthropology, but more fully to illustrate a complementarity between the studies each discipline produces. Yet the relationship between archaeology and anthropology is asymmetrical, and is likely to remain so – the point of this chapter is to appreciate where the rough, permeable and asymmetrical edges can fit together to produce useful patterns of enquiry rather than a symmetrical 'whole'. We understand the phenomena we study in a relational way: it is the relationships we draw between distinct phenomena that characterise our disciplinary understanding at any moment in time. What changes are the kinds of relationships that we recognise, seek, build and appreciate. One major goal of increased dialogue between anthropologists and archaeologists over personhood would be enhancement of the extent to which cultural comparisons can be made in order to consider what is similar and different between the comparators, and thereby for members of both disciplines to be aware of a wider range of human possibilities. In this endeavour, it would be important to differentiate between the kinds of understanding that an archaeological and an anthropological perspective provide. While they can be meaningfully compared and provide a point of reflection for one another, they are not fully isomorphic. Nonetheless, there is immense value in comparing differing ways of relating, and different forms of knowledge about these. Due to the decline in popularity of the grand narrative neither discipline might want to take responsibility for comparisons across the large scale and long term – but the extended project of a comparative synthesis of what we know about how personhood can be relational into a series of collages would allow us all to perceive many more 'partial connections' across cultural contexts.

## *Acknowledgements*

I would like to thank Duncan Garrow, Kevin Greene, Oliver Harris, Elizabeth Kramer and Tom Yarrow for their feedback on draft versions of this chapter. I would also like to thank John Chapman and an anonymous anthropologist who both provided reviewers comments.

### *Notes*

1 Strathern's *Partial Connections* was recommended by an anonymous anthropological reviewer of an earlier draft of this chapter – the book makes many vital points, and I found I had arrived at some parallel positions through reading other anthropological studies, including other texts authored by Strathern. I have brought some of the points in *Partial Connections* that have helped refine my current position to the fore, but other similarities remain implicit.

2 In some communities certain persons may magnify themselves and come to encapsulate the entire community or the entire cosmos. In some communities this expansion is temporary and limited, as with the Melanesian 'big man'. In others it is more enduring and expansive as with Polynesian chiefs or Mayan rulers (see Gillespie 2008: 130–132). The techniques for translation across scales vary.

3 One crucial feature of this period is Hodder's development of a contextual archaeology, where the meaning of an object is dependent on its context, and a context is composed out the relationships between its constituents (e.g. Hodder 1987). There are similarities here to the anthropological analyses of parts and collectivities carried out by Strathern, Mosko and others. Context, culture, community, person, etc. are not wholes in each analysis, they are compositions of parts which also extend into other compositions at other points in space and time. Each element depends on its broader context for its significance. Effectively, contextual archaeology recognises the way that meaning is relational.

4 Chapman and Gaydarska (2007: 143, 156) cite Clark (1991) and Reay (1959: 96–7) as discussing fragments of shell objects respectively kept as heirlooms and deposited with the dead. Melanesian funerals may symbolically fragment the person too. For instance, in Sabarl *segoiya* (Battaglia 1990) an assemblage of gifts that makes the person's relations manifest at the funeral is 'fragmented' amongst the assembled mourners (cf. Fowler 2004: 82–92).

5 I am grateful to Andrea Dolfini for discussing the use of metal and other materials in the Italian Chalcolithic with me (cf. Dolfini 2008).

6 There are some interesting and revealing exceptions, including Sax's (2002) ethnographic journey towards the Garhwal community he studies.

## *References*

Battaglia, D. 1990. *On the Bones of the Serpent: Person, Memory and Mortality in Sabarl Society*. Chicago: Chicago University Press.

Bickler, S. 2006. Prehistoric stone monuments in the northern region of the Kula Ring. *Antiquity* 80, 38–51.

Bloch, M. 1989. Death and the concept of the person. In S. Cederroth, C. Corlin and J. Lindstrom (eds) *On the Meaning of Death*, 11–29. Cambridge: Cambridge University Press.

Bloch, M. 1995. Questions not to ask of Malagasy carvings. In I. Hodder, M. Shanks, A. Alexandri, V. Buchli, J. Carman, J. Last and G. Lucas (eds) *Interpreting Archaeology*, 212–5. London: Routledge.

Bourdieu, P. 1970. The Berber house or the world reversed. *Social Science Information* 9: 151–70.

Bradley, R. 2002. Death and the regeneration of life: a new interpretation of house urns in Northern Europe. *Antiquity* 76, 372–7.

Brück, J. 2001. Body metaphors and technologies of transformation in the English Middle and Late Bronze Age. In J. Brück (ed.) *Bronze Age Landscapes: Tradition and Transformation*, 149–60. Oxford: Oxbow.

Brück, J. 2004. Material metaphors: the relational construction of identity in Early Bronze Age burials in Ireland and Britain. *Journal of Social Archaeology* 4, 307–33.

Brück, J. 2005. Fragmentation, personhood and the social construction of technology in Middle and Late Bronze Age Britain. *Cambridge Archaeological Journal* 16(3), 297–315.

Brück, J. 2006. Death, exchange and reproduction in the British Bronze Age. *European Journal of Archaeology* 9, 73–101.

Busby, C. 1997. Permeable and partible persons: a comparative analysis of gender and the body in South India and Melanesia. *Journal of the Royal Anthropological Institute* 3, 261–78.

Carsten, J. 2004. *After Kinship*. Cambridge: Cambridge University Press.

Chapman, J. 1996. Enchainment, Commodification, and Gender in the Balkan Copper Age. *Journal of European Archaeology* 4, 203–42.

Chapman, J. 2000. *Fragmentation in Archaeology: People, Places and Broken Objects in the Prehistory of South-Eastern Europe*. London: Routledge.

Chapman, J. and B. Gaydarska. 2007. *Parts and Wholes: Fragmentation in Prehistoric Context*. Oxford: Oxbow.

Clark, J. 1991. Pearl-shell symbolism in Highlands Papua New Guinea, with particular reference to the Wiru people of Southern Highlands Province. *Oceania* 61, 309–39.

Cummings, V., A. Jones and A. Watson. 2002. Divided places: phenomenology and assymetry in the monuments of the Black Mountains, southeast Wales. *Cambridge Archaeological Journal* 12, 57–70.

Dolfini, A. 2008. *Making Sense of Technological Innovation: the Adoption of Metallurgy in Prehistoric Central Italy*. Unpublished PhD Thesis, University of Cambridge.

Douglas, M. and S. Ney. 1998. *Missing Persons: a Critique of Personhood in the Social Sciences*. Berkeley: University of California Press.

Dumont, L. 1970. The individual as an impediment to sociological comparison and Indian history. In L. Dumont (ed.) *Religion/Politics and History in India: Collected Papers in Indian Sociology*, 133–50. Paris: Mouton.

Fowler, C. 2001. Personhood and social relations in the British Neolithic, with a study from the Isle of Man. *Journal of Material Culture* 6, 137–63.

Fowler, C. 2003. Rates of (ex)change: decay and growth, memory and the transformation of the

dead in early Neolithic southern Britain. In H. Williams (ed.) *Archaeologies of Remembrance: death and memory in past societies*, 45–63. New York: Kluwer Academic/Plenum Press.
Fowler, C. 2004a. *The Archaeology of Personhood: an anthropological perspective*. London: Routledge.
Fowler, C. 2004b. In touch with the past? Bodies, monuments and the sacred in the Manx Neolithic. In V. Cummings and C. Fowler (eds) *The Neolithic of the Irish Sea: Materiality and traditions of practice*, 91–102. Oxford: Oxbow.
Fowler, C. 2008a. Fractal bodies in the past and present. In D. Borić and J. Robb (eds) *Past Bodies*, 47–57. Oxford: Oxbow Press.
Fowler, C. 2008b. Landscape and Personhood. In *Handbook of Landscape Archaeology* (ed.) B. David and J. Thomas. Walnut Creek, CA.: Left Coast Press.
Fowler, C. In press a. From identity and material culture to personhood and materiality. In D. Hicks and M. Beaudry (eds) *The Oxford Handbook of Material Culture Studies*. Oxford: Oxford University Press.
Fowler, C. In press b. Personhood and the Body. In T. Insoll (ed.) *The Oxford Handbook of Ritual and Religion in Archaeology*. Oxford: Oxford University Press.
Fowler, C. and V. Cummings 2003. Places of Transformation: Building Monuments from Water and Stone in the Neolithic of the Irish Sea. *Journal of the Royal Anthropological Institute* 9, 1–20.
Geertz, C. 1973. Thick description: toward an interpretive theory of culture. In C. Geertz (ed.) *The Interpretation of Cultures*, 3–30. New York: Basic Books.
Gillespie, S. 2001. Personhood, agency and mortuary ritual: a case study from the ancient Maya. *Journal of Anthropological Archaeology* 20, 73–112.
Gillespie, S. 2008. Embodied persons and heroic Kings in Late Classic Maya imagery. In D. Borić and J. Robb (eds) *Past Bodies*, 125–134. Oxford: Oxbow Press.
Harris, O. 2006. *Identity, Emotion and Memory in Neolithic Dorset*. Unpublished PhD thesis: Cardiff University.
Herzfeld, M. 2004. Whatever happened to 'influence'? The anxieties of memory. *Archaeological Dialogues* 10, 191–203.
Hodder, I. 1986. *Reading the Past*. Cambridge: Cambridge University Press.
Hodder, I. 1987. Contextual archaeology: an interpretation of Çatal Hüyük and a discussion of the origins of agriculture. *Bulletin of the Institute of Archaeology, London* 24: 43–56.
Hodder, I. 2000. Agency and individuals in long-term processes. In M. Dobres and J. Robb (eds) *Agency in Archaeology*, 21–33. New York: Routledge.
Hoskins, J. 1998. *Biographical objects: how things tell the stories of people's lives*. London: Routledge.
Jones, A. 1999. Local colour: megalithic architecture and colour symbolism in Neolithic Britain. *Oxford Journal of Archaeology* 18, 339–350.
Jones, A. 2002. A biography of colour: colour, material histories and personhood in the early Bronze Age of Britain and Ireland. In A. Jones and G. MacGregor (eds) *Colouring the Past*, 159–74. Oxford: Berg.
Jones, A. 2005. Lives in fragments? Personhood and the European Neolithic. *Journal of Social Archaeology* 5, 193–224.
Joyce, R. 2001. *Gender and Power in Prehispanic Mesoamerica*. Austin: University of Texas Press.
Keates, S. 2002. The flashing blade: copper, colour and luminosity in north Italian Copper Age society. In A. Jones and G. MacGregor (eds) *Colouring the Past*, 109–27. Oxford: Berg.
Knapp, B. and P. van Dommelen. 2008. Past practices: rethinking individuals and agents in archaeology. With comments by C. Cobb, D. Saitta and J. Thomas and reply by B. Knapp and P. van Dommelen. *Cambridge Archaeological Journal* 18, 15–34.
LiPuma, E. 1998. Modernity and forms of personhood in Melanesia. In M. Lambek and A.

Strathern (eds) *Bodies and Persons: Comparative Views from Africa and Melanesia*, 53–79. Cambridge: Cambridge University Press.

McSherry, C. 2001. *Who owns academic work? Battling for control of intellectual property.* Cambridge, MA.: Harvard University Press.

Marcus, G. and Fischer, M. 1999. *Anthropology and Cultural Critique: an Experimental Moment in the Human Sciences.* Second Edition. Chicago: University of Chicago Press.

Marriott, M. 1976. Hindu transactions: diversity without dualism. In B. Kapferer (ed.) *Transaction and Meaning: Directions in the Anthropology of Exchange and Symbolic behaviour*, 109–37. Philadelphia: Institute for the Study of Human Issues.

Marriott, M. 1989. Constructing an Indian Ethnosociology. *Contributions to Indian Sociology* 23, 1–39.

Mauss, M. 1938. [trans. 1985, W. Halls] A Category of the Human Mind: the Notion of the Person; the Notion of the Self. In M. Carrithers, S. Collins and S. Lukes (eds) *The Category of the Person: Anthropology, Philosophy, History*, 1–25. Cambridge: Cambridge University Press.

Meskell, L. 1999. *Archaeologies of Social Life: Age, Sex, Class, Etcetera in Ancient Egypt.* Oxford: Blackwell.

Meskell, L. and R. Joyce. 2003. *Embodied lives: figuring Ancient Mayan and Egyptian experience.* London: Routledge.

Mosko, M. 1992. Motherless sons: 'divine kings' and 'partible persons' in Melanesia and Polynesia. *Man* 27, 697–717.

Munn, N. 1986. *The Fame of Gawa: a Symbolic Study of Value Transformation in a Massim (Papua New Guinea) Society.* Durham: Duke University Press.

Oliver, J. 2009. *Caciques and Cemi Idols: the Web Spun by Taino Rulers Between Hispanola and Boriquén.* Tuscaloosa: University of Alabama Press.

Owoc, M. A. 2002. Munselling the mound: The use of soil colour as metaphor in British Bronze Age funerary ritual. In A. Jones and G. MacGregor (eds) *Colouring the Past*, 127–40. Oxford: Berg.

Preston Blier, S. 1987. *The Anatomy of Architecture: Ontology and Metaphor in Batammaliba Architectural Expression.* Chicago: University of Chicago Press.

Ray, K. 1987. Material metaphor, social interaction and historical reconstructions: exploring patterns of associations and symbolism in the Igbo-Ukwu corpus. In I. Hodder (ed.) *The Archaeology of Contextual Meanings*, 66–77. Cambridge: Cambridge University Press.

Sax, W. 2002. *Dancing the Self: Personhood and Performance in the Pandav Lila of Garhwal.* New York: Oxford University Press.

Schwarz, M. T. 1997. *Moulded in the Image of Changing Woman: Navajo Views on the Human Body and Personhood.* Tucson: University of Arizona Press.

Smith, M. and Brickley, M. 2009. *People of the Long Barrows: Life, Death and Burial in the Earlier Neolithic.* Stroud: The History Press.

Strassburg, J. 2000. *Shamanic Shadows: One Hundred Generations of Undead Subversion in Mesolithic Scandinavia.* Stockholm: University of Stockholm Press.

Strathern, M. 1988. *The Gender of the Gift: Problems with Women and Problems with Society in Melanesia.* Berkeley: University of California Press.

Strathern, M. 1991. *Partial Connections.* Updated Edition, 2004. Walnut Creek, CA.: Altamira Press.

Strathern, M. 1992. *After Nature: English Kinship in the Late Twentieth Century.* Cambridge: Cambridge University Press.

Thomas, J. 1996. *Time, Culture and Identity: An Interpretive Archaeology.* London: Routledge.

Thomas, J. 1999. An economy of substances in earlier Neolithic Britain. In J. Robb (ed.)

*Material Symbols: Culture and Economy in Prehistory*, 70–89. Carbondale: Southern Illinois University Press.

Thomas, J. 2000. Death, identity and the body in Neolithic Britain. *Journal of the Royal Anthropological Institute* 6, 603–17.

Thomas, J. 2002. Archaeology's humanism and the materiality of the body. In Y. Hamilakis, M. Pluciennik and S. Tarlow (eds) *Thinking Through the Body: Archaeologies of Corporeality*, 29–46. London: Kluwer/Academic Press.

Tilley, C. 1996. *An Ethnography of the Neolithic: Early Neolithic Societies in Southern Scandinavia.* Cambridge: Cambridge University Press.

Tilley, C. 1999. *Metaphor and Material Culture.* Oxford: Blackwell.

Viveiros de Castro, E. 2003. Anthropology (and) Science. *Manchester Papers in Social Anthropology* 7.

Wagner, R. 1991. The fractal person. In M. Strathern and M. Godelier (eds) *Big Men and Great Men: Personifications of power in Melanesia*, 159–173. Cambridge: Cambridge University Press.

Williams, M. 2003. Growing metaphors: the agricultural cycle as metaphor in the later prehistoric period of Britain and North-western Europe. *Journal of Social Archaeology* 3, 223–55.

Whittle, A. 2003. *The Archaeology of People: Dimensions of Neolithic Life*. London: Routledge.

# 11

# No more ancient; no more human: the future past of archaeology and anthropology

*Tim Ingold*

## *Introduction*

The year is 2053, and the Association of Social Anthropologists is celebrating its centennial with a big conference.[1] As scholars are wont to do on such occasions, a number of contributors to the conference have been dwelling on the past century of the discipline with a mixture of wistfulness, curiosity and hubris, wondering why their predecessors hung on with such tenacity to forms of argumentation that now seem rather quaint. Everyone recognises that the title of the Association is a relic of past times. Social Anthropology is not what it was, for it is distinguished neither by a preoccupation with social phenomena, nor by the axiom that such phenomena are the exclusive preserve of a categorical humanity. The discipline has become, rather, a principled inquiry into the conditions and potentials of life in a world peopled by beings whose identities are established not by species membership but by relational accomplishment.

By this year of 2053, the term 'Archaeology', too, has become an anachronism, for the subject that still goes by that name has long since lost its association with antiquity. It is not that archaeologists have ceased to dig down for evidence of past lives, any more than ethnographers have ceased to participate in the lives that are going on around them, in what we call the present. But they have dropped the pretence that what is past is any older, or more ancient, than the present, recognising that the occurrences of the past are not deposited at successive moments while time moves on, but are themselves constitutive of that very movement. Between Archaeology and Social Anthropology, then, there is no longer any difference of principle. They have, in effect, converged upon a science of life whose overriding concern is to *follow what is going on*, within dynamic fields of relationships wherein the forms of beings and things are generated and held in place.

## *No more ancient*

In short, both the *archaeo-* of archaeology and the *anthropo-* of anthropology have lost their former appeal. To show why this has come about, I shall examine these disciplinary prefixes in more depth. Starting with *archaeo-*, we could pose the following question. What does it mean to ask how old something is? Or to put it another way, what kinds of assumptions do we make about a thing for such a question even to make sense? How old is a mountain, a river, a stone? How old is the wind, a cloud, a raindrop, or an ocean wave? How old is a tree, a person, a building, a pot, a piece of furniture? 'Ah, that writing desk', you exclaim with some relief, 'I can tell you *exactly* how old it is'. For you are a specialist in antiques, and an expert in such matters. A little bit of detective work allows you to deduce when it was made. Let us say that it dates from 1653. Remembering that we are now in the year 2053, you conclude that the desk is exactly four hundred years old.

But if we judge the age of a thing by the elapsed time from the moment it was made to the present, does this mean that for us to ask how old it is, the thing must at some time have been *manufactured*? Is 'how old is that?' a question that can only be asked of artefacts? Even if we answer, perhaps with some unease, in the affirmative, this only begs a host of further questions. The desk is made of oak, which was once hewn from a living tree and well seasoned before being cut into planks. Why should we not say that the desk is as old as the oak? After all, in substance if not in form, there is no more, and no less to the desk than the wood of which it is made. Then how old is the oak? The tree was not manufactured; it grew. Is it as old, then, as the acorn from which it sprang? Is the oak, in other words, older than the wood from which the desk was made? Then again, the desk has not remained unaltered by use. Generations of writers have worn and scratched its surface. Here and there, the wood has cracked and split, due to fluctuations of temperature and humidity, or been restored with filler and glue. How can we distinguish those alterations that result from use and repair, from those that are intrinsic to the process of manufacture?

The answer, of course, is that something is deemed to have been made at the point when its form matches a conception that is supposed to have pre-existed in the mind of a maker. The notion that making entails the bringing together of a conceptual form (*morphe*) and material substance (*hyle*) has, ever since Aristotle, been one of the mainstays of the western intellectual tradition. What goes for the writing desk also goes for the pot: when we ask how old it is, we count its age from the moment when form and substance were united in the allegedly finished thing. The clay, we suppose, is shaped in the potter's hands to a final form which, once hardened and fired, it retains in perpetuity. Even if the pot is now smashed, we identify its 'finishing' with the instant of original formation, not of fragmentation and discard.

So it is with the building, though at this point we might feel rather less sure of ourselves. What a difference, in English, the article makes! Building is an activity; it is what builders do. But as soon as we add the article and speak of *a* building, or even of *the* building, the activity is abruptly brought to a close. Movement is stilled, and where people had once laboured with tools and materials, there now stands a monument to human endeavour, solid and complete. Yet as all inhabitants know, buildings are never really finished. 'A "building"', observes the inventor and designer Stewart Brand, 'is always building and rebuilding' (Brand 1994: 2). The work of building goes on, in the day-to-day activities of repair and maintenance, and in the face of the inundations of animals, plants and fungi, and the corrosive effects of wind, rain and sunshine.

If, for this reason, it is difficult to state with conviction how old a building is, how much more difficult it must be once we turn from buildings to people! Of course, if you ask me how old I am, I can tell you right away. I was born in 1948, which means that since the year is 2053, I am presently 105 years old. But wait. In all probability, I died a few years ago, though I cannot tell you exactly when. Why, then, did you not start counting from the day I died? Why do we always count how old people are from their date of birth rather than death? Surely, at least for as long as people are still alive, they are not yet finished. Just as buildings are always building and rebuilding, and trees always budding and shooting, are not people always peopling, throughout their lives and even thereafter?

I think there is a reason why we count the years from a person's birth rather than from his or her death. It is the same reason why we count the age of the writing desk from when it was made, and the age of the oak from the germination of the acorn. There is a sense in which we believe that the person is finished even before his or her life in the world has begun. Though we conventionally date this finishing moment to birth, it would be more accurate to date it to that of conception. Indeed it is no accident that the inauguration of a new life should be known as a moment when the child is *conceived*, since it conforms to a logic identical to that of the Aristotelian model of making. According to this logic, a person is created in advance – or, as we say, *procreated* – through the unification of a set of ideal attributes with bodily substance. And if we ask where these attributes come from, the answer that social anthropologists would have provided, up to and even following the first decades of the twenty-first century, would have been: *by descent*. That is, each generation receives the rudiments of person-composition from their ancestors and passes them on, with greater or lesser fidelity, to their descendants. But the life of every person is expended *within* each generation, in being the person he or she is. For as we have seen, all the creative work has been done in advance, through the mutation and recombination of transmitted attributes.

What I have described is the essence of the *genealogical model*, namely that persons and things are virtually constituted, independently and in advance of their material instantiation in the lifeworld, by way of the transmission of ready-made but mutable attributes in an ancestor-descendant sequence (Ingold 2000: 136). I hope to have shown how closely this model is linked both to the idea that constitution involves the unification of form and substance, and to the possibility of asking – of both persons and things – how old they are. Returning to my original list, which ran from mountains, rivers and stones, through winds, clouds, raindrops and waves, to trees, people, buildings, pots and furniture, the tendency in thinking about antiquity has always been to start at the end and to push back as far as one can go. It is to think of things early in the list, like raindrops and clouds, as though they were part of the furniture.[2] Yet already with people and buildings, we run into the problem that this way of thinking cannot countenance how people build buildings, and buildings people, throughout their lives. Once we move on to things placed earlier in the list, such problems become insurmountable.

We are talking here of things that grow and wither, swell and abate, flow and ebb, whose forms emerge from the movements and circulations of earth, air and water. Yet these things are as much a part of the inhabited world as people and artefacts. One of the oddities of archaeology, as late as the first decade of the twenty-first century, was that it imagined the entire material world, barring the people themselves, as furnished accommodation. It was as though people, buildings and the artefacts to be found in them comprised *all there is*. In such a world, however, there would be no air to breathe, no sunlight to fuel organic growth, no moisture or soil to support it. Without these things, life would be impossible. And it was at the very moment when it began to dawn on archaeologists that the world they had imagined was crippled by inertia, but when they were still prisoners of the idea that things are constituted through the unification of form and substance (as in the classic concept of 'material culture'), that they came up with the notion of *agency*. The word was introduced to fix an insoluble conundrum: how could anything happen in a world of solid and immutable forms? The answer was to endow them with an intrinsic, but ultimately mysterious, capacity to act. Huge efforts and millions of words were expended in the futile search for this capacity. Fortunately, we can now put all that behind us.

For what has taken place, during the first half of the twenty-first century, has been a genuine sea-change in our thinking. One way of putting it would be to say that where before, the tendency was to start from the end of our list and work backwards, we would now – in 2053 – be more inclined to start from the beginning and work forwards. This is to think of a world not of finished entities, each of which can be attributed to a novel conception, but of processes that are *continually carrying on*, and of forms as the more or less durable envelopes or crystallisations of these processes. The shape of the mountain or the banks of the stream attest to processes of erosion that are still going on now, as they have done in the past. The rounded forms of pebbles on a shingle beach arise from their abrasion under the constant pounding of the waves, which are still breaking on the shore, even as sea-levels have risen and fallen. Ocean waves have the same basic forms now that they did hundreds, thousands or even millions of years ago, as do storm clouds and raindrops. We may say of these forms that they *persist*. Of a pot, however, or even of a body buried in a peat bog, we would say that it is *preserved*. It is the focus on persistence rather than preservation that distinguishes current archaeology from that of earlier times.

It would be fair to say that traditional archaeology was more interested in pots and bog bodies than in mountains or clouds. For only such things as were deemed to have been preserved qualified for entry in what was called the 'archaeological record'. It is a record comprised of fragments that, having once broken off from the flow of time, recede ever further from the horizon of the present. They become older and older, held fast to the moment, while the rest of the world moves on. But by the same token, the things of the archaeological record do not persist. For whatever persists carries on, advancing on the cusp of time. Waves continue to break, raindrops to form and to fall upon the mountainside, filling streams that continue to flow. In focusing on such things – persistent but not preserved, experientially ever-present yet ever absent from the record – current archaeology is interested not in their antiquity, not in how old they are, but in what we could call their 'pastness',[3] recognising them as carryings on along temporal trajectories that continue in the present. From the fixed standpoint of antiquity, what carries on also passes, and is thus ephemeral. If our interest is with pastness, however, it is the things that carry on that last, whereas the enduring constituents of the archaeological record, comprising the cast-offs of time and history, are ephemeral.

Persistent things have no point of origin. Rather, they seem to be originating all the time. For contemporary archaeologists, this is fundamentally the way things are. The world we inhabit, they say, *is* originating all the time, or undergoing what we might call 'continuous birth' (Ingold 2006: 3–4). And if that is true of mountains, rivers and clouds, then why should it not also be true of persons? Instead of comparing persons to buildings, pots and writing desks, and concluding that all are endowed with agency, we could compare them to mountains, rivers and clouds, recognising that all are immersed in the continuous birth of the world. This is to think of the life of the person, too, as a process without beginning or end, punctuated but not originated or terminated by key events such as birth and death, and all the other things that happen in between. And it is to find the locus of creativity not in the novelty of conception, to be unified with substance, but in the form-generating potentials of the life process, or in a word, in *growth*. And pushing this way of thinking as far as we can, we could wonder whether it might not give us a better understanding of things like buildings, pots and furniture. In so far as their forms, too, emerge within processes of material flow and transformation, cannot they also be said to grow? Even our writing desk could be considered as a phase in the pastness of oak!

## *No more human*

This is the point at which to return from the *archaeo-* of archaeology to the *anthropo-* of anthropology. I have already connected the time-honoured archaeological concern with antiquity, with how old things are, to the genealogical model of classical social anthropology. Of course the genealogical model was never *confined* to social anthropology, but was rather characteristic of thought across a range of disciplines. One of these was biology, reconfigured in the wake of the Darwinian revolution as the study of genealogically related life-forms, and concerned above all with tracing the phylogenetic pathways along which populations were understood to adapt through variation under natural selection. In the neo-Darwinian revival of the late twentieth century, the commitment to the genealogical model became ever more hard-line and explicit as living organisms came to be seen as the recipients and vehicles of digital information, their lives dedicated to the project of transmitting this information to progeny. Axiomatically, every organism was understood as the product of an interaction between genes and environment: the former introducing a character specification in the form of a suite of attributes or traits; the latter supplying the material conditions for their realisation. So far, so Aristotle.

Yet it is worth remembering that the one work widely credited with having launched modern biology had virtually nothing to say about human beings. This was of course *The Origin of Species*, by Charles Darwin. As he laid out the argument of his book, Darwin imagined himself as a spectator, watching the panorama of nature unfold before his eyes. Bringing the book to a close, he famously observed that 'there is grandeur in this view of life' (Darwin 1872: 403). But it is not a view available to non-humans. How was it, then, that human beings – or at least the more civilised among them – could reach such a transcendent position that they could hold the entirety of nature in their sights? How could they *know* nature in a way denied to other creatures, which could only *be* in it? Granted that Darwin could explain natural selection, could natural selection explain Darwin? It was in a later book, *The Descent of Man*, published in 1871, that Darwin set out to answer this question (Darwin 1874). Where *The Origin of Species* was a view, as it were, from the summit, *The Descent of Man* was an account of the climb (Ingold 1986: 49). And as everyone knows, his conclusion was that however great the gulf between the summiteers and the denizens of the lower slopes, the difference was one of degree rather than kind, and could be filled by countless gradations. The very notion of differences of degree, however, implies a common scale. By what measure, then, are some creatures high and others low?

It was a scale, in effect, of the balance of reason over instinct. Flying in the face of all that he had argued in the *Origin* about the ways in which species adapt along ever diverging lines and in manifold fashions to their particular conditions of life, Darwin now maintained that the relentless pressure of natural selection would drive an increase of 'mental power' across the board. Even in such lowly creatures as earthworms and fish one could observe a glimmer of reason, while at the other end of the scale, the residues of instinct could be detected in the most exalted of men (and still more so in women and savages of various descriptions). Contrary to the thinking of many but by no means all of his predecessors, Darwin insisted that the possession of reason – or the lack of it – was not an all or nothing affair distinguishing all humans from all non-humans. In evolutionary terms, he thought, reason advanced by a gradual, if accelerating ascent, and not by a quantum leap. Yet he never wavered from the mainstream view that it was man's possession of the faculty of reason that allowed him to rise above, and to exercise dominion over, the world of nature. In short, for Darwin and for his many followers, the evolution of species *in* nature was also an evolution *out* of it, in so far as it progressively liberated the mind from the promptings of innate disposition.

After a shaky start, Darwin's stock grew throughout the twentieth century to the point at which he had become a virtual saint among scientists. The celebration, in 2009, of the bicentenary of his birth spawned a glut of hagiography. We could not, it seemed, have enough of it. Yet the history of anthropology's flirtation with Darwinism had been far from glorious. Up until the outbreak of the Second World War, prominent physical anthropologists, drawing chapter and verse from *The Descent of Man*, were continuing to maintain that what were known as civilised and savage races of man differed in hereditary powers of reason in just the same way that the latter differed from apes, and that interracial conflict would inevitably drive up intelligence by weeding out the less well endowed groups. In 1931 Sir Arthur Keith, distinguished physical anthropologist and erstwhile President of the Royal Anthropological Institute, delivered a Rectorial address at my own institution, the University of Aberdeen, in which he maintained that interracial xenophobia was to be encouraged as a way of selecting out the weaker varieties. The war of races, Keith declared, is Nature's pruning hook (Keith 1931).[4]

But the second war in a century to break out among the supposedly civilised races of Europe, itself fuelled by xenophobic hatred, put paid to such ideas. In the wake of the Holocaust, what was self-evident to Darwin and most of his contemporaries – namely, that human populations differed in their intellectual capacities on a scale from the primitive to the civilised – was no longer acceptable. Darwin's view that the difference between the savage and the civilised man was one of brain-power gave way in mainstream science to a strong moral and ethical commitment to the idea that *all* humans – past, present and future – are equally endowed, at least so far as their moral and intellectual capacities were concerned. 'All human beings', as Article 1 of the Universal Declaration of Human Rights states, 'are endowed with reason and conscience'. To emphasise this unity, scientists reclassified extant human beings as members not just of the same species but of the same sub-species, designated *Homo sapiens sapiens*.

Yet if these beings are alike in their possession of reason and conscience – if, in other words, they are the kinds of beings who, according to orthodox juridical precepts, can exercise rights and responsibilities – then they must differ in kind from all other beings that cannot. *Homo sapiens sapiens*, then, was no ordinary sub-species. Doubly sapient, the first attribution of wisdom, the outcome of a process of encephalisation, marked it out within the world of living things. But the second, far from marking a further subdivision, registered a decisive break from that world. In what many late twentieth century commentators took to calling the 'human revolution' (Mellars and Stringer 1989), the earliest representatives of the new sub-species were alleged to have achieved a breakthrough without parallel in the history of life, setting them on the path of ever-increasing discovery and self-knowledge otherwise known as culture or civilisation. Human beings by nature, it was in the historical endeavour of reaching beyond that very nature that they progressively realised the essence of their humanity. Half in nature, half out, pulled in sometimes contrary directions by the imperatives of genetic inheritance and cultural tradition, their double-barrelled sub-specific appellation perfectly epitomised the hybrid constitution of these creatures.

It was with this cast of unlikely characters, known to science as 'modern humans' (as opposed to the 'archaic' variety, so-called Neanderthals, who had not made it through to the second grade of sapientisation), that the evolutionary anthropology of the late twentieth century populated the planet. The first such humans were portrayed as archetypal hunter-gatherers, people whom history had left behind. *Biologically* modern, they were supposed to have remained *culturally* at the starting block, fated to enact a script perfected through millennia of adaptation under natural selection. It was a script, however, that only science could read. Between the hunter-gatherer and the scientist, respectively pre- and post-historic, was supposed to lie all the difference between being and knowing, between the adaptive surrender to nature and its subjugation in the light of reason. In this scenario, it was the achievement of *cultural* modernity that provided science with the platform of supremacy from which, with no little hubris and profound contradiction, it asserted that human beings were part and parcel of the natural world.

Indeed by the late twentieth century it had become apparent that in this contradiction lay the very meaning of 'the human'. Referring neither to a species of nature nor to a condition of being that transcends nature, but rather to both simultaneously, it is a word that points to the existential dilemma of a creature that can know itself and the world of which it is a part only through the renunciation of its being in that world. Writing at the turn of our present century, the philosopher Agamben argued that the recognition of the human is the product of an 'anthropological machine' that relentlessly drives us apart, in our capacity for self-knowledge, from the continuum of organic life within which our very existence is encompassed (Agamben 2004: 27). To resolve the contradiction – that is, to comprehend knowing as being, and being as knowing – calls for nothing less than a dismantling of the machine. Far from tacking on a second *sapiens* to mark the onset of fully fledged humanity, it was necessary to move in a direction opposite to that of twentieth century science, and to attend to the generic *Homo* itself. And that was the direction anthropology took. By the first decades of the twenty-first century, it had become obvious that the concept of the human would have to go.

How come that anthropology was brought to such a pass that it had to relinquish the very *anthropos* from which the discipline had taken its name? The answer is that it came from thinking with, and about, children. In fact, children had always posed a problem for anthropology. Apparently delivered into the world as natural beings, devoid of culture and civilisation, they had somehow to be provided with the rudiments of identity that would make them into proper social persons. Childhood, wrote Goldschmidt sixty years ago, is characterised by 'the process of transformation of the infant from a purely biological being into a culture-bearing one' (Goldschmidt 1993:

351). As the offspring of human parents, the new-born baby was acknowledged as a human being from the start, but as one that had still to reach the condition of being human. On their way from infancy to adulthood, children appeared to be biologically complete but culturally half-baked. Indeed their status came closely to resemble that of prehistoric hunter-gatherers, likewise suspended in a liminal phase in the transition from a natural to a fully cultural life.

The resemblance is no accident. For in both instances the anthropological machine was at work, producing the human by regarding as not yet fully human an already human being (Agamben 2004: 37). Some humans, it transpired, were more human than others: grown-ups more than children; scientists more than hunter-gatherers. Moreover this same machine, dividing body and soul, generated a point of origin as the moment when these components were conjoined in the definition of a historical project, whether for the individual human being or for humankind as a whole. We used to speak, without batting an eyelid, of 'early man', and of the child's 'early years'. It was as though the antiquity of prehistoric hunter-gatherers could be judged, like the ages of pre-school children, by their proximity to their respective origins. Just as the child was deemed to be closer to its origin than the adult, so likewise, early humans were thought to be closer than later ones to that mighty moment when humanity began. Yet despite their best efforts, prehistorians failed to find this moment. And this was for the simple reason that it never existed. Nor indeed is there any such moment in the life of the child.

In reality, as we all know, children are not half-baked hybrids of biology and culture but beings who make their way in the world with as much facility and hindrance, as much fluency and awkwardness, as grown-ups. They are in the process not of becoming human, but of becoming the people they are. In a word, they are *growing*, in stature, knowledge and wisdom. But the child's life does not start from a point of origin, nor is his or her 'early' life closer to such a point than later life. Rather than being literally descended from ancestors, as posited by the genealogical model, children follow in the ways of their predecessors. They carry on. Of course there are key moments in life, but these are more akin to handovers in a relay than points of origin. And so it is with the history of the world. It, too, carries on, or persists, without beginning or end. Its inhabitants may follow where others have passed before, but none are more ancient than any other, nor others more modern. Or to put it another way, the world we inhabit is originating all the time. Yet the anthropological machine, as it drives the recognition of the human, also splits conception from materialisation, form from substance, and in so doing establishes the idea of their hylomorphic reunification in an original moment of procreation. Whenever we ask how old things are, the machine is operating in the background. To take it apart is thus to do away not only with the concept of the human but also with the question of antiquity. Abandon the concept, and the question disappears with it. No more human; no more ancient.

## *Afterword*

In 2009, the system of international finance that had fuelled the unprecedented prosperity of the preceding decades abruptly collapsed. It had always rested on shaky foundations, dealing as it did in a world of virtual assets, visible only on computer screens, which were ever more tenuously related to the material transformations wrought by real working lives. Once the pretence on which it rested was finally exposed, the whole apparatus fell like a house of cards. The fall was followed, in the immediately ensuing years, by the equally precipitous collapse of big science. For this, too, was found to rest on the pedestal of illusion and conceit. The particle physicists who believed that with one final throw of their collider, in the biggest and most expensive machine ever built, they would finally explain the structure of the universe, were pilloried as reckless and arrogant fools, like the bankers before them. And the bioscientists, who had abandoned the real world of living organisms for the computer-based modelling of large genetic data-sets, went the same way. It was a messy, bitter and contested implosion that cost many once distinguished careers. The funders of research were left in disarray.

Amidst the wreckage, however, a handful of small and adaptable disciplines that had never lost their footing began to thrive. Like tiny mammals in the dying days of the dinosaurs, they were ready to seize the opportunities opened up by the extinction of the megafauna that had once ruled the scientific world. They had a different strategy of reproduction. It was not to lay as many eggs as possible in the hopes that a tiny minority might survive in a fiercely competitive environment, but to treat the germs of knowledge with the same reverence as life itself, to be grown, nurtured and cared for. These mammalian disciplines recognised, as their reptilian predecessors had not, that knowing is itself a practice of habitation, of dwelling in a world undergoing continual birth. For them, knowledge grows from the ground of our engagement with the world. They saw that to be is to know, and that to know is to be. And among these disciplines, I am pleased to say, were anthropology and archaeology. That is why, in this year of 2053, we are still here to celebrate their success.

### *Notes*

1 This is the (somewhat revised) text of a plenary address presented to the 2009 Conference of the Association of Social Anthropologists of the UK and Commonwealth, on *Anthropological and Archaeological Imaginations: Past, Present and Future*, held at the University of Bristol, April 6–9.

2 In a famous painting, René Magritte highlighted the surreal consequences of this way of thinking about things by depicting a cloud making its entrance through the door of a room.

3 For this term, I am indebted to Cornelius Holtorf. In his presentation to the 2009 ASA Conference on *Anthropological and Archaeological Imaginations*, Holtorf argued that the 'pastness' of things depended not on the determination of a date of origin but on our being able to tell trustworthy stories linking them to the present. Of things preserved in the archaeological record, these would be stories of preservation, or perhaps of recovery.

4 Elsewhere (Ingold 2004) I have told the story of this lamentable episode in the history of anthropology at Aberdeen.

## *References*


Agamben, G. 2004. *The open: man and animal*, trans. K. Attell. Stanford, CA: Stanford University Press.

Brand, S. 1994. *How buildings learn: what happens to them after they're built*. Harmondsworth: Penguin.

Darwin, C. 1872. *The origin of species*, 6th edition. London: John Murray.

Darwin, C. 1874. *The descent of man and selection in relation to sex*, 2nd edition. London: John Murray.

Goldschmidt, W. 1993. On the relationship between biology and anthropology. *Man* (N.S.) 28, 341–359.

Ingold, T. 1986. *Evolution and social life*. Cambridge: Cambridge University Press.

Ingold, T. 2000. *The perception of the environment: essays on livelihood dwelling and skill*. London: Routledge.

Ingold, T. 2004. Anthropology at Aberdeen. *Aberdeen University Review* 60(3), 181–197.

Ingold, T. 2006. Rethinking the animate, re-animating thought. *Ethnos* 71(1), 1–12.

Keith, A. 1931. *The place of prejudice in modern civilization*. London: Williams and Norgate.

Mellars, P. and C. Stringer (eds) 1989. *The human revolution: behavioural and biological perspectives on the origins of modern humans*. Edinburgh: Edinburgh University Press.

# 12

# Commentary. Boundary objects and asymmetries

*Marilyn Strathern*

The invitation to offer some reflections on these papers is generous indeed. Growing up in Roman Kent, and escaping home to dig whenever I could, my early exposure to archaeology left a deep impression. Literally: for years after I ceased digging I remained absurdly proud of my excavator's thumb and worn down trowel. Indeed archaeology left an external mark on the body in the way ethnographic fieldwork in the Highlands of Papua New Guinea never did – except in the form of bodily protocols, such as finding myself in a room full of people sitting down and being squeamish about stepping over anyone's legs. But perhaps pride in a muscular thumb displaced a commitment to archaeology as a source of knowledge. It ceased to be an arena still to tussle with. I welcome the opportunity now.

By contrast, the tussle with anthropological problems became never ending, not least because objects of study are changing all the time. When a Highlands friend of mine visited Cambridge in 1999,[1] I had the pleasure of taking him to the Museum (Cambridge University Museum of Archaeology and Anthropology) and showing him some of the artefacts purchased from him 35 years previously. He was pleased to see them looked after and exclaimed at their pristine state. But I was conscious of an unspoken problem between us – that when he had accepted my invitation he assumed it would be to do with certain very pointed remarks (articulated in a letter a colleague wrote for him) about who plants the seeds of knowledge and who reaps the benefit. And while he no doubt saw some benefit to his people (as he put it) in being known through artefacts such as these, he indubitably saw much more benefit accruing to me/academia from the information he had given me over the years. The unspoken word was not so much recompense or compensation as measure – what measure of his worth, of his knowledge, of what he had given, would he find in Cambridge?

In a way we could almost say that he was hankering after a (re)description of what had gone between us earlier, imagining I would come up with a dazzling depiction – expressed materially or otherwise – of the ornamentation he had bestowed on me, to follow the thinking in Gosden's chapter. It was less the ineffability of experience that was the problem, than the fact that he was seeking to discern a transformation of values. (Indeed the redescription would have been that transformation.)

That desire unsatisfied, the unspoken operated as an awkward kind of boundary. It was a focus for apprehending something we had to do something about, lying between us yet locking us each into our separate worlds in very different ways. The concept of 'boundary object' pinpoints just such an imperative to do something – and in this case it was the knowledge (the words I had turned them into) rather than the artefacts I had procured that was the issue. Now the colleague who wrote down my companion's thoughts in the letter to bring with him had put his question into terms one would never have thought of invoking 35 years before, that is, in terms of rights to intellectual property. It was a reminder that objects of study change all the time not least because their global frameworks shift. This must be as true for archaeology as for anthropology,[2] and there is a point of interest here, I think, in reflecting on what lies between the two.

* * *

Intellectual property debates offer one arena in which the concept of a boundary object has been developed. I take from McSherry (2001) an interest in present-day scientific authorship and competing visions of how to interpret the rewards of scholarly work: is one dealing with a community of scholars who exchange gifts or with the justification of individual rights to the fruits of labour? The concept of the creative author of a work, she argues, itself bridges and reproduces both gift and market economies. For a boundary object is a construct or concept that 'holds different meanings in different social worlds, yet is imbued with enough shared meaning to facilitate its translation across those worlds' (2001: 69). To expand the particular example, scientific authors, in McSherry's view, can be seen as participating in a system of exchange premised on reciprocity, reputation and responsibility, in which the commodification of scholarship is immoral; or they can equally be seen as workers in the academic knowledge economy caught up in a system of capital accumulation and investment, where they should be exercising their rights to just reward.[3] The point is that both sides have a heavy investment in the boundary idea of the author as a creative agent.

We might recall arguments that emphasise the traffic of intellectual products in general, and the vocabulary that has sprung up around the notion of transactions across disciplinary divides. Hirsch (2004) has laid some of this out in his discussion of Galison's (1999) concept of trading zones where mediating languages (pidgins) spring up. The space or the zone emerges with a distinctive social character. There is an example of sorts in what has been called a 'recognition space' in the interaction of Australian law and Aboriginal law (Weiner 2006).[4] This is a legal facility that enables each party to recognise the other's space. Limited as this space is, it thus refers to an arena where Euro-Australian law is prepared for legal purposes to recognise Aboriginal claims to land. This recognition space is distinguished from substantive indigenous understandings, for it simply acknowledges that there can be an administrative assessment of such claims on the part of the Australian courts without ceding anything larger. It endorses neither the reasoning nor rationale of 'Aboriginal law' as such, only the admissibility of these claims. Here we might say that the notion of 'Aboriginal law' works as a boundary object. It can be transacted over without any encompassing understanding on what it might mean to either Aboriginal peoples or other Australians.

This could be a way of imagining a boundary between archaeology and anthropology. One could focus on objects in which both disciplines seem to have an investment without presupposing fuller understanding of what it might 'mean' from an archaeological or anthropological standpoint. Practitioners only have to find some meaning in it for themselves.

However, the limits of this formula are rather severe. Recognition space implies, Weiner argues, the notion of a culture with a boundary round it, so each is seen as an entity occupying a domain.[5] Indeed it serves to reinforce barriers. The recognition space becomes a creative after-thought to what already exists, a means of communication across a divide imagined as already there. Weiner offer an observation from a different standpoint: ontologically [his term] one cannot distinguish between a difference that emerges within a culture as opposed to a difference that emerges between two cultures. 'Why not start', he says, 'with "one world", wherein peoples, languages and more-or-less well understood "laws" contingently and praxically exist, and posit as our subject matter the differentiating activity that emerges from it and results in such categories as "indigenous" and "non-indigenous"?' (2006: 17, emphasis removed). The work of differentiation would be set against a background co-extensive with (anyone's) experience.

In other words, rather than concluding that whenever one talks of boundaries, one is talking about what must be enclosed within them, why not imagine boundaries as the point or juncture or moment at which differences are articulated? McSherry's boundary objects are entities at borders of discourses; they do not presuppose that a border is also an enclosure. (Boundary objects do not imply bounded objects.) Differences are created in the very attention being given to such objects. To think about archaeology and anthropology in these terms, would be to look for situations that generate the desire or need *to distinguish* the two disciplines.

* * *

This is in sympathy I think with the editors' intentions. As Yarrow says, the two disciplines face different sets of interpretive issues. In his and Garrow's words, the question is how such differences are created, including distinctions between discourses about the role of theory in analysis. It follows that I am also much in sympathy with Lucas's observation that rather than looking for commonalties it is only through looking at the discontinuities and fractures that proper bridges will be made. But how does one detect discontinuities and fractures? And what brings such distinctions to the fore? Why do some see that there is a bridge missing while others do not?

We are generally wary of being drawn into specialist discourse. So, for example, to talk about ceremonial exchange already presupposes anthropological models of interactions between people derived from present day observations, and from which the interpretation of archaeological material would be an extrapolation or extension; to talk of carbon dating implies a method whose techniques an anthropologist would have to take on trust, and so on. The asymmetries seem fairly obvious. By contrast it might seem that 'things' and 'persons' are generic entities available to archaeologist and anthropologist alike. I say this because several of the papers deal with (not necessarily agreeing with) persons and things as contrasts foundational to their (the archaeologist's and anthropologist's) divergence. The arguments tend less to the kinds of epistemic or analytical objects that the disciplines indicate by these terms than to their presence or absence as entities whose existence is already understood. 'Things' seem to be present for both disciplines, but (*pace* McFadyen) persons rendered as 'people' only in one.

I wonder, then, if one aspect of the asymmetry perceived to lie between the two disciplines is the habit of thinking that objects in the sense of things or artefacts are going to be what occupies (creates) the space between them. Simply put, in this view, the archaeologist finds the thing and the anthropologist adds context. The assumption on both sides may well be that one should be seeking the better definition or contextualisation of the 'found object' . Yet this cannot create a boundary term if the object as an unearthed artefact already belongs to archaeologist's world view and the notion of social or cultural context to the anthropologist's.

One of the sources power in the notion of (social or cultural) context is that it somehow puts the people back in, that is, creates them as having been an absence or lack. McFadyen properly objects to this depiction of archaeology. Indeed, rather like Weiner, Lucas argues that there is no difference in the absence of people from the archaeological record from the absence of many of the things they make – and then goes on to argue that we should also break down the contrast between (static) objects and (dynamic, people-filled) events. This supports one of Yarrow's critiques: he points to *ethnographic* practice and the absenting of people from the very accounts where one might have found them. Invariably the anthropologist instead ends up dealing with statements, memories, actions, ideas, rules, texts. If people are thus absent in a certain sense from anthropological accounts too, then their presence in other senses speaks to a theoretical status that cannot be taken for granted. And theories change. Several contributors point to new theoretical continuities between the terms (persons and things), not least in Fowler's analysis of changing depiction of personhood.

Here the innovative thread in these papers starts showing through. And here I find Filipucci's paper so useful: not things and people but divergence in modes of knowledge acquisition is her focus. As Lucas says, the difference is between different modes of scientific operation. But what might these be? Filipucci argues that the anthropologist's interest in narrative and representation will yield the practitioner an account of life that is no more nor less complete than the archaeologist's epistemological paradigm of traces. The interesting difference is the way the latter's notion that the past outstrips the present upturns the former's idea that the past is only known from the present. This means I think not that archaeology 'lacks' what anthropology can offer but that its interest in the past in fact englobes or encompasses anthropology. One might add that anthropology in turn seeks encompassment from other quarters, such as philosophy or social theory.

The point is echoed in Fowler's comments on the fragmentary nature of anthropological description. The kinds of accounts each discipline produces is as fragmentary *as* the other: but not *in relation* to the other. The asymmetries are differently construed, as Yarrow observes, the one appearing to endorse a knowledge deficit, the other seeing deficit elsewhere. The way archaeology produces different notions of deficit or loss is the lesson that Yarrow would hold out to anthropology. The fragment (epistemologically speaking, the trace) (Lucas) articulates an absence of a kind that anthropologists often only apprehend with considerable theoretical effort (e.g. Battaglia 1994).

What neither can hold is the theoretical (epistemic, analytical) object of the other discipline; persons and things do not look quite the same. However, boundary objects do not require symmetry. Suppose our boundary objects were the very entities that distinguish the two: their concepts and models. For the intellectual issue *between* disciplines is how to make their work of interest to others. What might render archaeology and anthropology interesting to each other could be the way in which differences emerge over the deployment of concepts, not ones that they share but ones that are dear to each. This means that there is more at stake than simply diverse 'points of view'. Nothing is gained by reducing the difference between disciplines to a difference in points of view when we should be being brought up against a difference in epistemology.[6] For the trick is to realise that 'points of view' itself captures an epistemological stance.

Enough queries have been raised already, but there remains an interesting issue that comes from focusing on things and artefacts as objects that require explanation or supplementation, as happens when the anthropologist comes up with the notion of context. The asymmetry is merographic: one entity differs from another insofar as it belongs to or is part of, is encompassed by, another entity (see what happens when you link archaeology to history rather than to anthropology). So contextualisation solves nothing, only introduces more deficits, gaps and thus more need for contexts (Schlecker and Hirsch 2001). And it is here that contexts start looking like so many 'viewpoints'. The points of view position is articulated by Edgeworth: it is the world within which we make our knowledge. It is a world where it is possible to take the viewpoint of another, to the extent of changing places with another, and a world full of singularities and pluralities (Mol 2002). Thus to think that the task is to contextualise reproduces the singularity of what has to be explained. And for as long as the entity is imagined as 'one' item to be tackled from 'multiple' viewpoints, no matter how many or how few are assembled, disparate viewpoints can never add up.

From beyond this worldview, from one not of perspectivalism but perspectivism, say, we might be able to describe it otherwise (Viveiros de Castro 2003): for example, while we constantly differentiate objects of knowledge, we could say that an anthropologist's critical attention works much like an archaeologist's, and in fact much like anyone else's. However, to turn to Gosden again, Euro-American scholars do not have sufficient words to give such a statement weight, for they do not themselves occupy this alternative world. Rather, for us as such scholars, it is the world of multiple views that will stay in place, offering its spread of infinite possibilities as so many differing viewpoints.

The infinite is not the same as the vague. On the contrary, (Euro-American) scholars are only going to engage with concepts and models that have some precision to them. The notion of a pidgin or creole that reduces the complexity of a model simply in order to make it communicable is not going to appeal. To introduce precision one already needs to know the object not as a singular thing but as a bundle of relations. It will require the specification of co-ordinates in relation to one another, rather like a grid location. We can think of the different axes of coordination as so many contexts (or domains or fields of knowledge). At the point of intersection the relationship between contexts fixes the object. By being able to specify that relationship, one has specified quite precise conditions under which one would recognise the recurrence of the object (Law 2004).

Conversely, what one created as a boundary object would serve to open up the relevant coordinates – that is, would expose the relations that kept its configuration of meanings in place – on either the archaeological or anthropological side. By first apprehending the internal relations and thus seeing how the concept is held in place for the archaeologist, say, one could then investigate the different relations that kept it in place for the anthropologist, and vice versa, arriving at a sense of the specific sources of interest that each had in the model. I thus return to the idea that we might take as a boundary object the disciplines' mutual interest in (precisely) their *own* concepts and models. What is brought together in such a move are the differences, the distinct grounds that each has in sustaining an object of some epistemological precision. And *that* might be of some interest to the other party.

* * *

Rowlands and Feuchtwang produce a topic that must surely have promise as another kind of boundary object – Gordon Childe's idea of civilisation, loosely integrated uniformities of behaviour and expectations over large areas – that could evoke complementary and reciprocal engagements from archaeologists and anthropologists alike. Here the epistemic objects are the kinds of temporalities or history of historicities that anthropology and archaeology would summon. It would be an exciting dialogue. And this collection points towards further examples, of which Robinson's discussion of Californian rock art offers a case already in dispute: made to be seen, the boundary object of a number of interpretative moves seems to be the art's local visibility. Edgeworth foregrounds the archaeological dig itself, which for the ethnographer opens up all kinds of issue to do with (Euro-American/scientific) knowledge practices, so 'fieldwork', that quintessentially archaeological habit, is taken beyond the practice of archaeology. One could offer other instances. In taking these papers together, however, which is the purpose of making a collection, the editors have fashioned a boundary object between the disciplines themselves. So if the search for symmetry has been so elusive to date, what is new in this collection? What is new is the way in which the contributors *also* let go of the notion of symmetry as involving some expectation of sharing in order to find it again in objectifying the differences that matter to each.

Joining the contributions to this volume,[7] Ingold's ethnographic report from 2053 hints wonderfully at what the outcome might be.

*Notes*

1 This was Ru Kundil (1993), now of Kuk in the Western Highlands, who has looked after anthropologists and archaeologists alike.
2 I refer to Social Anthropology, that is, not to an 'Anthropology' that (as it does for some) already subsumes archaeology as one of its fields.
3 Tremendous boundary work once went into represent the academy as a realm of non-property over and against the equation of academic freedom and authorial rights (McSherry 2001: 7).
4 Weiner refers to Noel Pearson's 'The concept of native title at common law', from the *Australian Humanities Review* (1997), as the source of the phrase.
5 I have drawn on this elsewhere (Strathern 2006). Weiner suggests that the anthropologist's cultural account is in effect a recognition space: accounts of those portions of the culture being described for which a fair translation can be achieved in another, notably the anthropologist's, language. This anticipates some of the comments about absences and gaps below, and Lucas's depiction of the anthropologist's for ever to-be-completed notions of 'culture' and 'society'.
6 See the quotation from Macdonald in McFadyen's chapter.
7 It is not without interest to note that the above was written before I had seen Ingold's piece.

## *References*


Battaglia, D. 1994. Retaining reality: some practical problems with objects as property. *Man* (NS) 29, 631–44.

Galison, P. 1996 Computer simulation and trading zones. In P. Galison and D. Stump (eds), *The disunity of science: Boundaries, contexts and power.* Stanford: Stanford University Presss.

Hirsch, E. 2004. Boundaries of creation: the work of credibility in science and ceremony. In E. Hirsch and M. Strathern (eds) *Transactions and creations: Property debates and the stimulus of Melanesia.* Oxford: Berghahn.

Kundil, R. 1993. *Biography of a Western Highlander*, translated by A. Strathern. Port Moresby: National Research Institute.

Law, J. 2004. *After method: mess in social science research.* London: Routledge.

Mol, A. 2002. *The body multiple: ontology in medical practice.* Durham and London: Duke University Press.

McSherry, C. 2001. *Who owns academic work? Battling for control of intellectual property*. Cambridge, Mass.: Harvard University Press.

Schlecker, M. and Hirsch, E. 2001. Incomplete knowledge: ethnography and the crisis of context in studies of the media, science and technology. *History of the Human Sciences* 14, 69–87.

Strathern, M. 2006. A community of critics? Thoughts on new knowledge, *Journal of the Royal Anthropological Institute* (NS) 12, 191–209.

Viveiros de Castro, E. 2003. (anthropology) AND (science). *Manchester Papers in Social Anthropology* 7.

Weiner, J. 2006. Eliciting customary law. In J. Weiner and K. Glaskin (eds) 'The (re)invention of indigenous laws and customs', special issue of *The Asia Pacific Journal of Anthropology* 7, 15–22.

# 13

# Commentary. Walls and bridges

*Julian Thomas*

Over thirty years ago, Sir Edmund Leach provided a broadly unenthusiastic commentary on a previous set of papers that addressed the relationship between archaeology and anthropology (see also McFadyen, and Yarrow, this volume). To a greater extent than most of the contributors to the present volume, he saw the two disciplines as incompatible. Archaeologists, he argued, were concerned with lifeless things, while anthropologists investigated conceptual and verbal categories (Leach 1977: 165). At best, artefacts in the ground were reflections of these categories, but the relationship between thought and expression was not sufficiently straightforward as to allow the former to be 'read off' from the latter. Clearly, though, Leach's account was informed by the understanding that ideas in the mind are not merely distinct from actions in the physical world, but logically precede them. Ideas are created in language and imposed onto tangible reality:

> The things that men make are 'projections', 'externalisations' of their inner selves and I would suppose that this had always been the case (Leach 1977: 168).

Where archaeologists appeared to be concerned with evolutionary or revolutionary processes played out through technology, ecology and resources, Leach saw historical disjunctures only in the thoughts that people think, while the people themselves were essentially changeless bearers of thought and language (1977: 170). For Leach, all human beings were 'people like us', in that they all thought in the same way, employing dichotomies between culture and nature, life and death, men and gods, raw and cooked, and identifying the boundaries between these categories with ambiguity and sacredness. He proposed that archaeology and anthropology might potentially 'meet up' over the things that they held in common: 'men', language and ideas. Archaeology should turn away from its focus on the objective physical environment, and consider instead how the world might have been conceptualised by past people. There is an argument that this is exactly what archaeology's 'structural turn' (e.g. Hodder 1982) attempted, although by this time the high structuralism that Leach advocated had been compromised by the impact of practice theories on both disciplines. Leach's distinction between an inner world of thought and meaning and an outer world of inert objects was inherited from the Cartesian/Newtonian revolution, which split subject from object and displaced the Aristotelian cosmos of animate substance in continual movement. Structuralism, then, was ultimately attributable to the "huge outbreak of dualisms" of the seventeenth century (Collingwood 1945: 100). Far from revealing the universal patterns of human thought, it imposed a modern western cosmology on 'the savage mind' and the past alike. Practice theories such as those of Bourdieu (1977) dismantled the opposition between mind and matter, by presenting culture as a means of engagement that is never fully spelt out, and not reducible to a set of abstract ideas held in the head.

The irony of the encounter between archaeologists and anthropologists documented in 1977 was that the protagonists were divided by their universalisms. The processual archaeologists of the time were in search of global laws of cultural behaviour, while Leach grounded his approach in the notion of universal structures of human cognition. While the former have generally proved illusive, it is questionable why we should trouble ourselves with investigating Leach's structuralist mammoth-hunters, if the outcome is only to discover that they were in all particulars indistinguishable from ourselves. One of the principal fascinations of archaeology lies in the way that it grants us access to worlds that were quite unlike our own, and which cannot be apprehended by any other means. It may be that the abandonment of these universalist aspirations has established the conditions for a more constructive dialogue between the two disciplines, although the papers in this collection lay much stress on an 'asymmetry' or 'trade gap' to the disadvantage of archaeology. Yet while from a British perspective the kind of archaeology that is presently being widely pursued appears to be heavily indebted to social/cultural anthropology, some American and Antipodean commentators have suggested that it is 'post-anthropological' (Bulbeck 2000: 44). That is, in drawing inspiration from philosophy and social science as a whole, 'post-processual' forms of archaeology are perceived as removing themselves from their embedding in 'four-field anthropology'. What makes archaeology more anthropological for one observer makes it less so for another.

What I take this to mean is that neither archaeology nor anthropology has a particularly fixed identity, and both are to some extent in flux – as Robinson argues they *must* be in his paper. It is for this reason that I find the spatialised metaphors of intellectual territories divided by walls or rivers and traversed by bridges that crop up throughout the papers a little unsatisfactory. Granted, academic disciplines periodically find themselves engaged in boundary-definition, but it is perhaps better to think of them as parallel traditions of knowledge-creation. These traditions are fuzzy around the edges, continually in motion, and having been nurtured by them provides each of us with the capacities that make an interdisciplinary conversation possible. We carry these traditions forward in our practice, rather than being contained within them. And as Edgeworth's paper elegantly demonstrates, because we are capable of occupying multiple subject positions, we can situate ourselves in relation to them in a variety of ways: now as ethnographer, now as archaeologist. It is not necessarily a problem that these positions may be incommensurate: they can still be mutually enlightening. Feuchtwang and Rowlands's contribution points out that archaeology and anthropology emerged from the common project of unilinear evolutionism. Their subsequent divergence has perhaps now been reversed to some extent, to judge from the recent re-embrace of the material world on the part of anthropologists. It is significant that this has to some extent been driven by social anthropologists who have some familiarity with archaeology, such as Danny Miller and Henrietta Moore.

Like Lucas, I think that we need to be cautious of the view that archaeology finds itself at an inherent disadvantage because it does not directly observe past people. This was exactly the argument that Leach made in 1977: anthropologists see social practice, archaeologists only see its residues. But his case was flawed, for while archaeologists were seeking 'the Indian behind the artefact', Leach's quarry was not the human beings themselves but the invisible symbolic systems and cultural grammars that hovered behind them. So for example, Griaule (1965) may have had direct access to his informant Ogotemmêli, but the structure of Dogon religious understandings that he pieced together was inferential, and just as conjectural as any archaeological interpretation. Several of the contributors here point out that ethnographic evidence is a partial and fragmentary as archaeological, and that the duration of the encounter with the informant is relatively limited. And as both McFadyen and Yarrow argue, the absences that archaeology contends with can be positive, and can bring forth creative thinking. Lucas brings these ideas together by citing three apparent failings of the archaeological encounter: missing people, a static record, and temporal distance. As he says, these three elements are linked by the theme of absence. What I would like to draw out of Lucas's account is the possibility that none of these is an absence in the full sense. Rather, they are all absent presences, and it is in this that the potential strength of archaeology lies.

People are not utterly absent from an archaeological site, and this accounts for the 'haunted' quality that Lucas notes. For the architecture and artefacts on any site owe their configuration and disposition to persons who are no longer present, and as such they continually draw attention to the *having-been-there* of those people (Heidegger 1996: 346). Moreover, archaeological sites are generally not devoid of people in the present: they are occupied by archaeologists. Edgeworth's observation that archaeological features are 'double artefacts' is crucial in this regard, for pits and post-holes are discovered through a repetition of the actions that created them in the first instance. Archaeological excavation is a re-inhabitation of a site, in which archaeologists negotiate spaces that were lived through by past people. In a sense these contemporary bodies stand as proxies or analogues for those of past persons, acquiring a familiarity with the place and its contents through engagement and practice. Similar claims have been made for 'phenomenological' forms of fieldwork that explore monuments and landscapes experientially (e.g. Tilley 1994). Something is going on here that transcends the observation of an archaeological object by a contemporary subject, because the practice of discovery is a performative one. A related argument covers the 'absence' constituted by temporal distance. For while the relationship between past and present can establish a useful discontinuity (for heuristic purposes, in setting up contrast and comparison), we are ourselves in time, and not observing from a position of 'apocalyptic objectivity' (Foucault 1984: 87; see McFadyen this volume). The past is gone, and yet we continue to inhabit the past, in the sense that the conditions we find ourselves amongst have been passed down to us. When we work on an archaeological site, our activity forms the most recent horizon in its history of occupation. Ingold's chapter echoes this theme by insisting that 'pastness' need not be equated with an abstract antiquity, since the world that we operate within is filled with things that are at once persisting and 'carrying on'.

Finally, it should be noted that the distinction between dynamics and statics is another aspect of the modern western conception of the world. In these terms, material things are considered inert, unless animated by human agency. The archaeological record is held to be composed of lifeless matter, things that have ceased to be animated, and which must be given meaning by human consciousness. Ingold notes, perceptively, that it is this emphasis on the static character of the archaeological record that has occasioned the archaeological concern with the agency of artefacts. His focus on life and growth shifts the emphasis away from the immanent qualities of things and towards their relational involvement in the process of the world. However, while we should expect neither agency nor pastness to be somehow contained within material things, the various ways in which they have been transformed, repaired, relocated and combined gives them the status of evidence. Our experience of material traces alerts us to a missing humanity that is distinct from our own.

Filippucci's paper provides a vibrant example of the immediacy that such absent presences can evoke. There is perhaps a tension between Lucas's view that archaeological remains 'are forgotten in an absolute sense', being related to no contemporary bearers of memory, and Filippucci's insistence that social memory can cohere around the things of the past even if they are being encountered for the first time. Her case is that the belief that memory is an internal individual capacity is a modern invention. When the past is drawn into the present through an encounter with a material trace it can be deeply felt, even if it relates to a time beyond personal experience. This is clearly the case when the memory of particular events has been kept alive by social tradition. No-one would deny the impact of relics of the Holocaust to the descendants of survivors. Equally, archaeologists have spent the past three decades coming to terms with the importance of ancestral human remains to Native American and Australian communities, even when they are many generations old. The question that Lucas is posing is whether traces of the past have a different kind of relationship with the present when they are not supported by the authority of tradition: when they relate to a past that is so remote that it is not remembered personally, socially or culturally. Can such traces produce a kind of constructed 'memory' of people who are wholly unfamiliar to us? At the very least, I would suggest that archaeology involves bearing witness to these people.

The case that I have been trying to make is that we need to reconsider the notion of 'presence', and recognise that human beings are not just objects that occupy a particular locus in space and time. The discussions of personhood that have been an important element of this volume have alerted us to the reality that the person is not bounded by their flesh. A human life is stretched over time, and spatially dispersed through interactions and effects. The human presence lingers in its absence after the biological death of the body. Taking these points into account, it is no longer possible to maintain that the distinction between archaeology and anthropology lies in the way that only the latter has direct access to human beings. On the contrary, we might want to say that the two disciplines concern themselves with human presences that manifest themselves in different ways. If there is an asymmetry, it lies in the degree to which we find ourselves attuned to these different kinds of presences. We might go so far as to say that archaeology remains difficult because we are still learning how to do it. Both archaeology and anthropology, as academic 'sciences', are extensions of our everyday skills for dealing with people and things. It may be their grounding in the immediacy of human presences and settings that affords both the 'mammalian' (as opposed to saurian) character that Ingold notes, valuing a knowledge that is derived from the contexts of lived experience. Yet the 'archaeological imagination', which gathers an awareness of other people by casting material things as evidence for their doings, is not easy to cultivate beyond the everyday level. This is possibly why archaeologists need to draw on anthropological observations in order to stimulate their own work. Fowler's commentary on the way that the two disciplines have studied personhood is an excellent example in this respect. It is not that personhood is unrepresented in the kinds of evidence that archaeologists study; it is that we need the prompting of anthropology in order to know what to look for. But to clarify: we are not seeking ways of finding past people, their consciousness or their agency locked inside material remains; we are developing a sensitivity to the way that those traces point toward absent presences.

Archaeology and anthropology investigate complementary aspects of human societies. Archaeology has the unique capacity of being able to study social practices that no longer exist, and which have no direct comparators in the contemporary world. In contrast to Leach's opinion, it is this distinctiveness of past communities, and what they have to tell us about the diversity of human experience, that makes them worth studying. However, this is not to say that if we could enter a time-machine and go back to interview past informants the enterprise of archaeological analysis would become redundant. The existence of 'archaeologies of the contemporary past' (Buchli and Lucas 2001) demonstrates that this is not the case. Societies 'look different' depending on whether we approach them through material traces or oral testimony. Neither of these modes of investigation is definitive, and each provides us with only a partial understanding of the whole. Archaeology needs the help of anthropology to stimulate its curiosity, but as Yarrow argues in his contribution, there should potentially be as much for anthropologists to learn from archaeology. It is not obvious whether the weakness of this reciprocal traffic should be attributed to the failure of archaeologists to communicate their insights to the other discipline, or to the insularity of anthropology. My guess is that it is a bit of both. However, the papers in this volume have done much to demonstrate the potential, and to provide us with optimism for the future development of the relationship.

## *References*

Bourdieu, P. 1977. *Outline of a Theory of Practice.* Cambridge: Cambridge University Press.
Buchli, V. and Lucas, G. (eds) 2001. *Archaeologies of the Contemporary Past.* London: Routledge.
Bulbeck, D. 2000. Post-anthropological archaeology. *Anthropological Forum* 10, 43–71.
Collingwood, R.G. 1945. *The Idea of Nature.* Oxford: Clarendon.
Foucault, M. 1984. Nietzsche, genealogy, history. In P. Rabinow (ed.) *The Foucault Reader*, 76–100. Harmondsworth: Peregrine.
Griaule, M. 1965. *Conversations with Ogotemmêli.* Oxford: Oxford University Press.
Heidegger, M. 1996. *Being and Time: A Translation of Sein und Zeit* (translated by Joan Stambaugh). Albany: SUNY Press.
Hodder, I. (ed.) 1982. *Symbolic and Structural Archaeology.* Cambridge: Cambridge University Press.
Leach, E. 1977. A view from the bridge. In M. Spriggs (ed.) *Archaeology and Anthropology: Areas of Mutual Interest*, 161–76. Oxford: British Archaeological Reports s19.
Tilley, C. 1994. *A Phenomenology of Landscape: Paths, Places and Monuments.* London: Berg.

# Index